William Wetmore Story

Roba di Roma

Fourth Edition. Vol. II

William Wetmore Story

Roba di Roma
Fourth Edition. Vol. II

ISBN/EAN: 9783744693790

Printed in Europe, USA, Canada, Australia, Japan

Cover: Foto ©ninafisch / pixelio.de

More available books at **www.hansebooks.com**

ROBA DI ROMA.

BY

WILLIAM W. STORY.

FOURTH EDITION.

IN TWO VOLUMES.—VOL. II.

LONDON:
CHAPMAN & HALL.

NEW YORK:
D. APPLETON & CO., 443 & 445 BROADWAY.
1864.

CONTENTS TO VOL. II.

CHAPTER XIII.
THE CAMPAGNA 1

CHAPTER XIV.
MARKETS 38

CHAPTER XV.
THE GHETTO IN ROME 53

CHAPTER XVI.
FIELD SPORTS AND RACES 88

CHAPTER XVII.
FOUNTAINS AND AQUEDUCTS 104

CHAPTER XVIII.
BIRTHS, BAPTISMS, MARRIAGES, AND BURIALS 120

CHAPTER XIX.
SUMMER IN THE CITY 153

CHAPTER XX.
THE GOOD OLD TIMES 165

APPENDIX 183

CHAPTER XIII.

THE CAMPAGNA.

THE Roman Campagna is a vast undulating plain stretching along the coast from Civita Vecchia to Terracina, a distance of about 100 miles, and extending in diameter from the sea across to the mountains which girdle it on the east about 40 miles. Along this plain, pursuing an irregular course from north to south, and marking the ancient boundaries between Latium and Etruria, hurry the yellow and turbulent waves of the Tiber; and nearly equidistant from Civita Vecchia, Terracina, and the mountains, perched on its seven hills, is the city of Rome. Looking from the lofty tower of the Capitol, you see on the east the long low shore of the Mediterranean stretching for miles, with here and there the little towns of Pratica, Ostia, and Ardea, darkly *silhouetted* above its line against the faint band of the flashing sea. Towards the south, swelling from the flat level in long and beautiful sweeps, rises the varied outline of Monte Albano, culminating in the cone of Monte Cavi, and then again sweeping gracefully into the plain. Along its lower slopes gleam the towns of Albano, Marino, Castel Gandolfo, and Frascati, with villas, gardens, and olive orchards stretching up the hill. Still higher, and resting on a little jutting ledge, like a rock-slide which has been caught and stopped in its descent, is the little grey town of Rocca di Papa. Green forests and groves girdle its waist and soften the volcanic hollows around the Alban lake; and high up on its summit, where once towered the temple of Jupiter Latialis, built by Tarquin, rising above the trees may be seen the shining walls of the Passionist convent of Monte Cavi, built by Cardinal York on the ruins of the ancient temple. Here on the spot whence Virgil tells us that Juno surveyed the ranks of the contending armies, "*Laurentum Troumque,*" and gazed upon the city of the Latins, you may stand and overlook the Roman world from Civita Vecchia to Naples

—and not disdain a stout coat to protect you in the evenings of summer. Where the Alban Hill again drops into the plain on the western side is a wide gap of distance, through which you look far away down towards Naples, and see the faint misty height of Ischia just visible on the horizon—and then rising abruptly with sheer limestone cliffs and *crevasses*, where transparent purple shadows sleep all day long, towers the grand range of the Sabine mountains, whose lofty peaks surround the Campagna to the east and north like a curved amphitheatre. Down through the gap, and skirting the Pontine marshes on the east, are the Volscian mountains, closing up the Campagna at Terracina, where they overhang the road and affront the sea with their great barrier. Following along the Sabine hills, you will see at intervals the towns of Palestrina and Tivoli, where the Anio tumbles in foam, and other little mountain towns nestled here and there among the soft airy hollows, or perched on the cliffs. At their feet, on three little hills that stand like advanced posts before the lofty mountains, are the half-ruined villages of Colonna, Zagarola, and Gallicano, which give their names to princely Roman families of to-day. Further along towers the dark and lofty peak of Monte Gennaro, that wears its ermine of snow almost into the summer, and the longer line of the Leonessa, where rose-coloured snow lies softly glowing against the sky as late as April. Beyond these, alone and isolated, in the north, rises out of the turbulent waves of the Campagna the striking and picturesque height of Soracte, swelling from the plain in form "like a long swept wave about to break, that on the crest hangs pausing." Sweeping now round by Rieti, Civita Castellana, and the mountains of Viterbo, we come back to the sea at Civita Vecchia.

Within this magnificent amphitheatre lies the Campagna of Rome, and nothing can be more rich and varied, with every kind of beauty —sometimes, as around Ostia, flat as an American prairie, with miles of *canne* and reeds rustling in the wind, fields of exquisite feathery grasses waving to and fro, and forests of tall golden-trunked stone-pines poising their spreading umbrellas of rich green high in the air, and weaving a murmurous roof against the sun; sometimes drear, mysterious, and melancholy, as in the desolate stretches between Civita Vecchia and Rome, with lonely hollows and hills without a habitation, where sheep and oxen feed, and the wind roams over treeless and deserted slopes, and silence makes its home; sometimes rolling like an inland sea whose waves have suddenly been checked and stiffened, green with grass, golden with grain, and gracious with myriads of wild flowers, where scarlet poppies blaze over acres and acres, and pink-frilled daisies cover the vast meadows, and pendent vines shroud the picturesque ruins of antique villas, aqueducts and tombs, or droop from mediæval towers and fortresses.

Such is the aspect of the Agro Romano, or southern portion of the Campagna extending between Rome and Albano. It is picture wherever you go. The land, which is of deep rich loam that repays a hundred-fold the least toil of the farmer, does not wait for the help of man, but bursts into spontaneous vegetation and everywhere laughs into flowers. Here is pasturage for millions of cattle, and grain fields for a continent, that now in wild untutored beauty bask in the Italian sun, crying shame on their neglectful owners. Over these long unfenced slopes one may gallop on horseback for miles without let or hindrance, through meadows of green smoothness on fire with scarlet poppies—over hills crowned with ruins that insist on being painted, so exquisite are they in form and colour, with their background of purple mountains—down valleys of pastoral quiet, where great *tufa* caves open into subterranean galleries leading beyond human ken; or one may linger in lovely secluded groves of ilexes and pines, or track the course of swift streams overhung by dipping willows, and swerving here and there through broken arches of antique bridges smothered in green; or wander through hedges heaped and toppling over with rich, luxuriant foliage, twined together by wild vetches, honeysuckles, morning glories, and every species of flowering vine; or sit beneath the sun-looped shadows of ivy-covered aqueducts, listening to the song of hundreds of larks far up in the air, and gazing through the lofty arches into wondrous deeps of violet-hued distances, or lazily watching flocks of white sheep as they crop the smooth slopes guarded by the faithful watch-dog. Everywhere are deep-brown banks of *pozzolano* earth which makes the strong Roman cement, and quarries of tufa and travertine with unexplored galleries and catacombs honeycombing for miles the whole Campagna. Dead generations lie under your feet wherever you tread. The place is haunted by ghosts that outnumber by myriads the living, and the air is filled with a tender sentiment of sadness which makes the beauty of the world about you more touching. You pick up among the ruins on every slope fragments of rich marbles that once encased the walls of luxurious villas. The *contadino* or shepherd offers you an old worn coin, on which you read the name of Cæsar; or a *scarabœus* which once adorned the finger of an Etruscan king, in whose dust he now grows his beans; or the broken head of an ancient jar in marble or terra-cotta, or a lacrymatory of a martyred Christian, or a vase with the Etrurian red that now is lost, or an *intaglio* that perhaps has sealed a love-letter a thousand years ago. Such little touches urge the imagination:—

> "Here are acres sown, indeed,
> With the richest royal'st seed
> That the earth did e'er suck in
> Since the first man died for sin.
> Here the bones of birth have cried ;
> Though gods they were, as men they died.
> Here are sands—ignoble things—
> Dropped from the ruined sides of kings.
> Here's a world of pomp and state
> Buried in dust, once dead by fate."

"What is that with which you are striking fire on your steel to light your pipe?" said a gentleman to a *contadino*, whom he had stopped to ask a question. "*Una pietra*—a stone I found here some months ago," he replied. "Would your Excellency like to see it?" and he extended to him a stone, the edge of which he had worn away on his steel. It was a magnificent *intaglio* in *pietra dura*, one of the rarest and largest of the antique stones that exists, and undoubtedly was the shoulder brooch of an imperial mantle worn by one of the Cæsars. For a few *pauls* the ignorant *contadino* sold an antique gem which was worth a fortune, and which had for its possessor no other value or use than a common flint.

Subterranean Rome is vaster than the Rome above ground. Almost every rising hillock has its *pozzolano* cave which stimulates your curiosity to explore. You enter and creep a short distance into the damp shadow of the earth, and then a shudder comes over you and you return—or else, finding your way blocked up by fallen earth and fragments of ruin, you are glad to turn back, and, after stumbling darkly over stones, to issue again into the warm sunshine. Some of these are entrances into the *arenariæ* or sand quarries of the ancients, which are burrowed far into the bowels of the earth. In these, hunted Christians in fear of martyrdom, robbers and assassins in ancient and mediæval days, emperors fleeing for their life from the insurrections of the Golden House, were wont to hide themselves. Into one of them, near the Esquiline gate, Asinius was decoyed and murdered, as we learn from Cicero. In another, Nero was recommended to take refuge when, with naked feet, disguised, and trembling with apprehension, he passed out the Nomentan gate with death at his heels, and shuddering, refused to bury himself alive in the sand-pit. And all along the Appian way they afforded hiding-places of thieves, who rushed out from them upon unwary travellers.

But besides the *arenariæ* and *latomiæ*, there are the dark labyrinthine galleries of the catacombs, intersecting everywhere the Campagna under ground with their burrowing net-work. Here in the black tunneled streets of this subterranean city is a mighty population of the dead. Tier above tier, story above story, in their narrow walled-up houses for miles and miles along these sad and silent avenues, lie the skeletons of martyred and persecuted Christians, each with his lacrymatory, now dry, and his little lamp, which went out in the darkness more than fifteen centuries ago. A few of these catacombs have been explored to a certain distance; but it is supposed that they extend as far as Ostia. Mr. Northcote, in his interesting work on the catacombs, says that the united length of all the streets in the cemetery of St. Agnes alone would be fifteen or sixteen miles, and reckons the length of all the streets in all the catacombs at no less than nine hundred miles. These vast subterranean labyrinths, where the sun never shines and the grass never grows, are densely populated by the dead, " each in his narrow cell for ever laid." On either side the tombs or cells are carven in the stone,—and for every seven feet of the dark streets Padre Marchi allows an average of ten sepulchral chambers, each with its dead occupant. According to this calculation, the Roman catacombs contain almost seven millions of graves.

Long before Æneas landed on the Latin shore cities had been founded there and flourished and perished; generations had come and gone; masterpieces of art had been executed, and all at last had been buried in almost indiscriminate decay. Rome itself was built upon the ruins of a far more ancient city, the very name of which has perished. Yet the wonderful *cloacæ* which drained that nameless city still remain, as perfect and solid as when they were laid, to drain the modern city of St. Peter and the Popes. These works are often attributed to the elder Tarquin, but there can be little doubt that they existed not only long before his time, but were of so old a date that even then it was not known by whom they were built. It is most improbable that Tarquin, whose whole territory extended in no direction beyond fifteen miles, and whose central city was of a very limited population, made up chiefly of herdsmen and banditti, should have constructed works of mere convenience and cleanliness exceeding those to be found in any other city; and the fact stated by Lactantius,[*] that a statue was found in these *cloacæ* by Tatius, representing an unknown person, to which such mystery was at-

[*] "Cloacinæ simulacrum id cloacâ maxima repertum Tatius consecravit, et quia cujus effigies esset ignorabat ex loco illi nomen imposuit." Lact., lib. i. ch. 20.

tached by him and his colleague that it was consecrated forthwith, and received the name of Venus Cloacina, would also seem to indicate that these works, so far from having been built by Tarquin, were ancient in his day.

Under the swelling mounds which rise everywhere around you in the Campagna are the galleries and foundations of ancient villas and the chambers of ancient tombs. It is but two years ago that Signor Fortunati undertook some excavations on the ancient Via Latina in hopes of discovering the remains of an early Christian church. Scarcely had he struck pick and spade into the earth, when he burst through the roof of two ancient tombs, which for ten centuries had lain there hidden from human eye. There stood the ancient sarcophagi, with the bones of their occupants. On the ceiling of one, perfect as ever, were figures and arabesques in *bassi rilievi* sketched with a master's hand in the wet plaster; and on the ceiling of the other were the fresh unfaded colours of Roman paintings of the early imperial days. In these tombs there was an air of peace and serenity which was very striking. Landscapes, fruits, musical instruments, birds, flowers, graceful figures, and masks were painted on the walls, and in the centre of the ceiling Jove wielded his thunderbolt. The aspect of everything was cheerful. On the sarcophagi were *alti rilievi* representing mythologic stories; and Death, instead of being impersonated by a grinning skeleton, hideous and frightful, stood in the shape of a youthful and winged genius with inverted torch. One could not but be struck by the contrast between the Christian catacombs, so sad, severe, solemn, and mournfully oppressive, and these pleasant and almost cheerful Pagan tombs. In the latter it seemed as if the family must have often gathered together in tender regret to remember the happy days of the past, and to be near the beloved ones who had once been with them in the body, with no misgivings about an infernal and hideous hereafter of perpetual agony. Built against one of these sepulchral chambers, and forming as it were a vestibule to it, was a tomb of a later date with several sarcophagi. On one of these was the following tender inscription:—

"C. Servienus Demetrius
Mar. F. Viviæ Severæ,
Uxori santissimæ et
Mihi Q. vixit mecum an-
nis XXII. Mens. VIIII. Dies V.
In quibus semper mihi
Bene fuit cum illa
Pancrati hic."

But even here the desecrating hand of some Goth had been, and through a hole broken in one corner had probably stolen the ornaments placed there by the pious hand of her husband.

When these tombs were discovered the whole world of Rome flocked to see them, and some modern barbarian, not contented with stealing the skulls and carrying off the fragments of marble and vases which lay profusely scattered over the ground, knocked off one of the most perfect of the stucco figures at the corner of the painted tomb and carried it off.*

Here also were unearthed the foundations of the early Christian basilica dedicated to St. Stephen, and built by St. Demetria, the first nun, at the instance of the Pope St. Leo the Great, who was the head of the church from A.D. 440 to 461. Bosio, the great explorer of Christian remains, had failed to discover it; but there it lay hidden under the grassy mould at the third mile-stone on the Via Latina, just as it was described by Aringhi two hundred years ago. It was in complete ruin, being razed to its foundations. Twenty-two columns of rare and beautiful marble, one of which is of *verde antico*, and several of *breccia* and *cipollino marino*, were found toppled down among its *débris*, as well as forty bases and more than thirty capitals, and numberless architectural ornaments attesting the richness of the old basilica.

Here too was exposed to view the old pavement of the Via Latina, worn into ruts by the narrow *plaustra* and *bigæ* of the ancient Romans, clearly showing that a drive was no joke in those days. At the side of the road are also raised walks for foot passengers, similar to those in Pompeii.

All these had lain under the smoothed mounds of grass for centuries, hidden from mortal eye; and here a month before the sheep had been peaceably feeding, and the shepherd dreaming on his staff unconscious of the world beneath his feet. Now we had broken through into the old life and death, and touched as it were past generations which were only dust and spirit, and read records of love and sorrow that had so long survived the hands that wrote and the lips that uttered them. Who was Vivia Severa, that made her husband happy for nearly twenty-three years? Was she as beautiful as she was amiable? and did Servienus Demetrius mourn her for a week and then marry again?

It was only the other day that a cry was heard in Rome, which would have sounded strangely enough anywhere else. "A new Venus has been found in a *vigna* on the Campagna about a mile

* Since this was written, all the stucco figures in this tomb have shared the same fate.

beyond the Porta Portese." The world of strangers, thrilled by curiosity, eagerly thronged out to see it, and the road for days was covered with carriages. Leaving the horses at a little *osteria*, you struck across an open vineyard a short quarter of a mile, when you came to the excavations, and there in the corner of a subterranean room belonging to an ancient villa stood the new Venus. Just risen, not from the sea but from the earth, somewhat grimed by the dirt in which she had made her bed for centuries, and with her arms and head lying on the ground at her side, stood the figure of the Paphian goddess with which we are all so familiar. But it is in all respects inferior in execution and finish to the celebrated Venus de' Medici, and not likely to disturb the old favourite in her " pride of place." The attitude of the two statues is the same with slight variations, and they seem to be copies of an original vastly superior to both. The legs and extremities of the new Venus are badly wrought, and the workmanship throughout is not of the first class ; but the *torso* is elegant in its contour, and the proportions slenderer and more refined than those of the Mediczan Venus. The head too, though battered, is larger and in better proportion to the figure than the small, characterless head of her rival.

The proprietor of the little *osteria* close by, under whose auspices and on whose *vigna* the excavations had been made, stood near, and smiled pleasantly on us and on his Venus; and when we congratulated him on his discovery, his rubicund face, bearing evidence of frequent libations to Bacchus, and adorned with a blazing nose that would have done no discredit to Bardolph, beamed with satisfaction. Willingly he answered all our questions. Oh, yes ! they had always known there was an antique villa here; but they had never thought it worth while to excavate it. *Si vede, che costa denaro.* But his business had prospered, *grazie a Dio*, and he required a cellar or grotto in which to store his wine; so he thought he would build it on this ground; it would be as cheap to make it here as elsewhere, and perhaps, *chi sa ?* he might find something to repay him. But, in an evil hour, an acquaintance had proposed to pay a certain proportion of the cost of the cellar provided he should have as his own everything of value that might be found in the excavations. A bird in the hand, thought Bardolph, is worth two in the bush, so he gladly accepted the proposal. But repentance followed close on the heels of his bargain; for scarcely had the first blow been struck with the pick, when the foundations of an ancient villa were disclosed; and upon pushing forward the excavations the workmen came at once upon a little room, the walls of which were still standing breast high ; and there in the centre lay the Venus we were looking at, fallen and covered with rubbish and loose dirt. At first the head and arms were wanting, but these also were found the next day in the same room. This success induced them to continue the excavations; and when I saw these, they had already opened a bathing-room of considerable size, where the ancient pipes and conduits still conducted the running water,—and were strongly in hopes of finding other statues and remains of value. Friend Bardolph, though the proprietor of a "*canova di vino*," seemed to have a very undeveloped knowledge or taste in sculpture, and apparently was not aware of the great value of the statue, but stood in a state of wonderment at the crowds of people who now flocked to see it. Though it was evident to him that he had lost by his bargain, he had made up his mind to his disappointment with an easy good-nature: at all events, for a week his *osteria* had been thronged with visitors, and he had made his profits out of the wine he had sold. The devotee to Bacchus did not transfer his homage to Venus. He was slow to accept new gods or goddesses. The value of wine he understood, *per Bacco;* but the value of statues he knew nothing about. As for old ruined foundations and bathing-rooms, they might be well enough in their way, but good, sound, well-built grottoes, capacious for butts of wine, were more tangible and solid in their advantages. So we bade him good-bye, and rejoiced as we passed to see that, around the stone tables and benches under the *pergola* of the *osteria*, a group of long-haired Germans were seated, with full flasks of his red wine before them, and drinking, smoking, and enjoying themselves, almost as much as if they were in Vaterland, and finding everything "*ausserordentlich gut.*"

A far better statue was lately unearthed in the grounds of the ancient Villa Livia, at Prima Porta, about nine miles beyond the Porta del Popolo. This villa, which was built by Livia Augusta, the wife of Octavius Cæsar, was formerly called *Ad Gallinas*, on account of a singular incident which happened to the empress on this spot, and in commemoration of which the villa was erected. Before she was married to Augustus, as she was sitting here one day, an eagle overhead dropped into her lap a white hen, with a branch of laurel covered with berries in its beak. An augury so striking as this could not fail to make a deep impression. The hen and its offspring were ordered to be religiously kept and tended, and the branch and berries of the laurel to be planted and carefully set apart. The branch of laurel took root and throve, and from it grew a grove, from which, ever after, the wreaths worn by the Cæsars at their triumphs were woven. But more than eighteen hundred years have passed since then; the imperial figures that walked there have fallen to dust and been scattered to the winds. The grove has left not a trace; and goats and sheep have for ages browsed over the green slopes which cover the ruins of the country-house. Suddenly, one summer day, the pick of the excavator breaks through the roof, and we enter the silent chambers where Livia and Augustus may once have lived and loved. The walls of these subterranean rooms are decorated with paintings which, despite the damp and dirt and rubbish of centuries with which they were found crammed to the ceiling, are almost as fresh in colour as if they had been painted but a year ago. On them may be seen green palms and pomegranate trees, that mingle together their intertwining foliage. The pomegranate trees are covered with blossoms and fruit in every stage of their growth, from the green bulb to the ripe and rose-stained shell; some of which are split open to show the carmine seeds. One little group of this fruit in the perfection of its ripeness is painted with remarkable freedom, truth, and brilliancy, and so vivid are the colours that it is scarcely possible to believe that they are not of this century. The chambers are small, without light and underground, and each visitor carries a little waxen taper, and examines with wonder these ancient paintings, while his imagination runs back to the long-vanished days.

Last spring (1863), all the world was flocking out to see these excavations, and the road was covered with long lines of carriages. As we drew up at Prima Porta, the first thing that met our eye was a colossal figure of Augustus, which had just been dug out of these grounds, and was lying on tressels in the shed of a little farm-house, facing upon the road. This statue, which is eight feet in height, is remarkable not only for its perfect preservation, only having lost the fingers of one hand, but also as being the most highly finished portrait-statue of the Roman school which has come down to us: indeed, both the paintings and the statue give us a high notion of the Roman art of that period. The emperor wears a cuirass, which is covered in front with beautifully-executed figures and groups in basso-relievo; over the loins and shoulders hang the fringed straps which usually decorate the Roman armour. He carries on his left arm a scarf, and in this hand he probably once held a sceptre— though it is now gone. The fringes on the loins and shoulders are finished with an elaboration and detail without parallel in any antique work; and the figures on the cuirass are beautiful in design and workmanship. In the centre of the cuirass, Cœlus is represented under the aspect of a majestic and full-bearded old man, surrounded by clouds, and overarched by a mantle blown out by the wind; beneath him, the charioteer of the sun, with flowing mantle dress, is driving forth his galloping steeds—and before him float two female figures, representing probably Herse and Aurora ; one with wide-spread wings, and the other with a veil streaming behind her and bearing a lighted torch in her hand. At the base of the cuirass is the goddess Tellus, in a recumbent attitude, her head crowned with leaves, her right hand resting on a cornucopia, and with two children standing near her. On one side above is Apollo with his lyre, seated on a winged griffin ; and behind him, Diana, with her quiver and torch, who rests upon a stag which she embraces with her arm. Both of these figures are beautiful in composition and execution. On the opposite side are the figures of two youths in tunics and mantles, one of whom carries a musical instrument, shaped into the head of a dragon ; and in the centre, between the Cœlus and Tellus, are two figures, representing, the one, a bearded barbarian, probably a Parthian, and the other an emperor or Roman general.

The nude parts are treated with equal care and finish. The head, which bears a very striking resemblance to the bust of the young Augustus in the Vatican, is wrought in a separate block of marble, and inserted into the statue at the junction of the cuirass. It does not seem to be of the same workmanship, and probably is by another hand. Indeed, it would seem questionable whether it originally belonged to the figure. The cuirass has been tinted with a roseate hue which still remains in many places, while the nude portions of the figure bear no such indications, and were evidently not coloured.

Here, too, in this same villa, other excellent works have been discovered, among which may be mentioned three busts—one of Septimius Severus—one of a female—and one of a youth of the imperial family.

At the western verge of the Campagna, at Ostia, they are now unearthing the antique city, opening its paved streets, and disencumbering its ruined houses and villas of the accumulations of ages under which they have lain so long concealed. Many of the streets are already cleared, and the pavement, worn into ruts by the ancient *biga*, with its high *trottoirs*, is exposed to sight. In some respects this disinterred city is even more interesting than Pompeii, where everything is on so small a scale that it seems almost like a collection of baby-houses. At Ostia, on the contrary, one gets a notion of space and size ; and one great palace which has just been opened comes fully up to our notions of the magnificence of Roman life. Wide corridors and galleries, adorned on either side with columns and marble statues, lead into a spacious *atrium* paved with a mosaic floor, that is wrought into a beautiful and graceful design.

The rooms are large, and portions of the rich and rare marble casing with which they were veneered still cover the base of the wainscot. The bath is luxurious, consisting of a deep basin of some thirty feet in length, surrounded by niches, in which still stand one or two of the marble statues with which they were once filled; and in an adjoining room are the conduits, pipes, and other arrangements for heating the water. Here, under the long, shaded porticoes, one could walk in the summer, and, gazing out between the marble columns and statues, see the blue Mediterranean; and here we can well fancy a worthy senator, trailing his *toga*, and discoursing with his friends, or reclining at his banquet and quaffing his cool Falernian, with ample room and verge enough.

Knowing that there are things like this in the dead city under your feet, it is impossible to walk over them in the upper air "without some stir at heart." A pensive, melancholy pleasure steals into the thoughts—you slide into the world of dreams, as you kick over the bits of marble with which the grass is strewn, or pluck the wild flowers that picture the sod and glow among the ruins. If you speak English, you quote Byron, and mutter to yourself, "Oh, Rome, my country! city of the soul!"—all of which will seem "quite absawd" to you when you are walking again in Regent-street.

Various as the Campagna is in outline it is quite as various in colour, reflecting every aspect of the sky and answering every touch of the seasons. Day after day it shifts the slide of its wondrous panorama of changeful pictures—now tender in the fresh green and ower-flush of spring—now golden in the matured richness of summer—and now subdued and softened into purple browns in the autumn and winter. Silent and grand, with shifting opal hues of blue, violet, and rose, the mountains look upon the plain. Light clouds hide and cling to their airy crags, or drag along them their trailing shadows. Looking down from the Alban Hill one sees in the summer noons wild thunder-storms, with sloping spears of rain and plashing blades of lightning, charge over the plain and burst here and there among the ruins, while all around the full sunshine basks upon the Campagna and trembles over the mountains. Towards twilight the landscape is transfigured in a blaze of colour—the earth seems fused in a fire of sunset—the ruins are of beaten gold—the meadows and hollows are as crucibles where delicate rainbows melt into every tone and gradation of colour—a hazy and misty splendour floats over the shadows, and earth drinks in the glory of the heavens. Then softly a grey veil is drawn over the plain, the shadow creeps up the mountain side, the purples deepen, the fires of sunset fade away into cold ashes—and sunset is gone almost while we speak. The air grows chill, and in the hollows and along the river steal long white snakes of mist—fires from the stubble begin to show here and there—the sky's deep orange softens slowly into a glowing citron, with tinges of green, then refines into paler yellows, and the great stars begin to look out from the soft deep blue above. Then the Campagna is swallowed up in dark, and chilled with damp and creeping winds.

Such is the Campagna of Rome: to me it seems the most beautiful and the most touching in its interest of all places I have ever seen; but there are those who look with different eyes. One Frenchman I knew who, on his return from a visit to Naples, was asked if he had seen the grand old temples at Pæstum. "*Oui, monsieur,*" was his answer, "*j'ai vu le Peste. C'est un pays détestable; c'est comme la Campagne de Rome.*" It is quite natural, however, that any one who has lived the greater part of his life in Paris, and only visited the country in its vicinity and formed his taste and patriotism there, should object to the Campagna. After that military landscape where low bounding hills are flattened like earthworks and bastions, and stiff formal poplars are drawn up in squares and columns on the wide parade of its level and monotonous plains, it is no wonder that the ever-varying graces of the Campagna, its rolling hills and vales and sheer mountains, should seem too free and unformalized, too wild and uneducated in their beauty. It is also a peculiarity of a Frenchman that he underrates everybody and everything except himself and his country. If, as is universally the case, he sneers at the Romans because they do not speak French well at Rome, though he himself speaks Italian not worse, but not at all, how is it possible that he should admit the beauty of the Campagna, it not being at all French? Let us be just, however, and admit that we also—we English and Americans —but too often call the Campagna by bad names, and speak of it as desolate and deserted, if not ugly. Others, however, are fairer in their estimate of things at Rome. I know one gentleman who had the liberality to say, "I do not *object*, sir, to the Carnival," and several who are equally liberal to the Colosseum and St. Peter's.

Really to see the beauty of the country about Rome, and the noble remains of its ancient grandeur, the traveller should go far out from the city into places not trodden to death by the regular tourist. Rome has now become a watering-place; and the stream of strangers that pours annually into the hotels and fills the streets, and overflows the houses, has washed away much of its original character. In the cities, the Italian is bastardized by foreign habits and customs. In the mountains, off the dusty highway of travel, he retains the hereditary qualities of his ancestors, and wears the ancient costume of his people. The occupation of the French soldiery has not improved the morals of Rome: the Gallic hat and bonnet and the curse of crinoline have invaded its streets; and the Rome of fifty years back scarcely survives even in the Trastevere quarter. Day by day, the sharp Roman traits are wearing out; and within the fifteen years that I have known it, much that was picturesque and peculiar has been obliterated. The costumes which Pinelli etched are fast going, but in the mountains there is no change. The habits, customs, and dresses which charmed the traveller centuries ago, still survive to delight the artist and form subjects for his canvas.

So, too, in the mountains may be seen some of the grandest and most affecting remains of ancient days. At Aquina, for instance, which is seldom visited, one may pass a charming day. This old city, the birth-place of Juvenal and the "Angelic Doctor," St. Thomas Aquinas, exists only in fragments and ruins, but they are all beautifully picturesque. The present village does not occupy the site of the ancient city; you turn off a few miles before reaching it, and drive or walk along a level valley girdled by magnificent mountains, over which at intervals are scattered the broken columns, arches, and ruined temples. There is the ancient gateway, and triglyphs, fragments and cornices, and huge blocks of stone and masonry everywhere strew the ground. Where once a noisy population thronged the busy streets with sacrifices, festivals, and triumphs, are now peaceful fields of grain, where only the *contadino* is seen as he drives his plough, or reaps his corn.

> "Nunc inter muros pastoris buccina lenti
> Cantat, et in vestris ossibus arva metunt."

Here, too, on the site of the ancient temple of Hercules, and built out of its ruins, stands the interesting old church "della Madonna Libera," itself now a deserted ruin, going rapidly to decay —weeds choke up its nave and aisles, the roof has fallen in, and the tower partially crumbled away. The very floor of the church is a cemetery, where you stumble over old sarcophagi, modern gravestones, and whitening human bones. The steps which once led to the ancient temple still remain in tolerable preservation, and on them you ascend to the church—and everywhere worked into the façade are antique fragments and cornices, and bits of sculpture worked into its walls.

But the most striking thing of all is the antique Arch of Triumph with its ornate Corinthian capitals, through which went the great processions of its glorious days. Half-choked up with débris and weeds, it now forms the sluice-way and dam, over which runs the mill-stream that turns the wheels of a factory a few paces beyond. Tall reeds and flowers nod and bend over the clear water that rises nearly to the cornice from which the arch springs, and the whole forms a strange, beautiful, and touching picture.

The system of agriculture differs in different parts of the Roman States. The long low district of the Maremma extending along the coast from the Tuscan frontier to Naples, the low marshy lands around Ferrara and Ravenna, and the Campagna in the immediate vicinity of Rome, known as the "Agro Romano," are divided into very large farms, owned by a few wealthy proprietors. The remainder of the Roman territory is for the most part subdivided into small farms, and cultivated on the *mezzeria* or *métayer* plan; the landlord furnishing the land, capital, and farmhouses, and making all necessary repairs, and the tenant giving his labour and supplying all the agricultural implements. The cattle, also, are the property of the landlord; the price of the seed for planting is equally borne by both; and for all extra labour in making improvements, such as building dykes, or cutting canals, or reclaiming waste land, the tenant receives wages. The net product of the farm is equally divided between them. This old system is destructive of all agricultural progress. The tenant lives from hand to mouth, and from season to season. His object is, by exploiting the land, to get from it its utmost every year; and having no capital, and being dependent for his living on the season's crops, he cannot afford to make experiments which look to the future, or to expend money upon betterments, though they promise to quadruple the value of his labour hereafter. Each season must pay for itself. He distrusts new courses, and becomes stolidly fixed in the old way; and his method of cultivation is precisely what his ancestors' was a thousand years ago. Of course the land, rich as it is, revenges itself upon the farmer by producing comparatively small crops; and, unable to support himself and his family on the fair profits of his industry without the closest economy, and sometimes not even then, he falls in debt to his landlord and is driven to dishonest courses in order to make up the deficiency. This same system prevails in Tuscany; but after a careful observation of it for years, I am persuaded that it is injurious to the landlord, the tenant, and the land. The proof that the system does not work well is clearly shown by the fact that, while land on lease returns generally five per cent. on the capital, land farmed out on a *mezzeria* contract rarely yields more than two and a half per cent. The result of this system is that the tenant spends as little as he can, allows no fallow time, scarcely manures at all, and impoverishes the land by his processes of exhaustion.

The plan of leases on fixed rents prevails on the Agro Romano; but the advantages which might thereby accrue to farmers are in great measure frustrated by the fact that the farms are so immense that only a wealthy agriculturist can afford to hire them. The Agro Romano is reckoned to contain about 550,000 English acres, and is divided into farms varying from 1,200 to 3,000 acres: some are, however, very much larger; and the famous farm of Campo Morto numbers no less than 20,000 acres, and is rented at some fr.25,000 a year. Of course such farms as these can only be hired by persons of large fortune; and accordingly we find that the vast Agro Romano is rented by only about 40 farmers, who, under the name of "*Mercanti di Campagna*," form a corporate body protected by government, and favoured by monopolies and special privileges. Meantime the smaller farmers, whose means do not enable them to pay such heavy rents, are forced to betake themselves to the marshes and the mountains, where they adopt the *mezzeria* system, and are crushed by it.

A curious crop of figures grows on the dominions of the Pope, at which it may be interesting here to give a glance before we look at the material products of the Campagna. The population of the Roman States is 3,124,668, and of these no less than a third part are cultivators and shepherds, while there are only 258,872 engaged in manufactures, and 85,000 in commerce, and affairs, and banking. That would look as if the great interest of Rome was agricultural, and, in fact, more than a million are shepherds and persons connected with farming. The *Catasto* of 1847 values at 870 millions the rural property under the Papal rule, without calculating the Province of Benevento; but the *Ministro dei Lavori Pubblici*, noting the fact that they cost less, values them at 610 millions. If this capital returned a good income, as it might under proper cultivation, there would be no need of great state loans; but in point of fact we find that the *gross* product of this capital is only fr.272,847,086, or ten per cent.; while in countries far less rich in soil and natural advantages, as in Poland, the gross income of the agricultural interest is at least double, or 20 per cent. on the capital. The consequence is that the state is saddled with a heavy public debt, on which the annual interest is 25 millions of francs: that debt, too, is constantly increasing. In 1857 a loan was negotiated with Rothschild of fr.17,106,565, and between '51 and '58, the government issued fr.3,000,000 of consolidated funds. It is a curious fact also, that may be noticed in this connexion, that the cost of foreign occupation by the French troops during the last ten years has exceeded the total expenses of the administration of justice by some 5,000,000 of francs, and amounted to more than six times the sum expended upon public instruction during that period.

The total number of landed proprietors in the Roman States is reckoned in the Census at 208,558. The Agro Romano, however, is held by 113 families and 64 corporations; six-tenths of it are in mortmain of the Church, three-tenths belong to the princely houses, and only one-tenth is the property of all the rest of the state. In the Province of Rome there is reckoned to be a population of 1,956 proprietors to about 176,002 inhabitants; that is, about one in ninety. Of the 550,000 acres of the Agro Romano, then, it seems that the corporations and princes, 177 in number, own 495,000 acres, or an average of 2,800 acres each; while all the remaining proprietors, amounting to 1,779, own only 55,000 acres; which gives to each an average share of about 3 acres. The mortmain of the priests gradually absorbs the free lands of the state at the rate of about 400,000 *scudi* a year.

In the provinces distant from Rome, and more out of reach of the Church, the proportion of landed property held by the people is far greater. Macerata, for instance, counts 39,611 proprietors in a population of 243,104; but here the farms are divided and cultivated on the *mezzeria* system. It is, however, only directly beneath the influence of the Church that agriculture languishes and dies.

The "*Mercanti di Campagna*," who are generally men of large fortune, hire the land of the Agro Romano from the Church and the princes. The Church, of course, does not pursue agriculture. The strong, able-bodied, fat, and healthy *frati*, numbering in the Roman State no less than 21,415, are an army of idlers, not of labourers; they do not spade and dig the earth, and plant and reap —"they toil not, neither do they spin"—nor probably was Solomon ever arrayed like one of them; but they carry round a begging basket to the farm-houses, or lounge through the vineyards and fill it at the expense of the owner, or lend the assistance of their countenance and conversation, and proffer a pinch of snuff to the hard-working mountaineers who live by the sweat of their brows. They give assistance after the fashion of one of the coast-guards of the Grand Duke of Tuscany, who, in a written report of a ship-wreck which had occurred during the night close to his station, stated: "I lent every possible help to the vessel with my speaking-trumpet, but, nevertheless, many corpses were found dead the next morning on the shore."* As the fashionable regiment of light-horse in the English service was reported to have once said, "The Tenth don't dance"—so "The Church don't work." It amuses itself with letting others work. It will not even dig up its own convent cabbage garden, but hires this labour to be done while it looks on. It naturally follows that it does not devote itself to the cultivation and tillage of its great Campagna farms.

The princes are a little in advance of the Church in their attention to agriculture. Some of them raise herds of cattle, breed horses, and pasture flocks of sheep on a part of their great domains. But the greater portion is let out to the "*Mercanti di Campagna,*" who take it on long leases, pay good rents, hire companies of *contadini* from the mountains to plough, till, sow, and reap, and finally, despite the taxes, put a large overplus into their pockets at the end of the year, and rapidly amass great fortunes. When the lease is long, the *mercante di Campagna* introduces reforms to some extent; builds barns, cuts canals, and drains and improves the land. Sometimes he visits the estate, but he never lives on it or personally superintends operations. This duty is left to his steward or *fattore,* who oversees everything, keeps the accounts, hires the peasants, and conducts the entire business of the farm. He is the "*imperium in imperio,*" and his word is law. He sometimes inhabits the great, grim, solitary *casale* with the head herdsman, who takes charge of the flocks of sheep or droves of cattle and horses, and they both almost live in the saddle. In the stable are generally a number of horses, ill-curried and rough-looking enough, but gentle, strong, and capable of enduring great fatigue, which are kept solely for their use. Armed with a musket or long-pointed pole, with a great green-lined cloak swinging from their shoulders, or buckled to their antiquated high-peaked saddle, the *buttero,* herdsmen, and cattle drivers may be seen galloping here and there over the plains with the *fattore,* and driving before them herds of cattle, their heads surmounted by a peaked black felt hat, their legs cased in solid leathern gaiters or leggings extending to the knee, and their iron-nailed shoes armed with long-curved rowels, that they plunge into their shaggy horses. Left to himself for the most part to organize affairs on these great farms, to make up accounts, and to purchase and sell, the *fattore* has a large liberty, and the *mercante's* eyes must be sharp indeed, or the *fattore's* skill slight, if he be easily detected in lopping the profits off at both ends for his own private behoof.

In like manner the Church leases to the *mercante di Campagna*

* "Ho prestato tutto l' aiuto possibile colla tromba marina—ma però, molti cadaveri erano trovati morti sulla spiaggia la mattina seguente."

the vast plains and valleys belonging to its various convents and ecclesiastical corporations. He takes the land naked, and supplies tools, cattle, labourers—in a word, everything needed for agriculture. But the Church is suspicious, and adheres to the established orders of things. It will not allow pasture land to be broken up into tillage and sown with grain, for fear that the land may be thereby impoverished; and the consequence is that the same ground is continuously subjected to the same treatment. As a general rule the arable land never goes to fallow grass; the pasture land is never broken up by the plough. Besides this, there is another great difficulty. By the canonical law leases of land belonging to the Church are prohibited for a longer term than three years. The *mercante*, if he could take the land on a long lease, would willingly lay out his capital on betterments of every kind, which would in the long run be advantageous to him and to his landlords: but on a lease of only three years he cannot afford to lay out much money in this way; for not only would his immediate profits be thereby diminished, but his subsequent rent would be increased. Most of these ecclesiastical lands are without the necessary barns and outhouses for the protection of cattle or the storing of hay and grain. These, of course, the *mercante* cannot afford to build on a three years' lease, and the good *frati*, penny wise and pound foolish, absolutely refuse to do this for him on the ground that they must look out for themselves and not for their successors. "We have no children to inherit from us," they say; "we are only a corporation of celibate priests. If the profits feed us during our life-time it will suffice us; and after us, chaos." This lack of proper barns for the cattle exposes the tenant to constant loss. Against the snows and icy blasts of winter, the rains of late autumn, and the fierce heats of summer, there is no refuge for his herds. They deteriorate, grow thin and sick; the cows yield a milk which is inferior in quality as well as quantity; as beef they are injured for the market, and many die in consequence of exposure. The hay, too, with which they are fed in the winter, must be carried to them and heaped upon the ground, and much is therefore trodden under foot and wasted.

A system like this is fatal to agriculture. It is like attempting to carry water from the fountain in a leaky bucket. Nothing is done on large principles; everything is effected by temporary expedients, and hand-to-mouth contrivances. No new inventions are introduced, no new experiments are tried, but all drags on in the old rut. The priests are so stupidly wedded to their system that it is impossible to change it, and so ignorant and bigoted in their doggedness, that they are open to no reasoning and argument. If the tenant desire to open canals for irrigation during a dry season, the priests cry out that this is flying in the face of Providence, who sends all the rain that is needful; and if the harvest be ruined in consequence of their obstinacy, they look upon it as a penance which it would have been irreligious to attempt to avoid. In the ten years previous to 1855, from want of proper shelter on the Campagna, it is estimated that the loss of cattle was from twenty to forty per cent.

Nothing can be ruder than the agricultural implements used by the Romans and Tuscans. The ploughshare is a triangular block of solid wood, pointed at the end and generally, though not always, armed at the point with a sheathing of iron. To compare it with the antique plough as described by Virgil would be an insult to the latter. In construction it is evidently more primitive and simple even than that of its antique progenitor. Two huge grey oxen, on whose yoke a heavy stone is hung to counteract its false strain and jerking leaps, slowly tug it along over the soft loam, the surface of which it scarcely scratches, while the *contadino*, blazing and dripping with perspiration, hangs all his weight on to the tail, and is knocked here and there sideways and sprung into the air constantly by its awkward and jerking plunges when it meets a root or stone. Slow enough is the progress of the plough and poor enough the result. One horse with a good American plough would do more and better work in an hour than this will do in three. As for a subsoil plough, the Roman agriculturists know as much about it as they do of the implements used in the planet Jupiter. All their tools are equally bad. Their spade is a triangular blade of iron with a long straight pole set into it without a handle, with which they can make little entrance into the ground. For all deep digging they employ a heavy mattock, shaped like a large blunt adze, which they use like a pick, wasting three-quarters of their force and their time in raising it over their head. It is melancholy and ludicrous to see them toiling with these wretched and inefficient implements, when they might save so much time, money, and strength by the use of tools which are universal in America. But in Rome there is no knowledge in respect of agriculture and no desire for improvement; nor do I believe there is a single utensil employed, even on the farms of gentlemen, that would not be jeered at by the most ignorant American labourer. As for sowing, and reaping, and mowing machines, the knowledge of their existence has never penetrated into the Papal States—agriculture has made no progress there since the days of the Georgics. The same usages, the same superstitions, the same implements still exist. Throughout Tuscany and Rome, little basket-carts, woven of stout osiers, and mounted on low wheels which turn upon wooden axles and scream as they go, may be everywhere seen, identical with the "*plaustra*" represented in ancient *bassi relievi*. It is not surprising that the ignorant *contadini*, who have no knowledge of what is going on in the world beyond the narrow limits of their own district, should adhere blindly to the old customs which have been transmitted from age to age; but it is amazing that the "*Mercanti di Campagna*," who are generally men of energy, ability, and education, instead of seeking to enlighten their minds, and of introducing proper agricultural implements and insisting upon their use, should make common cause with the *contadini* in their ignorance. This at least was not to be expected of them.*

I am well aware of the steady face which the Papal government sets against all improvements; but this is not a sufficient excuse for the continued use of tools and methods of cultivation rejected by all intelligent farmers. Efforts have, however, within a few years, been made to turn the public attention to agriculture as a science. Animated by a good spirit, certain landed proprietors demanded permission of the government to found an Agricultural Society; but it was refused, and their only method of arriving proximately at their end was by appending an agricultural branch to an already existing Horticultural Society. Under cover of this they have instituted an annual show of cattle and horses in the Borghese Villa, for the best of which they distribute medals of gold and silver. This is certainly a step in the right direction.

The principal products of the Campagna are hemp, grain, oil, wine, silk, and cattle. The vineyards are cultivated with care, but the crop is doubtful and the wine ill made, and in the best seasons the returns are inadequate. Within the last few years the grape malady has been felt very severely, and many a small vinegrower has been utterly ruined. But behold how this paternal government cares for its children! While the people are groaning under this

* In Tuscany an effort has been made of late years to introduce improvements in farming utensils, and to promote the study of agriculture. Societies have been formed for this purpose; and among the gentlemen who have taken a lead in this direction may be mentioned the Marquis Luigi Ridolfi, Count de Cambray Digny, Prof. Cuppari, Dr. Gustavo Dalgas, and Dr. Francesco Carega. Under their supervision, and edited by Dr. Carega, an "Annuario Agrario" is now published, full of instruction: but as yet little impression has been made on the country by their labours and counsel. The *mezzeria* system is repugnant to all improvements.

misfortune, Cardinal Antonelli seizes the occasion to lay a tax of 1,862,500 *lire* upon the grapes; and in default of payment by the vine-growers, this heavy tax is inflicted on the Commune. The wool being short, the shepherd shears into the skin.

The taxes upon agricultural products are heavy: all grain harvested from the Agro Romano pays 2¼ *scudi* the *rubbio;* which, as the *rubbio* is worth from 8 to 10 *scudi*, averages about 22 per cent. on its value. Everything grown upon the land pays an export duty of 22 per cent. and an import duty of 16 per cent. Cattle also are taxed to from 20 to 30 per cent. on their value, and 28 *lire* per head is demanded when they are driven to market. Horses also pay 5 per cent. of their cost every time they are sold, and this tax is paid by the buyer unless there be a special agreement to the contrary. Besides this, a regular tax of half a *scudo* a month is exacted upon all horses kept in the city.

Strange as it may seem, though nearly one-third of the population is engaged in agricultural pursuits, yet the government steadily discourages agriculture. By monopolies, improper privileges, heavy taxation, short leases, and dogged opposition to all improvements, it oppresses the farmer and peasant, and by the reaction of this oppression, injures itself. But it is upon the poor that this unwise policy lays the heaviest weights. Were a stimulus given to agriculture, were the lands of the Campagna under full cultivation, wages would rise, the people would begin to prosper and grow rich, the products of the country increase, and the state be lifted at once out of debt. But could the influence of the priest make head against the education and prosperity of the people? That is the vital question.

" One of the most striking features of the Campagna is the herds of cattle which are bred there, and roam over its hills and valleys. The oxen are estimated to number about 150,000, and magnificent beasts they are, with their soft greyish-white skins that, when well cared for, shine like silk, their enormous spreading horns measuring five and six feet in width, and their large soft eyes that Homer thought it no shame to give to Boöpis Here. They are as docile and obedient as they are majestic and powerful; and adorned with scarlet ribbons or bands, as they slowly drag along the heavy wains, no one could fail to notice them for their beauty. The *contadini* are very proud of them and treat them with the utmost kindness. With their natural love of colour they twine around their horns the wild flowers they pick along the road, and on *festa*-days deck them in wreaths and scarlet tassels and ribbons. The cows, when well stabled and protected from the weather, give abundant and rich milk; and the bulls, prodigious in their massive shoulders and knotted knees, would be no easy victories in a Spanish arena. Their horns, polished carefully, are sold in Rome as ornaments, to be placed over the doors as a protection against the evil eye; and, whether they subserve this purpose satisfactorily or not, they are beautiful enough in themselves to need no excuse of utility.

Buffaloes may also be seen in herds here and there. These beasts are still more powerful than the oxen, and are used to do all the hardest work. With their brutal low heads and turned-up snouts, their short-angled legs, wiry coats of shaggy hair, and rugged semicircular horns, they present a very savage aspect; but, though sulky, they submit to training, are very sagacious, and will drag enormous loads. Their eye is strangely melancholy and pathetic, and has the look of a creature which mourns over its unhappy lot, and sorrows at its own ugliness. But, though ugly, they are eminently picturesque; and tugging along through the hoof-deep sand of the coast, their rude carts laden with marble, travertine, or stone, under tall stone-pines that lean back from the constant strain of sea gales,—or wallowing up to their belly through the grass of the Pontine marshes —they form a very striking feature in the landscape. In these marshes they are used at certain seasons to clear the canals of the reeds, flags, and aquatic plants with which the summer has choked the stream. Driven into the water and urged on by drivers on either bank, who goad them with long poles, they stumble through the weeds, tearing them up with their breasts and hoofs, and sometimes with only their head and snout above water they snort along, blowing like hippopotamuses, and dragging with them tangled masses of grass that cling around their horns and broad black noses.* But though generally under control, their original savagery will sometimes break out under great irritation, and they will attack their drivers and trample them to death if they can get at them. All along the outer walls of Rome, at regular intervals, little pens are railed off with strong beams to afford refuge to any pedestrians in case they may chance to meet a drove of buffaloes or of oxen.

The flocks of sheep on the Campagna are estimated to amount to some 600,000. They are tended by shepherds, who, in their pointed hats adorned with gay cords and tassels or the eye of a peacock's feather—their short jacket of undressed sheeps' wool— their red waistcoats patched and faded—their breeches of goats' skin with the long shaggy hair hanging from them—their skin

* Mr. Rudolph Lehmann has made this scene the subject of a very clever picture.

sandals and *cioci*, laced over cloth under-leggings, which serve instead of stockings, are the modern type of old Pan. At their side they carry a yellow gourd of water, and in their pocket is stuffed a black wedge of bread and a few onions to lunch upon. All day long, leaning upon their poles which they plant diagonally before them, and spreading out their legs so as to form a tripod, they stand watching the herds, or gazing vacantly into the air, or going fast asleep. A great white dog of the St. Bernard breed always accompanies them. He is as intelligent as his master, thoroughly knows his business, and does all the active duty; keeping guard over the sheep, driving them here and there, preventing them from straying, and directing them in all their courses. So savage are these dogs that it is always well to be armed with a good stick in one's excursions off the main roads into the heart of the Campagna; for, in case the shepherd be out of the way, or asleep, they will instantly attack any one who approaches too near the flock. The sheep follow after the shepherd, and are not driven before him; and at nightfall, after his dog has gathered them all together, he leads them to their fold. It is a picturesque sight to see them then, all flocking along over the Campagna, with the shepherd marching gravely at their head. The fold, which is moveable, and pitched now in one spot and now in another, is made of a network of twine, stretched upon stakes planted at equal distances in the ground, and about three feet in height. It is the same sheepfold as that which was used in the Cæsars' time, and in an ancient *basso relievo* at Ince Blundel one of these "*retia*" may be seen inclosing some goats and pigs. The dormitory of the shepherd is a rude *capanna*, made of thick matted straw and sticks, just high enough for him to creep into on his hands and knees. There, on a straw bedding, over which he spreads his blanket, he sleeps. Sometimes, in case there are several shepherds, these *capanne* are built into a lofty cone, and here they cook their food and live together in a manner ruder than the American Indians. If you visit them you will find the warmest hospitality, and a native courtesy and good-breeding, without loss of independence of character, which no amount of oppression has been able to crush out of them. They are very ignorant, but delighted to learn, and look with wonder on all you say. Cicero they know by name; Julius Cæsar is an established fact; they are acquainted with St. Ovid, and they swear by Bacchus; but France, America, and England are nowhere in their imaginations, or loom vaguely up out of the distance like misty dream-lands. Rome is to them the world, the Tiber the king of rivers, and the Gran Sasso d'Italia their topmost Himalaya peak. They are glad, however, to hear that in England and America there are cities, and always ask whether there are mountains and rivers, with a certain air of patronage.

Some influence certainly falls upon them from the outward world in which they live; and they both love and appreciate the beauty of their own Italy. They will point you out the best views, freely criticise your work if you happen to be an artist, and often use poetic and imaginative phrases in speaking of nature, which show their native susceptibility to fine impressions. The old Roman pride, all overgrown with superstition and the rank growths of ignorance, still shows itself in their characters, as the cornices of the old temples peep out from the grasses and acanthus leaves and weeds in which they are buried. They would not change their country for any other in the world, and they look upon us as barbarians, or, at least, as coming from a barbarous, insignificant, and inferior world. Two of the *contadini* of one of the mountain towns near Rome, seeing an artist at work painting a picturesque lichen-covered rock, came up to him, and quietly looked over his shoulder. From his dress they took him for an Englishman, and, after having satisfied their curiosity as to his painting, one of them broke silence by saying to his friend, "*Non ci hanno sassi in paesaccio loro?*" (Have they no rocks in their miserable country?) "*Sassi ci sono, ma non c'è il sole*" (Rocks there are, but there is no sun), was the contemptuous answer.

The shepherds who come from the mountains are a very fine race of men, physically, and make admirable soldiers or bandits. In the army of Napoleon they were among his best troops—firm and courageous in battle, and faithful and enduring under the severest trials. Marco Sciarra, one of the most famous banditti chieftains of modern days, was an Abruzzese, and so was the well-known "Fra Diavolo."

As the summer comes on, the great heat renders the Campagna unhealthy for man or beast, and the sheep are driven to higher levels and cooler pastures among the mountains. Those who remain pay for it by the fever, and their flocks suffer even more than they.

A very considerable number of horses are also bred on the Campagna, and it is not unusual to see as many as three hundred collected together on one farm. Of late years much attention has been paid to their breeding, and attempts have been made to improve the breed by crossing them with imported horses; but thus far the result has not been satisfactory. The Roman horse is large, sturdy, and capable of enduring great fatigue; and in their power of withstanding the heat of the climate they are vastly superior to the

English horses, which it has lately become the fashion to import. Crossed with the English horse, the mixed breed becomes lighter and slenderer of figure, and therefore better for the saddle; but in harness it loses some of the best qualities of the native race. It deteriorates in stamina and endurance, becomes more fastidious in its feed, lengthens in the loins and fetlocks, and loses the iron hoofs which are the priceless gift of the real Roman horse. In this last particular the Roman horses excel all others, and such is the hardness of their hoofs, that it is the universal custom in Rome to leave the hind feet unshod, and only to shoe the fore feet with *demi-lunes*. As the pavement of Rome is made of a very hard volcanic stone that easily polishes, and as the city is built upon hills and declivities, a horse which is ironed on all his feet is liable constantly to slip and fall, and his value is greatly diminished if his hoofs will not resist the pavement without irons. For this reason alone the English horses are of less value in Rome than the native breed, and no one who does not wish to risk a sudden fall will trot an English horse, shod on all his feet, round the city.

Several of the Roman princes have interested themselves of late years in the breeding of horses, and among them may be named the Princes Doria, Borghese, Piombino, and Rospigliosi. Their breeds are, however, for the most part a cross of foreign and native horses, and, though handsome in figure, do not enjoy so high a reputation for strength and stamina as the pure Roman horses bred by some of the principal *mercanti di Campagna*. Among those who have been most successful in producing vigorous and noble native animals are the Signori De Angelis, Floridi, Piacentini, Serafini, Senni, and Titoni, and the Societies of Cisterna, San Pietro and Viterbo. Of the horses of mixed breed, those of Polverosi and Silvestrelli are considered as the best. The horses bred by Prince Borghese and Prince Piombino are gray in colour and of an average size; but the huge black horses which are used by the cardinals and *monsignori* to drag their lumbering gilt coaches are native horses, chiefly bred by Signori Floridi and Senni, and by the Society of San Pietro.

The Romans leave their horses entire, and have not the barbarous and absurd practice of docking the tail that is so frequently seen among the English and Americans. On the contrary, their massive tails and manes are left of their full length, and are esteemed as a great beauty. It is a universal practice here to brand the horses on the thigh, and sometimes on the shoulder, with the initials of the breeder's name, and, if he be of a noble family, with a coronet, so that the horses may be always identified.

The horses seen in herds on the Campagna are for the most part the mares—unbroken colts, or *poledri* as they are termed. The latter are generally left wild to roam about over the plains, all summer and winter, without shelter of any kind except what they can find under the trees. A huge *pilone* or receptacle for water is alone provided for them, and sometimes when the rains or the cold has utterly destroyed the grass, hay is scattered here and there in heaps for their sustenance, one half of which at least they tread into the mud and destroy. In this wild state they see nobody save the *buttero* or driver with his long pole, who visits them to guard against accidents. On the principal farms some fifty colts are bred every year. When their third year is past, the drivers go out together to catch them, as if they were wild animals. Approaching as closely as they can, and driving another horse with them as a decoy, they endeavour to drop over their heads a stout simple head-stall, which they extend on a long pole, and which is so constructed as to adjust itself at once and entrap them. This process is, however, often unsuccessful, and in case the horse they wish to catch is wild they have recourse to the lasso, which they are skilful in flinging over their necks. The colt thus caught is now dragged or driven home, and fastened to a stout pillar in the centre of a field, and his training begins; often, however, the colts are brought into the city and there broken.

I have never seen horses better trained than those at Rome—more completely in hand, more thoroughly docile and obedient—and I have almost never been eyewitness during many years' residence to any cruel treatment, or immoderate and passionate punishment of them. On the contrary, I know of no country where, on the whole, they are so well cared for or so kindly treated. The ferocious and unmanly beating to which they are often subjected in America and England is here almost entirely unknown. A "*mozzo*" always sleeps with them to guard against any accident at night. The stables are generally well ventilated and large, and they are never boxed up in narrow stalls to stifle with stench and heat as in that purgatory of horses an American livery stable. The Romans are never guilty of over-driving their horses. They are satisfied with a slow sure pace, and value bottom far above speed.

The goats are also a peculiar feature of the Campagna. These beautiful animals with their long white silken hair, yellow slanting beady eyes and snowy beards, may everywhere be seen leaping about among the ruins, mounted on broken walls, or cropping the hedges, and peering through them at you as you pass. They are large and generally of a yellowish white, though occasionally you may see black ones mixed among them. Every morning flocks of them are driven or led into the towns, where they may be seen crouching in the streets, while the goat-herd sells their milk fresh from the udder to his various customers, who come to the door and call for him. By ten o'clock they are all driven back to the Campagna, where they stray about all day long, forming picturesque groups among the ruins for the foreground of pictures.

Beautiful as is the Campagna, one cannot but mourn over the losses it has suffered. The great mother of nations has many dead children. The ancient cities and towns which once were scattered about on the plain around the eternal city have all vanished. Etruscan Veii, the great rival of Rome, was obliterated even in the days of Hadrian, so that its very site was forgotten, and only a few fragments and ruins show where it once flourished. Where, too, are Gabii, Fidenæ, Antemnæ, Sutri, Laurentum?—

> "Scis Lebedos quid sit? Gabiis desertior atque
> Fidenis vicus."

Where are the fifty nations which Pliny enumerates as belonging to early Latium, thirty-three of which were within the compass of the Pontine marshes? These vast meadows and grassy slopes now pastured on by cattle and sheep, and waving here and there with grain, were once thronged by cities, towns, villages, and villas. "And these," says Dionysius, "were so closely compacted together that if any one looking towards Rome should estimate its size with his eye he would be greatly deceived, nor would he be able to distinguish how far the city extends or where it ceases to be city, so are the buildings of the city and the country linked together without a break, and stretching out to an infinite length." *

There are great differences of opinion as to the population of Rome during its imperial days. According to Dionysius, it amounted to 84,700 in the time of Tullus Hostilius when the first census was taken. The population of Rome was, however, largely increased by the Albans, when Alba was conquered by Tullus Hostilius; and under Ancus Martius the cities of Medullia, Politorium, Tellinæ and Ficana, with all their inhabitants, were annexed. The census, it must be remembered, excluded from its total sum of *capita*, every slave, "*filius familias*," single woman and orphan—besides a large number who were struck from the register for unworthy conduct of any kind, and only included freemen who were Roman citizens. The numbers given on the tables of the censors therefore afford us only a proximate estimate of the real number of people in

* Dion. Halic. Antiq. Rom., lib. iv. ch. 13.

Rome. The city vastly increased during the period of the Republic and under the Cæsars, swollen by streams of people who poured into it from all sides as to a centre; so that, according to the estimate of Tacitus, the Roman citizens in the reign of Claudius amounted to no less than 6,000,000.

This, of course, embraced the whole number of Roman citizens existing throughout the provinces as well as in Rome. Taking this as a basis, and "after weighing with attention every circumstance that could influence the balance," Gibbon comes to the conclusion that there must have been in the Roman Empire "about 120,000,000 of persons,"—a degree of population which possibly exceeds that of all Europe, and forms the most numerous society that has ever existed under the same system of government. If we accept this statement and admit that the centralization of Rome was anything like that of London in 1820, we shall have as a result, that Rome and its suburbs contained about six millions. Whether, therefore, the statement of Tacitus be taken as applied to the total inhabitants of Rome and its suburbs, or to the Roman citizens throughout the world, the conclusion is about the same. But when this census was taken the population was by no means at its height in Rome. It continued to increase to the days of Aurelian. If, therefore, we reduce this calculation one-third, we still have no less than four millions of inhabitants in Rome and its suburbs; and this is the number at which, among others, the learned Justus Lipsius estimates it, after a long and learned examination of the question. It can scarcely be deemed that the centralization of the city of ancient Rome was extreme: it was as Athenæus calls it, an "Uranopolis," containing entire nations; into it the whole Empire poured; the walls of the ancient city were so embedded in it that they could scarcely be traced; and Pliny and Dionysius state, for a length of from ten to fifteen miles the Campagna was covered with so dense a mass of buildings that the city could not be distinguished from the country, the whole shore being crowded with houses. Let us add to this that the term Rome was applied, like that of London, not only to the city itself, but to all the adjacent towns which it had swallowed up; that the streets were very narrow and the houses of an extreme height, rising six and seven stories and perhaps more, so that Augustus was forced to fix 70 feet as a limit, above which they should not, for the future, be built; or to use the words of Cicero, "*Roma cœnaculis sublata et suspensa, non optimis viis, angustissimis semitis;*" and if we then take into consideration also the statements of Athenæus, of Vitruvius, Lampridius, Varro, Lucan, Claudian, and many others who speak of the size of Rome—or merely that of Pliny, who after describing Babylon, Nineveh, and Thebes, says that "if any one considers the height of the roofs, and forms a just conception of its size, he will confess that no city in the whole world could be compared to it in magnitude"—we shall perhaps come to the conclusion that this population of four millions, enormous as it seems, is not an exaggerated number to be contained in a city called by Martial—

"Terrarum dea et Gentium, Roma,
Cui par est nihil et nihil secundum."*

Within a century of the conversion of Constantine, Alaric swept down with his desolating hordes from the north. Genseric followed him, and then came Ricimer, Vitiges, and Totila; and not only no grass grew under their feet, but palaces, temples, houses, villas, aqueducts, crumbled to ruin and dust before them. The whole northern portion of the Campagna, over which the stream of barbarians poured, is utterly razed of its buildings, so that scarcely a vestige now remains of those closely populated streets described by the ancient historians as extending even to Ostia. Here and there is still to be seen a broken bridge tangled and buried in luxuriant weeds and ivy, or the shattered foundations of some ancient villa, but these are rare. Over their ruins the dust of centuries has gathered, and they are hidden from sight beneath smoothed mounds of grass. The old Etruscan cities along the coast are utterly gone; and the Roman cities founded on their ruins have also so entirely disappeared that their very sites are now disputed by antiquarians.

After the irruptions of the barbarians, Rome sank into desolate silence. Then Nature itself frowned upon her in her degradation of Popes and Anti-popes, and scourged her with calamities. Earthquakes shook over the plain, the Tiber rose not to "mantle her distress," but to increase it with destructive inundations. Famine and pestilence depopulated her more than even the sword of the barbarian. The Popes and Anti-popes, fighting for supremacy with the German emperors, or disputing with each other for their succession, had no time to lend her a helping hand. Everything rotted rapidly and crumbled away. Then came the bitterest of all her scourges, the Normans under Robert Guiscard, who ruthlessly laid waste the city itself with fire and sword, demolishing the splendid remains of antiquity, and carrying ruin everywhere. What was left undone by them was completed by the soldiery under the Constable De Bourbon in 1527, whose ravages were worse than those of Genseric and

* See Appendix for a fuller discussion of this question.

Totila. Desolation followed his footsteps over the Roman ground, and monuments of his barbarity stand everywhere on the southern side of the Campagna. The great Roman families made fortresses of the tombs and monuments of their ancestors, and the Popes tore down the splendid remains of Roman Empire to build out of their *débris* hideous churches. Adrian I. destroyed the Temple of Ceres and Proserpine to erect the ugly church of Sta. Maria in Cosmedin. Paul V. overthrew the entablature and pediment of the Forum of Nerva to make a fountain on the Janiculum, and took the last column of the Basilica of Constantine for the statue of the Virgin in the Piazza Sta. Maria Maggiore. The Colosseum was used as a quarry for the stones of the Barberini Palace. The brazen plates of the Pantheon were melted into the grotesque *baldacchino* of St. Peter's. The Farnese Palace was built by plundering and destroying the Theatre of Marcellus, the Forum of Trajan, the Arch of Titus, the Temple of Antoninus and Faustina, and the Colosseum; and Urban VIII. threatened to tear down the tomb of Cecilia Metella because he wanted its blocks of travertine. The church and the nobles vied with each other in the work of destruction, and Rome suffered more from them than from the barbarians.

After such treatment as this the only wonder is that anything now remains. That the splendour and size of Ancient Rome was not a boast, the fragments and bones of her gigantic skeleton still existing on the southern side of the Campagna is an ample proof. Wherever we step a ruin arrests the eye; wherever we dig we strike the foundations of villas and tombs.

The destruction of the villas and habitations about Rome, the desolation of fields and gardens, and the annihilation of agriculture entailed a terrible evil upon Rome. The malaria stalked in the footsteps of ruin, and rose like a ghoule out of the graves. Looking at the ruins which are scattered everywhere about, and considering how thickly the Campagna was once populated, it is impossible to believe that in the early days of its prosperity it was stricken by this malady, which now renders it unhabitable. Why should these noble villas have been built there if the malaria then existed? Is it possible that the wealthy Romans should have chosen the Campagna in preference to all the mountain districts as a site for their country-houses if in so doing they risked their health and lives? Or it is not more probable that the fever which now threatens it is an evil spirit evoked in later days by neglect and abuse?

Listen to Pliny. "Such," says he, "is the happy and beautiful amenity of the Campagna that it seems to be the work of a rejoicing nature. For truly so it *appears in the vital and perennial salubrity of its atmosphere (vitalis ac perennis salubritatis cœli temperies),* in its fertile plains, sunny hills, *healthy woods,* thick groves, rich varieties of trees, breezy mountains, fertility in fruits, vines and olives, its noble flocks of sheep, abundant herds of cattle, numerous lakes and wealth of rivers and streams pouring in upon it, many seaports in whose lap the commerce of the world lies, and which run largely into the sea as it were to help mortals."

Compare this picture of the Campagna with its present condition. Nature is beautiful as ever, but the healthy forests are gone, and no one can now praise "the vital and perennial salubrity of its atmosphere."

As late as the middle of the 14th century, if we may trust to the expressions of Petrarca, the scourge of the malaria was unknown in some places which are now wasted by it. In a letter to the Cardinal Giovanni Colonna, written from Capranica, a little town some thirty miles from Rome, where he was detained by the dangers of the road for sixteen days, he says, " *Aer hic, quantum breve tempus ostendit saluberrimus.*" Yet this air now is very far from perfectly salubrious—what has brought about this change?

Cicero in his "Republic,"* speaking of Rome, says that Romulus chose a place for the city abounding in fountains, and healthy in a pestilent region. (*Locum delegit et fontibus abundantem et in regione pestilenti salubrem.*) In this passage he apparently refers to the Palatine, for there Romulus founded the city. But in point of fact the Palatine was in the days of Cicero not accounted peculiarly healthy, and was certainly less so than the surrounding hills, of one of which, the Esquiline, Horace speaks as "*Esquiliis salubribus.*" Indeed, it was on the Palatine that a temple was consecrated to the Goddess of Fever, which plainly indicates that it did not enjoy the reputation of being peculiarly healthy. He must, therefore, probably have intended to refer to the whole city as it existed in his day, and to have meant by the pestilent region about it the Pontine marshes. This is rendered probable also by a previous passage in the " Republic," in which he says that the position of the city was selected "*incredibili opportunitate,*" a phrase he would not probably have applied to a city immediately surrounded by a pestilent plain, into which it could not extend itself.

Besides, we have every reason to believe that the Agro Romano was not in his time pestilential. Strabo, who wrote in the reign of Tiberius, speaks of the delight with which the Romans frequented the Latian coast, and of the many villas they built there for summer residence, and cites as unhealthy places only the suburbs of Ardea, Lavinium, Antium, and a part of the Pontine marshes. Yet this

* De Rep. lib. xi. s. 6.

unhealthiness could not have been very great, for we know that Antium was a most important town, and that the whole district around it, and down as far as Ostia, was covered with villas, where the Romans of wealth and position went to pass their summer months. Here were the famous villas of Mæcenas and Cicero, and, in a letter to Atticus, Cicero says that he finds his residence here delightful, and that the inhabitants are men of cultivated minds and prefer their native city to the metropolis. Here, too, Lucullus, Lucretius, and Atticus often resided. Augustus was living here when he received his title of "*Pater Patriæ*." Here Nero was born, and here, after his return from Greece, he insisted on first celebrating his triumph before going to Rome. The importance of the place, and the class of persons who lived along this shore, is attested by the remarkable remains of art which have there been discovered, among which may be mentioned the Fighting and Dying Gladiators, the Apollo Belvidere, and a noble statue of Esculapius. Agrippina the younger had a villa here, with delightful gardens extending down to the sea. Hadrian, too, had a magnificent palace here, as well as on the plain under Tivoli; and here came Antoninus Pius, Vespasian, Commodus, Septimius Severus, and, in a word, nearly all, if not all, the emperors up to the time of Constantine. It is difficult to believe that "with all the world before them where to choose," they should have voluntarily selected a spot to live in which was peculiarly unhealthy; and we are forced to the conclusion that this coast, now so stricken with malaria, must once have been wholesome. As it is now, who would pass the summer months there?

There is not, perhaps, a more pestilential spot anywhere near Rome than the neighbourhood of Ostia, where stretch the grand pine forests of Castel Fusano. The place is now almost uninhabitable. Yet here, or in this vicinity, Pliny built his famous Villa Laurentina, where he sometimes spent the summer, and of which he says, "*Hæc jucunditas ejus hyeme, major æstate.*" Nor was he alone in this taste. The shore was crowded with villas, so as to present the appearance of a series of cities: "*Litus ornant varietate gratissima, nunc continua nunc intermissa tecta villarum, quæ præstant multarum urbium faciem, sive ipso mare, sive ipso littore stare.*"* Indeed, it was to Laurentum that the emperor was counselled by his physician to betake himself during the summer, so as to avoid a pestilence then raging at Rome—a plain indication that this was then considered as a peculiarly healthy place.

Alsium (now Palo), again, is now so desolated with fever that no

* Letter to his friend Gallus.

one who could avoid it would willingly pass a night there. Yet this was precisely the spot where Julius Cæsar, Pompey, and Marcus Aurelius built their villas and passed the summer months, and Fronto speaks of it as a place of delights.*

In face of these facts, it is difficult to contend that the Campagna of Rome was considered by the ancient Romans to be unhealthy. Fever and ague there undoubtedly were in some places, but not to such an extent as to render even these uninhabitable; and in general the very fact that the Campagna was covered with villas and houses of the rich seems clearly to show a different condition of healthiness from that which now exists.

There can be little doubt, also, that the climate of Rome has greatly changed since its ancient imperial days. Snow, which now very rarely falls at all on the Campagna, and never in such quantity as to cover it, or to be visible for more than an hour or two, used formerly to fall to a considerable depth, and to remain long on the ground. Pliny† speaks of the long snows as being useful to the corn, and Virgil, Livy, and Horace mention the freezing of the rivers, a phenomenon now unheard of.‡ Pliny also says that the bay would rarely live without shelter through the winter, either at Rome or at his villa at Laurentum.§ Nor, if we may trust Fenestrella, was the olive cultivated until the time of Tarquin.‖ This seems surprising and almost incredible, when we think that now the olive and bay are everywhere seen; and that so far from their not being able to resist the climate, even roses bloom in the open air all the year round in Rome. It becomes, however, quite intelligible, when we read of the severe frosts and snows of ancient times, and hear that in the winter of 355 the Tiber was choked up with ice, the snow lay seven feet deep where it was not drifted, and many men and cattle perished in it; and that not only the fruit-trees were destroyed, but many houses were crushed by the weight of the snow upon them.¶ St. Augustine also gives us an account of another year when the snow remained forty days on the ground, and trees perished, cattle died of hunger, and wolves, emboldened by famine, came into the streets of the city, and dragged a dead body out in the Forum, where the snow was very deep. Martial also mentions that in his time a child was killed by a piece of ice which fell from the portico of Agrippa. These, of course, were exceptional winters

---

* Fronto, i. 179. † Hist. Nat. xvii. 2.
‡ See Daines Barrington, 58 vol. Philosoph. Transact.; Gibbon's Miscel. Works, vol. iii. p. 246; Livy, v. 13.
§ Epist. ii. 17. ‖ Plin. Hist. Nat. xv. 1.
¶ Livy, v. 13; Dionys. xii. 8, Fragm. Mai.

even then, but it may be fairly said that they would be unheard-of phenomena now.

Many are the theories propounded to account for the malaria which now prevails over the Campagna. It is asserted by some to result from want of ventilation: the mountains shutting off the wholesome northern winds which would purge the dead air of the plains, and blocking up the exit of the *scirocco* which blows over it from the open sea. But this was always the case. Some attribute it to the exhalations and miasma generated from the ground itself; but it is difficult to understand how this can be, since the land is by no means low and marshy, but, on the contrary, rolling, hilly, and dry in the greater part of its extent. Others, again, allege that the great forests, which were held sacred by the Romans, and served as a barrier to the Pontine marshes, being now destroyed, the miasma generated there is blown by the winds over the healthy portions of the Campagna, and infects it with contagion. But even here on these very marshes Pliny tells us that there were once no less than twenty-three cities, and we learn from Livy that they were portioned out to the Roman people and cultivated by them, and looked to as the resource of Rome in times of scarcity. Camillus, too, fixed his camp on these very plains in his war with the Arunci in B.C. 405. These facts prove that the Pontine marshes, now considered so deadly, were then so innoxious that an army could with impunity encamp upon them. An army which should try the same feat there at present would be decimated in a day. How did it then happen that the Romans could do this? Simply because the plain was populated and cultivated. Wherever there is a thick population, and the air is well stirred and beaten, the malaria disappears. In the low, dirty, damp Ghetto, which the Tiber inundates on the least rise of its waters, fever and ague are rarer than in any other part in Rome, simply because the people are more crowded together. Great grain fields feed upon miasma—it is their sustenance. The beaten-up ground becomes purified by tillage; it is only when left utterly to itself, encumbered year after year with dead and rotting vegetation, that it generates miasma.

But these great Pontine swamps, which cover no less than 13,000 acres, are now left to stagnate in the sun. Over their soft slimy bottoms herds of buffaloes, stags, wild boars and porcupines run, and their green and "gilded pools" are only troubled by wild ducks and geese, marsh birds and water snakes. Here and there are solitary pot-houses, and around them groups of fever-stricken *contudini*, gaunt, sallow, and shaking in the sun, tell the sad tale of the malaria. Yet the road lies over a beautiful country. Grand mountains look softly down upon it. Tall poplars stretch out and out for miles, and this infected air is sweet to breathe as if it had the very elixir of Hygieia in it.

The restoration of the Pontine marshes to their pristine condition now looks hopeless. They can only be conquered by the united assault of a mighty army of labourers, backed by government and enforced by millions of money. It is of no use to attempt reclamation on a small scale. Those who attempt it will be sacrificed without any beneficial result. But if any army of 100,000 labourers could be turned into it together, and directed by science, without regard to the prime expense, the foul fiend who shakes his foggy mantle of fever over the country might be driven out of his stronghold. But the first efforts should undoubtedly be made on the Agro Romano, for then the result would be quicker and surer.

Despite all the different theories by which the malaria has been accounted for, it seems to be agreed on all sides that the true remedy is cultivation, drainage, and population. The Church, persuaded of this, has at divers times made short and efficient efforts in this direction. Boniface VIII. in the 13th century made the first attempt to restore health to Rome by draining the Pontine marshes. His example was followed by Martin V. and Sextus V., but it was not until Pius VI. put his hand to this good work that anything effectual was accomplished. He laid out on the canals and drainage no less than 1,622,000 *scudi*, and certainly vastly improved by these noble labours the health of all the adjoining districts. The Campagna also felt the beneficial influence; fever manifestly decreased, and has ever since continued to retreat with every new step towards cultivation. Pius VI., not satisfied with his work, ordered somewhat arbitrarily, but with a clear understanding of the case, that 20,000 *rubbie* should be annually cultivated on the Agro Romano, intending to bring it all by degrees under tillage. In this design he found a worthy successor in Pius VII. This Pope traced around Rome a circle of one *kilomètre*, which he commanded the proprietors to cultivate. Beyond this, another and another circle was to be made, until the whole Campagna, brought into complete cultivation, should "blossom like the rose." Groves and woods were to be here and there laid out to render the air wholesome and fend off the bad winds. But he died before the second circle was drawn. The marsh of bigotry and ignorance is not so easy to drain, and his great project was never advanced a step by his successors. The 16,000 *rubbie* he reclaimed have shrunken under Pius IX. to 5,000, and everything is going the old pig's way—backward.

Leo XII. also laid out a vast plan of operations, which, had it been carried into operation, would have changed the whole aspect of the Campagna and of the Roman world. He proposed to transport into this uncultivated district a population of 100,000 labourers, who were to be divided into a hundred bands. The proprietors of the Campagna were then to be ordered to deliver over their lands to a company, on long leases, the government guaranteeing the revenue thereof. But this scheme met with violent opposition, and sectarian fears and jealousies rendered its adoption impossible. One part of the state could not be depopulated to furnish labourers for another portion. The import of a hundred thousand Protestants was not to be thought of, and the difficulty was to find such a number of voluntary emigrants from any Catholic country. They might perhaps have been collected from France, Germany, and the Swiss cantons; but diplomatic jealousies intervened, and this great enterprise was abandoned.

The present condition of the Campagna finds favour, however, in the eyes of some Catholics. The Abbé Gerbet, in the introduction to his elaborate work, "Esquisse de Rome Chrétienne," in speaking of these noble efforts of Pius VI. and Leo XII., finds consolation for the failure of their schemes in words which deserve quotation:—
". . . Je crois qu'il est moralement utile que des foyers de population avec tous les mouvements qu'ils entraînent, surtout dans notre siècle, ne se multiplient pas aux portes de Rome. . . . Il ne faut pas raisonner de Rome comme d'une autre ville; les convenances sont d'un ordre tout à fait à part. La ville théologique a besoin comme un monastère d'avoir autour d'elle un enclos paisible; la ville hospitalière qui tient à offrir à toutes les grandes infortunes, à celles du cœur comme à celle du trône, une retraite pleine de majesté et de tendresse, la ville des ruines, qui n'a pas seulement des musées, mais qui elle-même est un musée gigantesque, serait très-mal à l'aise, très-sottement assise dans l'atmosphère enfumée et bruyante de Birmingham ou de Manchester. . . . Il ne faut pas tout mesurer de l'utile matériel, même dans l'empire de la matière. L'industrie qui a le globe devant elle pourra bien se passer de bouleverser, d'une manière irréparable, le parc de Rome. Le monde est grand—et Rome est unique."

Such is the poetry with which learned abbés settle the great question of the industry of a people.

CHAPTER XIV.

MARKETS.

UNDER the shadow of the Pantheon is the principal market of Rome. It is held chiefly in the open streets leading from the Piazza della Rotonda to the Piazza St. Eustachio, the meats being exposed for sale in little booths planted against the walls of the houses, or a little in front of them, where they are swung upon hooks under their awnings or spread upon sloping counters. These are generally made of wood, though marble slabs are now beginning to take their place. All the arrangements are shabby in the extreme, and there is not much picturesqueness to make up for the want of nicety. The boards on which the meats are laid are swashed constantly with water, and swept with wet brooms, so that all "above board" is really clean, however it may look; but below, the booths are grimy with a thick paste of water and dust, and floating down and feathers scattered by the wind about the market here find a resting-place, and lie heaped in the corners or plastered on the posts. Yet under these most uninviting benches beggars at night make their bed upon these feather couches—nay, more, this was the familiar resting-place by night of a "holy man" who, within a few months, has received the honours of beatification in the Catholic Church. I beheld the splendours of that ceremony in St. Peter's, when thousands of candles were lighted, and prayers were said, and masses were chanted, and books were circulated in his praise; and in answer to my inquiries as to his history, I learned that he was remarkable for a most amiable and charitable disposition, and for extreme personal filthiness; that he never changed his clothes, and generally slept under the benches in the market; that he begged all day in the street, gave the money to the poor, and never washed; and that if the "odour of sanctity" was in his person it was not an agreeable odour.

Until within a few years there was no special place set apart for shambles in Rome. The cattle were driven into the city in herds, and slaughtered by the butchers at their shops. The Campagna oxen and buffaloes are not a gentle race of beasts, and driven along by the *butteri*, who pricked and goaded them on with long pikes, they sometimes became enraged and made fierce onslaughts upon persons who happened to be passing. Inside the city every one retreated into some shop or *portone* when he heard the ringing of the *bufalaro's* bell announcing their approach; but outside, under the walls, there was no resource but to turn on your heels and flee, unless you chose to run the risk of your life. The *mandriani* and *butteri* who guided them did their best with long poles and pikes to protect the unfortunate passer, but the herd, irritated by dust, heat, and fatigue, and pricked by pikes, sometimes lowered their horns and made furiously at him. To afford a refuge for those who were thus caught, pens of stout planks were set at intervals around the walls, and herein one could be safe from their attacks. Any one walking round the walls will still see them, and sometimes even now will gladly avail himself of them when an accidental herd is driven by. Pope Leo XII., among other admirable works for the improvement of Rome, prohibited herds being driven into the city or slaughtered there, and established public shambles outside the Porta del Popolo, where all the cattle are killed to supply the market. But this enlightened Pope was cut short in his career, with many noble projects unfulfilled, and the circumstances of his death, to say the least, arouse very ugly suspicions. Certain it is that Monsignor Peraldi, in view of those circumstances, proposed that henceforward, upon the death of any Pope, a thorough examination into its causes should be made obligatory on the government, adding, that by this means the sacred college of cardinals would avoid the necessity of so frequent elections.

But though living cattle are not now driven into the city to be slaughtered, their carcases, piled into carts, are to be frequently seen passing through the streets. Generally, however, they are brought in a covered cart, not particularly inviting in its aspect, and driven by a butcher in a dirty frock stained shockingly with the colour of his trade.

In the market itself you will see the carcases of pigs, calves, goats, and sheep, strained across the door of the butchers' shops in all their ghastliness, and these are often spotted here and there with fragments of gold leaf and tinsel to attract purchasers. The shambles outside the walls are only for cattle, smaller animals being frequently killed in the interior of shops, almost within the reach of any eyes that pass.

In the market, no attempt is made to keep the disagreeable parts of the animal out of sight. The Italians do not seem to think any part is disagreeable. Horrible scarlet blood puddings, enough to frighten a delicate stomach out of a week's appetite, are ostentatiously exhibited to catch the eye, and all the insides are hung about the market, or grouped together, as if they were the most attractive of things. There is in their minds nothing which is refuse. Every part is kept and finds its purchaser. The subdivision of even the poultry is also a curious feature of the Roman market. You need not buy the whole even of a chicken, but any part you like will be sold separately, be it liver, gizzard, breast, wing, leg, or head. Even the combs of the poultry are sold by themselves, and when cooked whole or cut up in pieces in little *vol-au-vents* form a constant dish on the Roman tables.

Through all the streets of the market you hear the cackling, gabbling, crowing, and screeching of cocks, hens, turkeys, ducks, and geese: some of these are kept in pens, some packed in great baskets covered with net-work, some run about and guzzle in the gutters, or step daintily round to pick up what they can find. Beside the booths are seated men and women who are busy plucking these unfortunate creatures, and cramming their feathers into a great basket. As soon as one is thoroughly plucked, he is blown up so as to look of an amazing obesity, swung on the hook for sale, and another unsuspecting victim is seized from his companions, and at once converted by a summary process into meat.

The Roman market is rich in game of all kinds. Here may be seen the brown rough hide and snarling snout of the wild boar, the smooth "leathern coats" of slender deer, and the black and white quills of the "fretful porcupine." Here too are many varieties of feathered game—brilliant pheasants, partridges and ducks, hundreds of woodcocks, quails, thrushes, larks, sparrows, ortolans, *beccafichi*— in a word, flying creatures of every size and appearance, from the wild goose to the smallest and most familiar garden bird; for there is nothing an Italian will not shoot, and nothing he will not eat. In the latter respect he is the very cousin of "Poor Tom"—not even despising such cheer as the combs and legs of cocks, and even cats, frogs, "rats, and such small deer."

You fear that I am stretching a point—but I am not. The cat is here esteemed a delicacy among the lower classes; and if you happen to own a particularly large and fat one, you must keep a sharp look out, or you will lose it. Entering the studio of an acquaintance once, I found his workmen in an excited state gathered about the corpse of an unfortunate cat, which had paid the penalty of its life merely for indulging a natural curiosity to behold the interior of a sculptor's studio. An animated discussion was going on as to which of the hunters should have the body after it had suffered the fate of Marsyas. "But what do you intend to do with it?" I innocently asked. "*A mangiarlo, sicuro*" ('To eat it, of course), was the instant answer. "*E un cibo eccellente*" ('Tis an excellent dish).

But to return to the Roman market. At a few paces from the streets where meat is sold, you will find gathered around the fountain in the Piazza della Rotonda (for so the Pantheon is called by the people of Rome) a number of bird-fanciers, surrounded by cages in which are multitudes of living birds for sale. Here are Java sparrows, parrots and parroquets, grey thrushes and nightingales, redbreasts, yellow canary birds, beautiful sweet-singing little goldfinches, and gentle ringdoves, all chattering, singing and cooing together, to the constant plashing of the fountain. Among them, perched on stands, and glaring wisely out of their great yellow eyes, may be seen all sorts of owls, from the great solemn *barbagianni*, and white-tufted owl, to the curious little *civetta*, which gives its name to all sharp-witted heartless flirts, and the *aziola*, which Shelley has celebrated in one of his minor poems:—

> "Sad Aziola! many an eventide
> Thy music had I heard
> By wood and stream, meadow and mountain-side,
> And fields and marshes wide,
> Such as nor voice, nor lute, nor wind, nor bird,
> The soul hath ever stirred:
> Unlike them, and far sweeter than them all.
> Sad Aziola! from that moment, I
> Loved thee and thy sad cry."

And many a night listening to them, as they called plaintively to each other over the Sienese slopes, have we all remembered Shelley, and quoted his words.

The principal fruit and vegetable market of Rome is held every Wednesday and Saturday in the Piazza Navona, and on these occasions it presents a most animated, picturesque, and characteristic scene. Hundreds of booths and stands of every description are then erected, and into the lap of this capacious piazza the Campagna and kitchen gardens pour their treasures. The way is everywhere blocked up. Heaps of delicate crisp lettuces and celery, enormous cabbages and pumpkins big enough to make Cinderella's carriage, creamy cauliflowers, bristling artichokes, clusters of garlic and onions, red tomatoes, and monstrous red and yellow fingers of beets and carrots, are tumbled on to the pavement. Huge baskets run over with potatoes, yellow *cocuzzi*, and infant pumpkins or *zucchette*, and, in a word, with every one of those vegetables of which Cav. Marino proposes in his Fischiata to weave a garland in honour of Murtola.* In some of these baskets may be seen dried mushrooms, of which the Italians make great use in the winter, and excellent truffles to cause the epicure's mouth to water. These grow in great quantities in the country round Rome, and especially at Spoleto, and used to be very cheap before the French bought them up so largely for the Parisian markets. Here and there great cauldrons, where one or more of these vegetables are boiling, pour forth their unsavoury steam; and beside them heaps already cooked are lying for sale. At certain seasons, these cauldrons bubble with hissing oil, into which chopped vegetables and fritters are dropped and ladled out all golden, and garnished with fried pumpkin flowers, upon shining platters. Here, too, sacks gape with wide mouths, and show within them thousands of the great brown Roman chestnuts. All the winter long little portable furnaces smoke wherein they are roasting, to be sold at twenty for a *baiocco*, and many an old wife sits by " with chestnuts in her lap," whose husband, perhaps, has " to Aleppo gone, master of the Tiger." If you would really know how good these roasted chestnuts are, split them and eat them hot with a little butter and salt.

In the summer, as we pick our way along, we run constantly against great baskets of mushrooms. Here are the grey *porcini*, the

* " Honor dell' insalata, inclite herbette,
Rose vivaci, cavoli fronzuti,
Lupin, poponi, baccelli gusciuti,
Finocchi forti ed acetose agrette,
Rustiche e grosse rape, alme zucchette,
Porri ritorti, carcioffi barbuti,
Agli spicchiuti, torti e ben gambuti,
E carote vermiglie e ritondette,
Tartuffi incitativi e signorili,
Radici lunghe, branche e tenerelle,
Spinaci oscuri, e capperi gentili,
Melon a volta, malve e mercorelle,
Ceci, baccelli, e voi cicerchie umili,
E tremule e crinite pimpinelle,
   Voi saporite e belle
Mente, scalogni, cipolle scorzute,
Voi crispe indivie, e lattughe costute,
   E voi zucche panciute,—
Tessete voi la laurea trionfale
Onde ne faccia il Murtola immortale."

foliated *alberetti*, and the orange-hued *ovole*; some of the latter of enormous size, big enough to shelter a thousand fairies under their smooth and painted domes. In each of these baskets is a cleft stick, bearing a card from the inspector of the market, granting permission to sell them; for mushrooms have proved fatal to so many cardinals, to say nothing of Popes and people, that they are naturally looked upon with suspicion, and must all be officially examined to prevent accidents. The Italians are braver than we in the matter of eating, and many a fungus which we christen with the foul name of toadstool, and ignominiously exile from our tables, is here baptized with the Christian appellation of mushroom, and eagerly sought for as one of the cheapest and most delicious of vegetables.

The fruits are as plenty as the vegetables. Apples, pears, plums of every size and hue, nectarines and freckled apricots, peaches, lemons, and oranges abound. Early in the spring you will find baskets heaped with green almonds, which are to be eaten, shell and all, and great quantities of the little high-flavoured wood strawberries, which are brought in fresh from the gardens morning and night, and are sold at from five to six *baiocchi* the pound. The apricots, cherries, and plums, too, are particularly good, and are very cheap. Here, late in the winter, hang great clusters of delicious grapes strung on a thread, and all the late summer and autumn loll out of over-heaped baskets to tempt the eye and the palate. But the most popular fruit is the water-melon. As long as it lasts, in every piazza in Rome, you will see dripping wedges of it ranged along on stands and sold for a half-*baiocco*. The Piazza Navona is its head-quarters. Here heaps of water-melons are piled up on all sides, like great green bomb-shells, and near by each is a bench, behind which, flourishing a long sharp knife, and shouting "*Belli cocomeri—cocomeri belli, chi vuole*," at the top of his voice, stands a man who tosses them in the air, raps them with a sharp fillip, and then slicing them into even wedges, spreads them on his bench. Who can refuse them as they glow there, fresh and juicy, the black seeds spotted on their rosy flesh? Flies, bees, and wasps pursue them with pertinacious avidity, and in the intervals of sale the *bagarino* has his hands full in driving away these creatures with his busy wisp. Around the bench are constant customers—thirsty, heated men, who wipe away the perspiration from their foreheads, and seizing the rosy wedges, plunge their faces into them, until the juice spurts and drips over the pavement. Flinging the rind to the ground, he seizes another, while a dirty little scamp secures it, and gnaws away the faint pink edge he has left down into the green.

The people care far more for the water-melon than for the grape. They make parties out of the gates to eat them, and cannot restrain their appetites at the sight of them. At the time of the cholera, several years ago, when the government prohibited them from being brought within the gates, for sanitary reasons, the Romans murmured and growled more than if a tax had been laid upon them. One remedy there was—they could eat water-melons outside the city, and there they poured in crowds to devour their favourite fruit. In one of the companies of "come outers" was a stout athletic carter, who, as soon as he had left the Porta Portese, bought two water-melons and sliced them up, and slipping one wedge into his mouth, cried, "Sir Cholera, will you let me eat this slice of water-melon? *Via, via*—Come, come, Sir Spiteful, this one slice?" This finished he seized another, and cried, "Just one more, Sir Cholera, and long life to you! And this one more still because, '*sai*,' it's so particularly good—and this one more for the sake of your beautiful phiz—and this, for the whiskers of the doctors who have given you your passport for Rome." And thus with a new salutation to each slice, and amid the laughter of his friends, he ate the whole of both the water-melons. But that night he was carried to the *lazzaretto*, and the next day to the cemetery.

The next greatest favourite to the water-melon are figs. Of this luscious fruit, which grows in great quantities all around Rome, there are many varieties—green, yellow, purple, hyacinthine, and almost black. They are brought into the market heaped up in baskets, and set out on the benches of the Piazza di Navona for sale. There you will see the *zuccaiuoli, garaoncini, calavresi, brogiotti, castagnuoli, pisinelli, grasselli, zuccherini, lardaiuoli, verdini,* and *dottati*; and of these the best are the *brogiotti*, a large purple fig; the *dottati*, a long, light-green fig; the *zuccherini*, a small, flat, and very sweet fig; and the *verdini*, which is a late fig with a green skin and carmine in the inside.* There are two crops of figs on each tree. The first, which ripen in July, and are called *fichi-fiori*, or flower figs, are little esteemed and have not much flavour; but the second figs which ripen later, though smaller, are far richer and better. When the latter are ripe, in September, the Roman people gather in the evening in the Piazza Navona to enjoy their fig-feast, or, as they

---

* The ancient Romans knew many other figs; and in his Saturnalia, Macrobius, on the authority of Cloatius, enumerates no less than twenty-six different kinds,—called *Africa, albula, arundinea, asinastra, atra, palusca, angusta, bifera, carica, caldica alba, nigra, Calphurniana, Chia, cucurbitina, duricoria, Herculanea, Liviana, ludia, leptoludia, Marsica, Numidica, pulla, Pompeiana, precox, Tellana,* and *atra*.

call it, the "*Magnata de' Fichi.*" Parties of five or six unite together, purchase one of the great baskets, and, seating themselves round it, make very short work of its contents. First they select the ripest fruit, the thin silken skin of which looks as if it had been scratched by a cat, and is sticky with the rich juice oozing through its rents. These they swallow at a mouthful without peeling them. Then come the poorer figs in succession down to those which are young, thick-skinned, and milky round the stem. After this a glass of *aqua vitæ*, or a *fiasco* of red wine, is taken "for the stomach's sake." It is wonderful what quantities a true Roman will eat at one sitting. A not uncommon meal for a peasant is his hatful, and on these special occasions more are eaten than I should like to say. Of all fruits, however, there is none more easy of digestion than figs, and the *magnata* is seldom followed by any after-pangs under the ribs.

And here let me advise travellers, and particularly invalids, who come to Rome to pass the winter, to have their cooking done in their own houses, and not to live on dinners sent in from *trattorie*. The market itself is capital. Mutton is not esteemed by the Italians, and is not generally good; but lamb is excellent, and so are kid (*capretto*) and beef; and no better pork and veal can be found in the world. Rome has been always celebrated for its game; wild boar (which should be cooked with an *agro dolce* sauce), woodcocks, hares, snipe, and quails (which in the season cost only five *baiocchi* apiece), not to speak of thrushes, larks, and *beccafichi*, are very plentiful and cheap. *Capriuole* (roebuck) are also to be found, and there is no better eating. Nor is there lack of fishes; as, for instance, the *spigola*, mackerel, and red mullet, lobsters, and crawfish, as good as can anywhere be found; very fair shad from the Tiber, fresh delicious sardines, millions of little *alicetti* which closely resemble whitebait, and are nearly as good; and *sepie*, which are not to be scorned when well-cooked; and besides, there are legions of the fish that Cleopatra put on the hook of Anthony, of the first quality. I know that it is the common talk of the English, that there are no fishes worth eating in the Mediterranean; but I am not of that opinion; and I remember, only a short time since, hearing one ruddy Englishman at dinner deliver a long discourse on this subject, during which he declared that the finest fish, in his opinion, in English waters was the red mullet, "which is not to be found in the Mediterranean," he added; and at that very moment there was a dish before him filled with red mullet, which he had refused to take because it was only a "Mediterranean fish." He who would eat a truly Roman dish of fish, should go to the Palombella, or some other *osteria* in the Trastevere, and order a "*Zuppa alla marinara.*" When it comes on to the table he will scorn it, and with a laugh, will timidly taste the first spoonful; but, fifty to one, he will send back his plate to be helped a second time, admitting that, "after all, it is not so bad." In this connexion let me also recommend the little salted anchovies, called "*alici*" or "*acciuge,*" which—split, cleaned, and put for an hour or two under oil and vinegar—are an excellent whet to the appetite, and are eaten by the Italians immediately after soup.

But whoever has regard for his palate or his health should not for a long time live on dinners furnished from *trattorie*. It is undoubtedly less troublesome and cheaper to have one's meals sent in than to cook them at home. The first week they will seem excellent for the price. Then they will begin to fall off in quantity and quality. You will complain to the *traiteur*, and he will promise to do better. Gradually, however, you will lose your appetite, and nothing will taste good to you; and, finally, your stomach will be out of order, your system in general not quite right, and you will begin to accuse the climate and the market, when the fault is really in the *trattoria*. My advice, then, is not to depend on a *trattoria* for any length of time; and you can follow it or not, as you please. How is it possible that a dinner can be furnished from a cooking-house, which shall at once be cheaper and better than that which you can cook at home, and also give a profit to the *traiteur?* The meat, though it may be good, can never be of first quality; but the sauces, the soups, the gravies, the condiments, what must they be? This is an unpleasant question to ask; but after three months' experience your stomach will answer. You will be a less agreeable person than you were when you first came to Rome; will enjoy the churches, ruins, galleries, and climate less, and will probably betake yourself to blue-pills if you are English, and think it necessary to go to Naples for a change of air. What you really want, however, is not a doctor nor a change of air, but a cook and a change of kitchen.

Besides the booths of vegetables and fruits which are to be seen on market-day in the Piazza Navona, there are many others on which are spread old books, the off-scourings of libraries and auction-rooms, among which may sometimes be found very curious and valuable works. Mostly, however, they consist of old theological works in folio and quarto, bound in vellum and well-thumbed and greased; odd or imperfect volumes, school-books with which the fingers of dirty boys and girls have had more to do than their eyes, pamphlets, effete treatises on scientific subjects, old prints and designs torn from books, histories of the wars of Napoleon, and sheets of costumes and outlines of Roman history by Pinelli. Around these are groups chiefly composed of fathers of families, who come to purchase the second-hand school-books, and priests who pour over the others by the hour. If there happen to be a curious or rare book, it is snapped up early in the morning by the priests, antiquaries, and proprietors of old libraries, who regularly come to market for this game, and have a keen scent. It is, however, quite common to find here copies of the classics and of quaint old Latin treatises of the 15th century, printed in the Italic type by the Venetians, which can be purchased for a *paul* or two.

In other booths there are all sorts of woollen and cotton cloths for sale, where women of the city or country are for ever chaffering with the Jewish seller and beating down his prices. In the winter all the market-women carry a *scaldino*, or little earthen pot filled with burning charcoal, which they place under their dress when they sit down, or carry about in their hands to keep them warm; and gathered round the booths they gesticulate violently with one hand while they grasp their *scaldino* with the other. Hats, too, of every kind may here be bought, and brilliant stamped pocket-handkerchiefs; and the *contadino* may be seen bearing his newly-purchased hat mounted on top of the old one, while his wife sturdily tramps at his side with a great new glaring handkerchief folded over her neck or worn as an apron.

More curious than these booths are the old rickety benches strewn with riffraff, which are planted here and there in the piazza. A miserable shaky old man generally tends them, and occupies himself in placing and replacing his wretched store of wares so as to attract purchasers. He has odds and ends of every kind for sale—old brass buttons, broken knife-handles, scissors ground down to almost nothing, odd steel forks, dirty old beads, bits of smashed cameos, old glass phials, rusty nails, fragments of locks, brass plates for keyholes, shattered candlesticks, old tooth-brushes—in a word, all the dirty, wretched riffraff which has been thrown away as useless. Among these things is always a little plate, on which are huddled together a quantity of old beads and fragments of cornelian. Look well at that, for in it you may find an antique *intaglio* of great value. You will not find it the first nor second time; but if you have patience and go as the antiquaries go, every market-day early in the morning, you will be sure, sooner or later, to be rewarded. The wretched old man who stands shaking behind the bench, with a bead-like drop at the end of his nose, does not know the value of his *intaglio* if he have it, and will willingly sell it to you for a *paul*. He has bought it of some ignorant peasant who found it in the Campagna, and was glad enough to turn it into a half-*paul*, or perchance he purchased it among a quantity of rubbish into which it had fallen. Some years ago, a poor priest was looking over one of these benches, and saw a large cut-glass bead which pleased his fancy, so he bought it for a few *baiocchi*, carried it home, and placed it among other little nicknacks on his mantel-piece: one day a friend came in and, looking over these things, he took up the glass bead.

"What is this?" he said, after carefully examining it; "and where did you get it?"

"Oh!" answered the priest, "that is a glass bead I bought some time ago at the Piazza Navona. It belonged to a chandelier, I suppose. Pretty, isn't it?"

"Glass bead!—chandelier!" cried his friend. "Why, *caro mio*, it's a diamond."

And so it proved to be, not only a diamond, but one of great value. If you wish to see it, you must ask the Emperor of Russia, to whom it now belongs, to show it to you. And I wish at the same time you would inquire what became of the priest, for I have been unable to learn his history subsequent to the discovery of the diamond. As he was in orders, he could not have married the emperor's daughter; otherwise that would have been the natural finale of his fortunes.

The time has gone by in Italy when masterpieces of Titian and Raffaelle, and gems and *intagli* of great value, were to be picked up for nothing. The world has opened its eyes, antiquaries and curiosity collectors swarm, and no little shop in the darkest street can conceal a curious or valuable relic for a long time from their prying search. Early in the mornings of *festa*-days, when the piazzas of Rome are thronged with peasants, they are to be seen slipping round in the crowd and inquiring for the *roba* that has been found by chance on the Campagna; and one must "get up airly," if he means to secure a prize without paying for it. There are doubtless opportunities for those who are on the alert, but they are not "plenty as blackberries." I am well aware that hundreds of "your Raffaelles, Coreggios and stuff" are annually purchased by my accomplished fellow-countrymen at a bargain, but clever men who have made Art the study of their lives, and who are "toiling all their life to find" them, rarely have the same good luck.

Gasparetto himself was something of an antiquary: he had rubbed against a good many foreigners, and was always on the alert to find some "curiosity" which should make his fortune. At last his time came. He was one day by chance in the palace of the Cæsars, when one of the peasants, whose occupation it was to work among the cabbage beds, showed him a treasure he had just unearthed. It was a little pocket spy-glass, covered with rust and bearing evident marks of having lain who knows how long in the ground. It was summer time, the peasant wanted money and could not wait for foreigners. Gasparetto pooh-poohed the thing, of course, as valueless, though all the while his heart beat fast; but he managed well, and at length secured the prize for a matter of two or three *scudi*. Fired with joy, he ran at once to one of his antiquarian friends. His face was beaming with an air of importance as he entered the shop, where several experts happened to be present. " *Che cosa di nuovo?* What news ?" cried his friend, for he saw that something of interest was coming. "Look," said Gasparetto, and showed his spy-glass. "Well?" inquired his friend, "what of it?" "That spy-glass," answered Gasparetto, "was found in the Golden House of Nero. Nero, as you know, set Rome on fire, and this may have been the very spy-glass he used to look at the flames of Rome. I will make my fortune out of it."

"Bravo! bravo!" was the shout of all present. "*Proprio un tesoro unico*—that is a treasure indeed!—the spy-glass of Nero! Don't sell it for less than a thousand pounds."

But do not laugh at poor Gasparetto—Jones himself was no better off. A short time ago he was remarking a singular mouthpiece, in which Mac, who is curious in such matters, was smoking his cigar. "It *is* singular," said Mac, wickedly, "and its history is wonderful. The original of this was found in an old Etruscan tomb on the mountains; it was made of gold, and probably was the mouth-piece in which some old Etruscan king once smoked his cigar."

"Gad! that is remarkable," said Jones; "what a wonderfully clever people those Etruscans were! they beat us at making everything! But how did you know it was a cigar-holder?"

"Oh!" said Mac, "we found the ashes in it."

If you wish to buy antiques or curiosities of any kind, it is as well to know something about them; so I would advise you to study up the matter before you trust your judgment. One other bit of advice I will give you—do your own bargaining, and don't trust your courier to speak for you.

"Bless me! that's a very fine picture, that Sibyl," said Robinson. "*Frangsaw*, ask the man there who painted it."

"He saysh it ish a Domenichino. You see von like him in Palazzo Borghese: dat ish copy, dis ish originale."

"It is a very fine picture, *Frangsaw;* ask him the price."

So *Frangsaw* turns to the dealer, and talks somewhat at length with him. The amount of the conversation is this:—

"Milordo wishes to know the price."

"Oh, the price? Tell him it's a very rare picture!"

"*Che! Che!* rare picture—what's the price?"

"Why, you see, I ought to have four hundred dollars for it, at least."

"Four hundred devils! I shall tell him no such thing. *Via*—what will you really sell it for? Don't talk nonsense to me; I know who painted it, and all about it."

"Well if you will get him to pay 300 *scudi*, I will let it go."

"And for me?"

"Well, for you—if you will get 300, I will give you 20 *scudi*."

So *Frangsaw* addresses his patron again:—

"He saysh, sir, he let him go, becaush you see he ish a friend of mine; he let him go for 400 *scudi*."

"But that's a very large price."

"Yash, sir, it ish; bot he rare picture—originale. I try make him give him 350 *scudi*."

"Yes, do, *Frangsaw*; tell him I'll give him 350 *scudi* and no more."

So *Frangsaw* turns again to the dealer:—

"He won't give more than 250, and thinks that is too much; but I can make him give that."

"*Troppo poco*—too little," says the rather depressed dealer.

"Nonsense, it isn't worth 100. Come, let us have it for that price. You never 'll get more."

"*Bene*—but you see then I only get 230, if I pay you the 20 *scudi*."

"Well, that's 130 more than it's worth."

So *Frangsaw* again comes to his master:—

"Well, sir; I beat him down to 350 *scudi*; he let him go for that."

"Tell him I'll take it, and tell him to send it to my house. Shall I pay him now?"

"No, sir; I come pay him when he give picture."

So *Frangsaw* makes out of both parties the little sum of 120 *scudi*; and Robinson is delighted to get possession of the original Domenichino, which a clever young Italian in the next street painted last year on an old canvas, and hung up his chimney to smoke and dry, and then ironed it out to sell; and Robinson says to all his friends who come to visit him in London: "Seen that Domenichino of mine? Magnificent picture! Got it at a perfect bargain. Came out of Cardinal Fesch's gallery. Worth five hundred pounds at least. You see, if you're only up to the dodge of it, you can get jolly good things for almost nothing. No use to buy modern pictures, and that sort of thing. Costs such an infernal price. Don't catch me at that."

But in the meantime we have strayed round the whole piazza, and stumbled over the old iron that is strewn everywhere in heaps, and wound in and out among the crockery, and earthenware, and glass, and smelt garlic enough to suffice for a week. But before we go let me tell you of a curious custom of the place, which is called, " *Il possesso di Piazza Navona.*"

Before any one can be admitted to the high honour of *bagarino* of this piazza, which enables him to peddle and sell at retail within its limits, he must have so distinguished himself by his sharpness in bargaining as to be entitled to the degree of *Dottore di Piazza Navona*. Throughout Rome this title is given by general consent to any one who is particularly plausible and slippery; but before he can exercise the functions of *bagarino* there, he must formally graduate and receive the *possesso* or "freedom of the piazza."

His investiture is a solemn ceremony. First he must agree to surrender his real name, and accept a nickname, selected by the "*sensali e capoci di piazza.*" These names are always descriptive of some peculiarity, either of person or mind. For instance, one long, lean, dried-up fellow goes by the name of *Baccala*—salt fish; another rough-bearded fellow is called *Orso*—bear; another, with projecting teeth, *Cinghiale*—wild boar; another, with a great round head, *Cocomero*—water-melon; and another, a little hunchback, *Gobbetto*. The women also have their names. There is the *Bianca*, the *Rossa*, the *Sermolina*, who sells lemons; the *Fringuella*, who sells endive near the theatre; and the *Ciliegia*, who sells beans, peas, artichokes, and tomatoes; all of whom are only known by these nicknames.

The induction to the "*possesso*" takes place on a *festa*-day, when the piazza is crowded. There is a tumultuous rushing of the crowd to and fro, and then suddenly above their heads, lifted on the shoulders of stout porters, you behold the figure of the *bagarino* who is to receive the degree of Doctor. Amid roars of laughter, cries of salutation, clapping of hands, and waving of handkerchiefs, he is borne along. After he has thus made the circuit of the fountain, two stalwart fellows leap on its rim, and one seizing the Doctor by the shoulders and the other by the feet, they give him three dips into the running stream, crying out, "*Cavaliere bagnato*," while the crowd shriek and yell, and beat iron pans, and shake their rattling balances, till the old piazza echoes with the din. This over, the dripping candidate for these high honours is placed astride the neck of one of the porters, who, holding him by the hands to steady him, bears him aloft in triumph, the crowd all whistling as he goes, to the steps of St. Agnese, where the senate of the Piazza Navona awaits him. A circle is then made about him, and the chief magistrate makes an oration to him, complimenting him in the name of his brethren, and finishes by saying :—

"The most noble order of go-betweens (*sensali*), pedlars, porters, fruiterers, vegetable sellers, ragmen, sellers of grain, old-iron mongers, earthenware sellers, and of all sorts of merchants of dried seeds and fruits, to-day, in their boundless magnanimity salute thee as their fellow-citizen, and establish and engraft upon thee the most exalted and praiseworthy appellation of 'Salt-fish.' Therefore be it known and ordained that henceforward, by all the matriculated order of the piazza, thou shalt be called no longer by the original name of Alessandro, but by thy substituted name of Salt-fish. In exchange thou shalt be Salt-fish ; in all sales, Salt-fish ; in all purchases, Salt-fish—and, *Viva* Salt-fish !" As he finishes, the cry of "*Viva* Salt-fish !" is taken up by the crowd and echoes all over the piazza.

Then comes the formal investiture of the *bagarinato*. One by one come forward the chief *sensali*, and present him in succession with a huge cabbage-head, a cauliflower, a bunch of endive, lettuce, celery, beets, and carrots; a handful of chestnuts, beans, lupine seeds, and chick-peas ; a platter of pears, apples, grapes, prunes, oranges, figs, and whatever other fruits are in the market; and finally the bystanders scatter over him a snow and hail of grains, small seeds, flour, meal, and barley, till his shirt, pockets, and throat are filled with the dust, and his hair is powdered with white and yellow.

Two heralds then proclaim with stentorian voices: "Salt-fish now takes possession of the Piazza Navona—clear the way !" and in a twinkling "Salt-fish" is seated on the topmost step of St. Agnese, and pulled by his feet down from stair to stair until he is landed, thoroughly bumped and sore, on the pavement of the piazza ; then he rises, makes a long salutation, receives a wild cry of applause, and in his new quality of *Bagarino, Dottore di Piazza Navona*, invites all his friends to drink with him at the Osteria del Pellegrino.

CHAPTER XV.

THE GHETTO IN ROME.

" Quid mereare Titus docuit, docuere rapinis
Pompeianæ acies, quibus extirpata per omnes
Terrarum, pelagique plagas tua membra feruntur.
Exiliis vagus huc illuc fluitantibus errat
Judæus—postquam patria de sede revulsus
Supplicium pro cæde luit, Christique negati
Sanguine respersus commissa piacula solvit,
Ex quo priscorum virtus defluxit avorum."
Prudentius, Apotheosis, line 538 *et seq.*

HEREVER the stranger takes his lodging in Rome, he will scarcely have unpacked his trunks before his ears are saluted by a peculiar cry, not frank, open, and given with the full force of Southern lungs, like the usual street cries, but suppressed, sorrowful, and seeming almost as if it came from some one in pain. It is a human voice, uttering some indistinct words in a high, monotonous, veiled tone, prolonged at the close, and dying down through a mournful chromatic into a final squeak or sigh. Vainly he endeavours to catch the words. He cannot match the sounds to any of the articles enumerated in his conversation phrase-book, which he has been steadily studying all the way from Genoa. Melancholy as the tones are, the voice at times seems to be calling out "*Appe ve*"—as if some sad and exiled cockney were announcing the fact that he (in the plural) is not so wretched as you might imagine,—and at times to be struggling to cry "*Roma Vecch—,*" as clearly as is consistent with a violent cold in the head and a decided thickness of enunciation which always cuts him short in his attempts.

"What's that?" cries our English friend; "I say, by Jove, there's a man crying out *Roma* something. I shouldn't wonder if that's a poetical way of offering models of the ruins," for he has heard a good deal of the poetical forms of speech used by the

Italians. Pleased with his own ingenuity, he rushes to the window to verify his supposition. Alas! the mystery vanishes, the poetry dissolves into very flat prose, the picturesque incident which would have made such a pretty text for the private journal he is writing for his friends is not at all worth recording. He sees below a very shabby, ill-dressed, and unpoetic person; sometimes with a superabundance of hats, and always with a lean gray sack slung over his shoulder, who slowly slouches and shuffles along the pavement, looking inquiringly up and down at all the windows. Now and then he pauses to utter his painful cry, straining out his head and neck, then stares at the houses on either side from garret to ground-floor, and if no responsive "*Pst*" is heard, indicating the possibility of a bargain, shifts his sack higher on his shoulder and shuffles on again. It is only a wretched old Jew such as you have seen a thousand times in London. But what is he crying?

Did you think, oh my friend, that he could not see you behind your half-closed blind? Those black, long-slit eyes were made to peer through crevices. They note you at once—an unmistakeable nose turns up (if such a nose can be ever said with propriety to turn up) in your direction, an interrogative finger is lifted, and a low, snuffling, submissive voice solves the riddle for you, and acquaints you at once with his profession, as he says clearly enough now, and rather confidently too, "*Roba Vecchia!*"—old clothes?

You are rather fierce at first, and answer the descendant of Moses with as much of a scowl as you can induce your curved eyebrows to make; but Mary Anne, who when this incident occurs is engaged in writing a long letter home full of hard statements against the Italians as a "nasty, dirty, cheating, miserable set"—her opinions being founded upon an extended acquaintance of three or four days with her courier "*Frangsaw,*" the porters at Leghorn, the postilions and beggars at Civita Vecchia and along the road, and the snuffy old servant of her *padrone di casa*—has a good laugh with you afterwards over the old Jew, and adds the incident to her letter in a postscript as characteristic of the stupidity of the Italians, "who really think that we have come abroad to sell our old clothes. Just fancy!" Let me, however, do Mary Anne justice. She does think Rome is "*so* nice," though it is "*so* nasty," and says it is "so jolly to have such lots of picture-galleries and churches to see, and the models on the steps are so nice, and it's so nice to have so much sun, and the ruins are so nice too, and everything is so nice, excepting, of course, the people, who are not nice at all: John says they are all 'a rotten old lot of beggars' here, and you know, Byron says, that art and men, and all that sort of thing (I don't exactly remember what the words are) fail, but nature still is fair. And so it is, to be sure. Just fancy!"

The poor old Jew meanwhile goes down the street. Shall we follow him into the Ghetto, where he will empty his sack of all the *roba vecchia* he has gathered, and after cleansing, scouring, shifting, turning, sewing, patching, changing, brushing, and renewing, will finally expose it again for sale, at a hundred times its cost, and twenty times its value. Shall we beard the Hebrew in his den?— the Moses in his stall? It is a curious place, I assure you, and well worth looking into.

The way is plain. You live in or near the Piazza di Spagna, of course. Take the Corso and go straight to the Capitol, thence through the Via de' Cerchiari to the Piazza Montanara, and you are on the very confines of the Ghetto. Let us pause here before entering. It is useless to hope to go straight to any place in Rome without being drawn a little out of the path we have proposed to ourselves, or stopped on the way by some object of interest which we cannot pass by,—and in going to the Ghetto you can scarcely avoid lingering a few minutes at least in the Piazza Montanara. Every Sunday you will find it thronged with peasants from all the mountain towns in the vicinity, who come down from their homes to labour on the Campagna. As they are generally hired by the week, they return to the city every Sunday to renew their old engagements or enter into new ones. This piazza is one of their chief places of resort, and Sunday is their day of 'change. Here they make their petty purchases, transact their small business, make merry together in the pot-houses, lounge about in the streets and sun themselves, and go to the puppet theatres, where there are at least two performances every day. Men, women and children, in every variety of costume, crowd the place, some with their rude implements of husbandry, some with the family donkey, on which they will return, "ride and tie," to the Campagna towards nightfall, making very picturesque "flights into Egypt" along the road, and some carrying their whole wardrobe on their head in a great bundle. Most of them are stalwart, broad-shouldered, and bronzed with the sun, but here and there may be seen the bleached, saffron face of one who has been stricken down by the fever and whose smile is pale and ghastly. The men are dressed in home-spun blue cloth, and wear on their legs long white stockings and small-clothes, heavy leathern gaiters strapped up to the knee, or the shaggy skins of white goats. As the cold weather comes on, a huge blue cloak with a cape is flung over the shoulder, and the peasant, firm as an old Roman, stands like a statue for hours in the piazza. The women are dressed in the vivid colours of their town, with scarlet bodices and snowy cloths on their heads, broad-shouldered, full-bosomed, straight-backed, large-waisted, and made to bear and to endure. Their faces beam with health like russet apples glowing in the autumn sun, and the circulation is decidedly good. So, too, is the digestion, if one judges from the appetite with which they eat their raw onions and salads, and bite great curves out of their wedges of black bread.

Here, seated in the open street, you will see a peasant holding under his chin a basin with a curved notch to fit his neck, from which the piazza barber is rubbing lather over his face with his hand, preparatory to reaping the thick black stubble of his beard. On the opposite side you will hear the snapping of scissors, where sits another peasant, whose round bullet-head has just been cropped close to the skin; or another, on whom the operation is now completed, and who, as he rises from his chair, passes his hand over his head with a grin of satisfaction, and puts on his new hat that he has just bought in the piazza.

At the corner of the piazza, in the open air, with a rickety table before him, on which are a few sheets of paper, and an inkstand, sand and pens, is the *scrivano* or letter-writer, who makes contracts and writes and reads their letters for them. He is generally an old man, bearded, and with great round iron-rimmed spectacles on his nose. Ah! into his ear how many confessions have been made, how many a declaration of passionate love has been whispered, how many a tender and affectionate phrase has been uttered for the ears of distant friends and lovers! Italian letters are almost invariably expressions of feeling or sentiment, and not, like English letters, filled with news and incidents, and descriptions of persons and places; and the memory of this old man has many a love romance hung up within its secret chambers that we shall never know. Look at that peasant girl, who, leaning on both her hands over the table, is dictating to him in a low voice, while a group out of ear-shot stand behind her patiently awaiting their turn. See! how the blood mantles in her rich brown face as she utters words which are to pass through his ears into the heart of her lover, far away in the mountains. Her heavy braids of blue-black hair shine in the sun, her great gold earrings shake against her neck, her bosom throbs against the stiff scarlet bodice, her lips are parted with an eager expression as she watches the trembling hand of the letter-writer (trembling from age, not passion), who mysteriously conveys to paper "the perilous stuff that weighs upon the life." An open letter on the table under her hand shows that she is dictating an answer to that.

What a picture it is, out there in the open air! what colour! what light and shade! what expression!

Or look at that young peasant behind, who turns over and over the letter he holds, vainly endeavouring to decipher the black mysterious lines that the old man will interpret for him into heartbeats from home as soon as he has finished the letter in hand. His face now illuminates, for the old man's task is done—he has folded the letter, sealed it with a wet red wafer, directed it, and given it to the girl, who pays him two or three *baiocchi*, and, saying to her friend "*A te*," turns away with a contented smile to run and drop it in the post.

Nor only this will you see. Sometimes, instead of smiles, tears —hot, burning tears—drop on that old rickety table. Death has been busy, a life's hope crushed,—and the old man's spectacles are dim with mist. He places his hand gently on the shoulder of the writer and says—"*Pazienza! Cosi vuole Iddio. Come si fa?*"

What a magic lantern that old man's memory would be to peep into! what comedies, farces, and tragedies, one might see on its shifting slides! Even the table itself, could it but speak, might thrill us with many a strange story and drama that has passed over its boards.

But our way lies towards the Ghetto, and we must not linger here too long. Look up! There are the giant remains of the once splendid and still famous Theatre of Marcellus, built by Augustus, and dedicated to his youthful nephew, "*Heu! miserande puer*," whom Virgil has immortalized in his verse. There still stand some of those magnificent Doric and Ionic columns, which Vitruvius and Palladio considered as worthy models of the best style of their orders. But a terrible change has come over them since the Augustan times. They are all built into the walls of the Orsini Palace, a huge, ugly, characterless structure, that frowns over the Piazza Montanara, and darkens along the narrow street. Halfburied under ground are the Doric columns of the lower story, and the rude doors of dark dirty shops, in which all sorts of riffraff are sold, reach nearly to the crumbling cornice. Windows, pierced here and there irregularly, mere holes in the wall, look out between the upper columns. The middle ages have overgrown and defaced the antique beauty. The theatre of the brilliant days of Augustus, has, in turns, become a feudal fortress and a barricaded palace, and finally yielded its lower stories to miserable shops and shabby lodgings. Yet even in its degradation it is one of the most imposing and picturesque of the Roman ruins.*

* Among the admirable photographs of Mr. Macpherson, of Rome, none is more striking than that of this Theatre of Marcellus.

Let us pass round this gigantic hulk that towers and glooms over the low, miserable houses near it, and we are in the Ghetto. We have entered, appropriately enough, into the Piazza del Pianto—the Place of Weeping—for sorrow and tears have been the heritage of the children of Israel ever since their splendid city was destroyed, and they were scattered to the four winds of heaven. On the very spot where we now stand, or within a short distance from it, this Roman colony of Jews have lived for more than eighteen centuries, despised and degraded—the pariahs of Europe and the Church. Through all the sad vicissitudes of these ages of ignominy, here they have clung with a pertinacity which is unaccountable. No savagery of persecution has been able to drive them away from the place where they have suffered most. Enslaved, and thrown to the wild beasts of the arena as sport for the imperial populace, outlawed and denied all intercourse with Christians by the Popes, branded with infamy, oppressed by cruel laws, irritated by constant insults, banned from the city, and crowded in wretched and unwholesome houses, they have hovered about Rome as moths round the lamp that burns them, and are now the oldest unbroken colony of Jews in Europe. Close by the side of the Papal Church, which claims to have been instituted by Christ, the Jewish Church, dedicated to Jehovah, has stationed itself, and maintained the laws of Moses with unflinching faith. Persuasions and threats have been tried on it in vain. Under the unremitted burden of their woes, the Jews have obstinately resisted conversion, and on the ruins of the Pagan temples, and within the precincts of the city dedicated to Jove, the two churches of Moses and Peter have held their hostile camps. In the temples of Jove and Juno the Catholic priest has preached in vain for centuries to the disbelieving Hebrew. There is something sublime in this loyalty of allegiance. While the descendants of the poor fisherman have made broad their phylacteries, sat in the high places and glorious temples, and given law to the world, the chosen people of God have herded like swine in the Ghetto. Yet, despite the enormous temptations held forth to seduce them from their faith, instances of conversion have always been rare. The history of such a colony cannot but be interesting, and I propose to set down a few notes thereupon.

But first let us take a glimpse of the Ghetto. Its very name is derived from the Talmud Ghet, and, signifying segregation and disjunction, is opprobrious, and fitly describes the home of a people cut off from the Christian world, and banned as infamous. Stepping out from the Piazza di Pianto, we plunge at once down a narrow street into the midst of the common class of Jews. The air reeks with the peculiar frowsy smell of old woollen clothes, modified with occasional streaks or strata of garlic, while above all triumphs the foul human odour of a crowded and unclean population. The street is a succession of miserable houses, and every door opens into a dark shop. Each of these is wide open, and within and without, sprawling on the pavement, sitting on benches and stools, standing in the street, blocking up the passages, and leaning out of the upper windows, are swarms of Jews—fat and lean, handsome and hideous, old and young—as thick as ants around an ant-hill. The shop-doors are draped with old clothes and second-hand *roba* of every description. Old military suits of furbished shabbiness—faded silken court dresses of a past century, with worn embroidery—napless and forlorn dress-coats, with shining seams and flabby skirts—waistcoats of dirty damask—legs of velvet breeches—in a word, all the cast-off riffraff of centuries that have "fallen from their high estate" are dangling everywhere over-head. Most of the men are lounging about and leaning against the lintels of the doors or packed upon benches ranged in front of the shops. The children are rolling round in the dirt, and playing with cabbage ends and stalks, and engaged in numerous and not over-clean occupations. The greater part of the women, however, are plying the weapon of their tribe, with which they have won a world-wide reputation—the needle—and, bent closely over their work, are busy in renewing old garments and hiding rents and holes with its skilful web-work. Everybody is on the look-out for customers; and, as you pass down the street, you are subjected to a constant fusilade of "*Pst, Pst*," from all sides. The women beckon you, and proffer their wares. At times they even seize the skirts of your coat in their eagerness to tempt you to a bargain. The men come solemnly up, and whisper confidentially in your ear, begging to know what you seek. Is there anything you can possibly want? If so, do not be abashed by the shabbiness of the shop, but enter, and ask even for the richest thing. You will find it, if you have patience. But, once in the trap, the manner of the seller changes—he dallies with you as a spider with a fly, as a cat with a mouse. Nothing is to be seen but folded cloths on regular shelves—all is hidden out of sight. At first, and reluctantly, he produces a common, shabby enough article. "Oh, no, that will never do,—too common." Then gradually he draws forth a better specimen. "Not good enough? why a prince might be glad to buy it!" Finally, when he has wearied you out, and you turn to go, he understands it is some superb brocade embroidered in gold—some gorgeous *portiere* worked in satin—some rich tapestry with Scripture stories—that you want, and with a sigh he opens a cupboard and draws it forth. A strange combination of inconsistent and opposite feelings has prevented him from exhibiting it before. He is divided between a desire to keep it and a longing to sell it. He wishes if possible to eat his cake and have it too,—and the poor ass in the fable between the two bundles of hay was not in a worse quandary. At last, the article you seek makes its appearance. It is indeed splendid, but you must not admit it. It may be the dress the Princess d'Este wore centuries ago, faded but splendid still—or the lace of Alexander VI., the Borgia—or an ancient altar cloth with sacramental spots—or a throne carpet of one of the Popes. Do you really wish to buy it, you must nerve yourself to fight. He begins at the zenith, you at the nadir; and gradually, by dint of extravagant laudation on his part, and corresponding depreciation on yours, you approach each other. But the distance is too great—the bargain is impossible. You turn and go away. He runs after you when he sees that you are not practising a feint, and offers it for less—but still the price is too high, and he in turn leaves you. You pass along the street. With a mysterious and confidential air, another of the tribe approaches you. He walks by your side. Was it a gold brocade you wanted? He also has one like that which you have seen, only in better condition. Would your Signoria do him the favour to look at it? You yield to his unctuous persuasion and enter his shop; but what is your astonishment when, after a delusive show of things you do not want, the identical article for which you have been bargaining is again produced in this new shop, and asserted stoutly, and with a faint pretence of indignation, to be quite another piece! This game is sometimes repeated three or four times. Wherever you enter, your old friend, Monsieur Tonson like, makes its appearance,—and you are lucky if you obtain it at last for twice its value, though you only pay a twentieth part of the price originally asked.

All the faces you see in the Ghetto are unmistakeably Hebraic, but very few are of the pure type. Generally it is only the disagreeable characteristics that remain,—the thick peculiar lips, the narrow eyes set close together, and the nose thin at the junction with the eyebrows, and bulbous at the end. Centuries of degradation have for the most part imbruted the physiognomy, and all of them have a greasy and anointed look. Here and there you will see a beautiful black-eyed child, with a wonderful mass of rich tendril-like curls, rolling about in the dirt; or a patriarchal-looking old Abraham, with a full beard, and the pure Israelite nose hooked over the moustache, and cut up backward in the nostrils. Hagars, too, are sometimes to be seen, and even stately Rebeccas at rarer intervals stride across the narrow street, with a proud, disdainful look above their station; but old Sarahs abound—fat, scolding, and repulsive—who fill to the extreme edge the wide chair on which they sit, while they rest their spuddy hands on their knees, and shake all over like jelly when they laugh. Almost all the faces are, however, of the short, greasy, bulbous type, and not of the long, thin, hook-nosed class. No impurity of breed and caste has sufficed to eradicate from them the Jewish characteristics.

As it is with the faces, so it is with the names. The pure Hebrew names have in great measure disappeared, or been intermarried with Italian surnames. These surnames are for the most part taken from some Italian city, or borrowed from some stately Italian house, with a pure Jewish prefix; as, for instance, Isaac Volterra, Moses Gonzaga, Jacob Ponticorvo. So also their speech is Roman, and their accent thick and Jewish. It is seldom that one hears them speak in their original Hebrew tongue, though they all understand it and employ it in their religious services.

The place and the people are in perfect keeping. The Ghetto is the high carnival of old clothes, the May-fair of rags. It is the great receptacle into which the common sewers of thievery and robbery empty. If a silver salver, a gold watch, a sparkling jewel, be missed unaccountably, it will surely run down into the Ghetto. Your old umbrella, your cloak that was stolen from the hall, the lace handkerchief with your initials embroidered in one corner, your snuff-box that the Emperor of Russia presented you, there lurk in secret holes, and turn up again after months or years of seclusion. In this *columbarium* your lost inanimate friends are buried, but not without resurrection.

Crammed together, layer above layer, like herrings in a barrel, the Jews of Rome are packed into the narrow confines of the Ghetto. Three of the modern palaces of Rome would more than cover the whole Jewish quarter; yet within this restricted space are crowded no less than 4000 persons. Every inch has its occupant; every closet is tenanted. And this seems the more extraordinary in spacious and thinly-populated Rome, where houses go a begging for tenants, and where, in the vast deserted halls and chambers of many a palace, the unbrushed cobwebs of years hang from decaying walls and ceilings. With the utmost economy of room, there is scarcely space enough to secure privacy and individuality; and, herded together like a huge family, they live in their sty. The street is their saloon, where they sit and talk, in loud snuffling voices, across from shop to shop, and from pavement to the opposite garret. The houses are all connected together on the upper floors;

so that, in case of inundation, the inhabitants may freely traverse the place without setting foot in the street. Dr. S—— assures me that, when called to visit professionally one family in the Ghetto, he has repeatedly been conveyed from chamber to chamber, from one end of the street to the other, giving advice all the way, and receiving pay as for one visit; and he also added that the best houses of the wealthiest Jews were never free from a certain odour abhorrent to the Christian nostril. Were you transported blindfold to this place, you would at once recognize it by this sign. Fortunately the level of the Ghetto is so low that, whenever the Tiber rises and overflows its banks, as is frequently the case in the autumn and winter, the whole quarter is under water. This is inconvenient perhaps, but the inhabitants owe a deep debt of gratitude to old Father Tiber, who thus washes out at intervals this Augean stable. At times the waters rise so as nearly to fill the lower stories in the Fiumara, and in 1846 the houses were inundated even to their ceilings.

Despite this purgation the place reeks with foul odours. But if confidence can be placed in the statements of some old authors, there is no remedy for this defect so long as the Jews adhere to the faith of their forefathers.

It is, however, an extraordinary fact that, despite the filth and bad drainage of the Ghetto, it is on the whole one of the healthiest places in Rome. The average of deaths is small, fever is rare, and in the year 1837, when the cholera raged in Rome, fewer died in the Ghetto than in any other part of the city. This is certainly a corroboration of the prevalent idea in Rome, that fever avoids places where the air is much beaten by a constant concourse of people, and that the denser the population the safer the residence.

The method of cleansing the Ghetto indicated by the learned authors just quoted is not, I fear, a very available one. The Jews pertinaciously resist it, despite the tender invitation held out constantly before their eyes every time they issue from the Ghetto by the Ponte Quattro Capi, where they may read in Latin and Hebrew text this sentence from Isaiah (ch. lxv. ver. 2), inscribed in large letters over the portals of a little church: "I have spread out my hands all the day unto a rebellious people, which walked in a way which was not good after their own thought." This inscription was the happy idea of a converted Jew, who thus showed his zeal for his new religion. Its results have not, however, been as yet very striking, and perhaps, *Chi sa?* the Jews apply it to the Christians and not to themselves.

Once a year the papal Church, on the Saturday before Easter, baptizes into the Christian faith a recanting Jew, giving him with one sprinkle salvation and the "odour of sanctity;" but a certain extraordinary resemblance of features is often to be marked between the converts of successive years, and it is to be feared that the holy Church is sometimes deceived, or—is not:—

> "Lo! Micah—the self-same beard on chin
> He was four times already converted in."

When this ceremony does take place, it is performed in the Church of San Giovanni in Laterano with great ceremony. The proselyte, covered with a white veil, and holding a burning wax candle in his hand as a symbol of enlightenment, is anointed on the neck and head, and sprinkled with holy baptism from the great porphyry vase, in which Rienzi bathed in rose-water. The procession then returns to the church, the cardinal blesses the convert at the altar, and then makes a long sermon at the expense of the new Christian and his old friends in the Ghetto. This concluded, he retires, extricated from the claws of the devil, and, if Fortunatus be correct, "surpassing ambrosial dews with the sweetness of his breath."

At earlier periods there have not been wanting converts of eminence at rare intervals, and it has even happened that a regenerated Jew has seen his son admitted to high honours in the Church, and, had his life been sufficiently prolonged, might in his old age have beheld him in the chair of St. Peter wielding the thunders of the Vatican. This was the case of a certain Pietro Leone, who in the eleventh century renounced Judaism, and together with his son was baptized by Leo IX., and assumed his name. Both these Jews were most honourable and excellent persons. The father was very rich and learned, and was held in high consideration by Pope Leo. His son also enjoyed the favour of Paschal II., and was made governor of the Castle St. Angelo. The son of the latter devoted himself to literature, and seems to have been much esteemed in his first years of manhood. He was made Cardinal by Calixtus II., and sent legate to France; but here, on the death of the Pope and the election of Cardinal Gregorius under the title of Innocent II., he was seduced by the party opposed to this election, and was elected Anti-pope under the title of Anaclet II. After this, his conduct seems to have been far from satisfactory. He despoiled the churches, drove Innocent II. from his seat, which he held to his death despite of excommunication, and at last, abandoned by nearly all his partisans save Ruggero Duke of Sicily, to whom he had given his sister in marriage, he died in 1138.

But let us continue our walk through the Ghetto. Passing down the Fiumara and turning at a sharp angle to the left, we enter the Piazza di Santa Maria in Pescheria, and see before us the church from which it receives its name. This uncouth structure occupies the site of the ancient temple of Jove or of Juno (there is some doubt which), and is barnacled upon the ruins of the once splendid Portico of Octavia by which these temples were surrounded; a few of the beautiful Corinthian fluted columns of its vestibule are still standing, cracked and crumbled by fire, and defaced by time and abuse. Some of these are built into the walls of the wretched houses. One or two stand alone, braced by iron bars and supporting fragments of the old cornice, and the two centre ones fronting the piazza are connected by the lofty brick arch which Septimius Severus threw between them to support the entablature after the fire by which the portico was injured in the reign of Titus. Within the enclosure stands the church, and on the arch are the peeling frescoes of a Christian age, dropping daily with the decaying mortar. Nothing can be more melancholy than this spectacle. Everything has gone to ruin. Low miserable houses surround this splendid relic of antiquity. The noble columns are broken, stained, and walled up. The splendour of imperial Rome has given place to the Pescheria—the fish market. Step under this arch and look up that narrow, dirty, but picturesque street on the left—that is the Pescheria. Stone slabs, broken and grappled by iron hooks, stretch out on either side into the street, and usurp it so as to leave no carriageable way between them. If it be market-day you will see them covered with every kind of fishes. Green crusty lobsters, squirming crawfish all alive, heaps of red mullet, baskets of little shining sardines, large *spigole*, sprawling, deformed cuttlefish—in a word, all the inhabitants of the Mediterranean are there exposed for sale; while the fisherman, standing behind them, slashes now and then a bucket of water over the benches and cries out his store. Is the market over—the street is deserted, the marble slabs are crusted with scales of fish, the purchasers and the purchased are gone, but the "ancient and fish-like smell" remains, a permanent bequest, to haunt the place, and mingle in companionship with the other odours of the Fiumara. Great dark holes open into the houses behind, begrimed with dirt and smoke. Above stretches an arch supported by black beams, over which is reared a series of chambers; here juts out on its iron arm the lantern which illuminates feebly the street at night; and here, in a grimed corner, is placed a Madonna-shrine with an onion-shaped lamp burning before it. Do what the Jews may, they are forced to accept the Virgin. Here, reposing from his labours, sits a Jew behind one of the stone slabs. He tends the empty bench, with a green cravat on his neck, and a huge gold watch-chain hanging out of his waistcoat pocket. Behind him, grim with filth, is a great square door. Look at it close—it is antique, of the age of Septimius Severus; its lintels are carved in the egg and cup pattern, and it now serves as the door of his shop, unaltered save in its use. Everywhere crop out of the walls fragments of columns, architraves, and defaced capitals, and from the windows old petticoats dangle and flap about among them.

Please to remember that this place which I have been describing was once the Portico of Octavia, and then shut your eyes a moment and let your fancy carry you back to the ancient days. Here on this very spot where we are now standing stood the Cupid of Praxiteles, the Diana of Ciphesiodorus, the Ludovisi Mars, the Phidian Venus; just behind us rose the Temple of Juno; and here the Romans of the Augustan age sauntered between the acts at the Theatre of Marcellus. This was the spot whence Titus and Vespasian led forth their splendid triumph after the destruction of Jerusalem. Through these very columns that stink with fish passed their glittering train, gorgeous with gold, gems and ivory, flaunting Syrian robes of purple embroidered with gold, with richly-caparisoned elephants and dromedaries, then new to the Roman eye; bearing hundreds of statues of every metal, and the "*spolia opima*" torn from the great Temple of Jerusalem. Yes, over this very ground, where the sons and daughters of Zion drive their miserable trade in old clothes, and where the Pescheria breathes its unsavoury smells, were carried in pomp the silver trumpets of the Jubilee, the massive golden table of shewbread, the seven-branched candlestick of gold, the tables of the law, the veil itself from behind which sacrilegious hands had stolen the sacred utensils of the altar—and in their rear, sad, dejected and doomed, followed Simon the son of Gorias, loaded with clanking chains, and marching in the triumphal train of his victors to ignominious death at the base of the Capitol. Shut your eyes and see the procession go by—statues, crowns, elephants, purple robes, flashing figures, laurel-crowned legions, and at last, the chariots, with four milk-white horses abreast, bearing the Emperors Vespasian and Titus, stained vermilion, and dressed in purple and gold tunics, to the Temple of Jupiter Capitolinus;—and when the last robe has fluttered away, and the last brazen clang echoed through the double rows of marble columns, open them again, and behold the Fiumara and the Pescheria, and listen to the strain taken up after seventeen centuries. It is no longer "*Io triumphe*," but "Ogh clo'"—*Roba vecchia.* "To what base uses we may return!"

Shut then your eyes again. Thirteen centuries have passed since that vision of triumph. Under the temple of the Jews, close by the spot on which you stand, a boy has been born, and grown to man's estate. To the walls of the little church of St. Angelo in Pescheria he has affixed an allegorical picture, and you hear his voice describing it. There is a great fire, with kings and subjects burning therein; and among them a matron (who represents Rome) dying in the flames. On the right is a church, from which issues an angel in white robes, bearing a naked sword in one hand, while with the other he drags the matron from the fire. High above on the church tower stand St. Peter and St. Paul, and cry, "Angel, angel, succour our protectress!" Descending from the sky many a falcon (which are barons) has fallen into the flames, while others are pouncing upon a beautiful white dove that bears in his bill a myrtle crown. The dove gives it to another bird hunted down by the falcons, that he may place it on the matron's head. Beneath is written: "I see the time of the great judgment, and do thou expect that time." The voice which speaks and explains the picture is that of Cola di Rienzi. You open your eyes to catch a glimpse of the last of the Romans. There is no one near but an old Jew, and by no means the last of them, who shows you a bad mosaic of which he wishes to make a dispensation to you, "for a consideration," and looking on the walls for the picture, you only see a marble slab forbidding the playing of any game in the piazza.

But shut your eyes again, and you will hear a trumpet sound, and see Rienzi marching out of the church clad in armour, with his head uncovered, and surrounded by the papal vicar and a goodly retinue of followers with allegorical standards of Peace, Liberty, and Justice. They are going to establish the "good estate," for which he paid with his life.

Brushing away these cobwebs of the fancy, you open your eyes again. The church is still there, but Rienzi has gone, never to reappear. It is not worth while to enter the church,—there is nothing of note in it; or, if there be, any Jew boy about the place will be your Murray. He will also tell you, if he happen to know the fact, that for many years the Jews were forced to listen therein, once a week, to a sermon delivered by a Christian upon the text of their perversity. It was of course a converted Jew, named Andrias, who first conceived so happy a thought; and Pope Gregory XIII. was well pleased to carry it at once into execution. He therefore ordained that at least 100 men and 50 women, which number he afterwards raised to 300, should attend this Christian service. Every Sunday came the *sbirri* into the Ghetto, and drove the wretched inhabitants with the crack of their whips, like veritable overseers of a slave plantation, into the precincts of the church. Guards stood at the door to make sure that the appointed number were there; and the *sbirri* within, if they caught a poor devil of a Jew asleep or inattentive, brought him to his bearings at once by a lash of the whip over his shoulders. The sermon was delivered by a Dominican priest, upon the very text which had formed the theme of Jewish discourse the previous day in the synagogue. The effect does not seem to have been satisfactory, for very few of the Jews were whipped into Christianity, though the lashes were laid on with an unsparing hand. Nevertheless, this practice lasted for more than two centuries and a half, and was only abandoned within the reign of the present Pope. The sermon was at first delivered in the church of San Benedetto, but at a later date St. Angelo in Pescheria was substituted.

Passing through the Pescheria and turning to the right we enter the Via Rua, which is the Corso of the Ghetto. Here a better set of shops may be found, for here are established those of the Jewish colony who have amassed a fortune, or at least are on the way to do so. Everything here is shabby enough, but far better than those of the lower part of the Ghetto, and here you will find all kinds of linen, cotton, and woollen cloth piled away on the shelves.

Crossing again the Piazza di Pianto, we pass into a little irregular place called the Piazza della Scuola, where the synagogue stands. The building is very simple, and offers a special contrast in this respect to every other church in Rome. It is rather singular in its architecture, and in front there are two ugly pillars, and a golden inscription in Hebrew, by which you know it to be the synagogue. All synagogues have a striking family resemblance internally; and I shall not occupy your time and mine with describing the seats below for the men who always honour God by keeping their hats on during their religious ceremonies, nor the seats far above in the well-like cupola, where the daughters of Israel look down through a grating upon the altar below. When you are in it you feel that the Romish Church has had no hand in making it, and that quite a different worship takes place there on its hard regular benches. However, if you are not satisfied without a full description of it, I refer you to a most interesting chapter on the Jews in Rome in the "Figuren" of Ferdinand Gregorovius, where you will find considerable information on the subject.

One bit of information I may be permitted here to give, inasmuch as the stranger will not find it in the pages of Murray. The piazza receives its title della Scuola from the fact that the synagogue unites in itself five *scuole* or schools; namely, of the Temple, Catalana, Castigliana, Siciliana, and of the new school. Each of these represents a parish or ward, which is devoted to a particular class of Jews, according to their nationality, and each has its school in which children are taught to read and write and reckon (the last being of special importance to a people whose law is Numbers).

I the more readily ask you not to linger in the synagogue, for there is matter much more attractive in that great irregular building, half-palace, half-barracks, which stands over opposite to it, and has already attracted your attention. That is the famous Palazzo Cenci. Can anything be more appropriate than that the Palazzo Cenci, which, being interpreted into the vernacular, signifies "the Palace of Rags," should crown the highest ground of the Ghetto. There it stands, lifted on a rising mound, which is formed of the *débris* and ruin of the Theatre of Balbus, now only an informal mass of rubbish, and looking down over the Piazza di Pianto. Yes! the Cenci Palace most fitly looks down into the Place of Weeping. The very name has already awakened in your heart a confused feeling of sorrow and indignation. The painful, melancholy, terrible story we all of us know has risen like a nightmare before your imagination. The place is hideous to you, for it embalms the most tragical of all earth's tragical histories. Shall we ascend the slope that leads to its *cortile?* This is the back entrance. The scene has strangely changed since Francesco Cenci, like a demon, ranged its rooms. One now sees French and Roman soldiers looking out of its windows, where they have their barracks, and hears the discordant trumpet-practising that echoes through its halls and shakes the rattling panes. Through that door we used to ascend to Overbeck's studio, which was open to the public every Sunday; and as if the spirit of contradiction possessed the place, it was here that he created his outlines of the New Testament history, and gave all his genius to the adoration of the Madonna and the saints. A ghost-like man he was, ascetic and dry in his manner and look, with long hair piously combed behind his ears, solemn in his voice and gesture—a sort of outline himself with almost no flesh and blood in him, who walked about his studio in a long priestly sort of dress, and explained his charcoal outlines. His figure was in form like one of the dryest of the early Siena school, without any of that gorgeous colour in which the primitive painters loved to indulge, but which Overbeck considers to be too sensuous for spiritual art. He is no longer to be found in the studio which he occupied here for so many years; and the pencil has given place there to the musket.

This is the back of the palace; it fronts on the Piazza Cenci, a dreary and deserted place enough. Look up at it. Over a high narrow archway juts out an iron balcony, from which Beatrice may have looked with those sad eyes, that were friends with grief. It is easy enough to see her there still, if one have a lively imagination. Underneath her gapes the great black hole of entrance, looking like a fit vestibule to some horrible inquisition, or even, if possible, to some worse place. *Per me si va nella città dolente* might be inscribed over it, so grim and ugly is its aspect. Sooty, grimed with the dirt of ages, and doorless, it seems like the passage to Acheron; nor is the illusion dispelled as you ascend its ruinous slope of brick stairs, and pick your way along its filth and ordure; for, glancing down doorways on the right, you see long black passages leading down and down into subterranean depths, that stretch out of sight into darkness. Glad enough are you when you have passed the obscenity and stench of this passage to issue into the light of day in the *cortile*, and see the sunshine playing on the granite columns, and antique friezes, and open corridors of arches. But on the pavement here are open gratings, through which you look down into subterranean *oubliettes*, the caverns probably of the old Theatre of Balbus, where God knows what crimes may have been perpetrated in barbarous ages. A sort of ugly horror seems to possess the whole place, which even the sunshine cannot quite dispel.

As you stand in this *cortile* you see directly before you a little church, founded in 1113 by Cencio, Bishop of Sabina, and rebuilt by Francesco Cenci in expiation of his atrocious crimes, or rather as a bribe to the church for absolution. Let us read its inscription: "*Francescus Cencius, Christopheri filius, et ecclesiæ patronus templum hoc rebus ad divinum cultum et ornatum necessariis ad perpetuam rei memoriam exornari ac perfeci curavit—anno Jubilei MDLXXV.*" Think what the church must have been of which Francesco Cenci could dare to call himself "patron." It is fitly dedicated to the unbelieving St. Thomas.

We have now gone through the Ghetto; and it remains for me to set down a few notes relative to the history of this little colony of Jews, and of the oppression under which they have suffered.

Among the heathen Cæsars the Jews had been forced by imperial decrees to perform three sacrifices for every new emperor. First on his installation; then on the occasion of any illness; and third, in case of any war undertaken by him. These it was not only incumbent upon the Jews in Rome to perform, but, after the taking of Jerusalem, upon the whole people wherever it might be.

When the Popes took the place of the emperors, and Christianity assumed the purple robes, the forms of sacrifice were changed, but the homage was exacted. Upon the installation of the Pope a deputation of Romish Jews were obliged to present themselves to his holiness on the public way of his triumphal procession, singing songs in his praise, and carrying on their shoulders a copy of the Pentateuch written on parchment, bound in gold, and covered with a veil, which on bended knees they offered to him, beseeching his protection. The successor of Peter took the book, read a few words from it, and then putting it behind him said, "We affirm the law, but we curse the Hebrew people and their exposition of it." Having thus graciously accepted their homage, he proceeded on his way; and the deputation, full of fears for the future, retired to their humble quarters in the Ghetto, saluted on all sides by the cries and scoffs of the populace.

It was Calixtus the Second who revived the old usage, and re-created it in this form in the year 1119; and his successors were so much pleased with it that they continued it thenceforward for nearly four centuries.

The spot on which this homage was generally offered was at the Bridge of Hadrian, the second destroyer of Jerusalem, but sometimes it was performed on Monte Giordano. The ill-treatment to which the Jews were subjected by the mob in these public places at last became so excessive, that in 1484 Innocent VIII., taking compassion on them, received them in the enclosure of the Castel St. Angelo. Burkhard, the master of ceremonies of the Pope, gives us the address of the Jews, and the response of the holy Father, in these words. Extending the copy of the Pentateuch, the chief of the deputation said, in Hebrew, "Most Holy Father, we Israelites beseech you, in the name of our synagogue, that the Mosaic law given by Almighty God to Moses, our priest on Mount Sinai, may be conceded and allowed to us, as by other eminent Popes the predecessors of your holiness it has been conceded and allowed." To which the Pope replied, "We concede to you the law, but we curse your creed and your interpretation; for he of whom you said, 'he will come,' has already come, our Lord Jesus Christ, as is taught and professed by our Church."

On one occasion Pius III., in the year 1503, being ill, received this deputation in a hall of the Vatican. But Julius II. immediately remanded the ceremony to the Bridge of Hadrian, where he made a long sermon on the occasion, and his physician, the Spaniard

Rabbi Samuel, also spoke with eloquence. His successor, Leo X., received this homage with still greater pomp and circumstance, as is evident from the description of the occasion by his great master of ceremonies Paris de Grassis. This worthy person tells us that the Jews stood before the door of the Castel St. Angelo on a wooden scaffold covered with gold brocade and silken carpets, and bearing eight burning wax candles. There they held up the tables of the law, and while the Pope rode by on his white horse, fat, sensual, and repulsive (for surely, if the portrait Raffaelle has left us of this voluptuary be faithful, nothing could have been less spiritual than his appearance), the Jews made their customary humble appeal, and this holy figure, differing somewhat from that of the chief of the apostles, made the usual response. What a picture it must have been! Perhaps Adrian saw it with a satirical eye, thinking little better of the Pope than Mosheim, who places him in the list of atheists, or than the Venetian ambassadors, who give accounts of his gross excesses and vices of a nature to scandalize the lowest rake of this century. However this may have been, certain it is that the ceremony was discontinued by honest, pious, and ascetic Adrian, and was not again renewed.

Yet it was not to be permitted to the Jews to be absolved from humiliations, and, though the homage was not exacted, they were obliged to cover with costly stuffs and carpets a portion of the street over which the papal procession took its way. At the installation of Gregory XIV., the steps of the Capitol and the Arch of Septimius Severus were adorned by them; but by a refinement of annoyance worthy of a papal court, they were subsequently bound to decorate with their richest tapestries, silks, and embroideries, the detested Arch of Titus, built to commemorate their own degradation and the destruction of their holy city, as well as the whole road leading thence to the Colosseum. These tapestries and hangings bore upon a gold ground embroidered emblems designated by the Pope, with Latin texts taken from the New and Old Testament. The emblems, generally twenty-five in number, and expressive of every sort of fantastic allegory, were woven by the Jews themselves in their dirty Ghetto, and doubtless had hatred and indignation enough wrought into their texture to give a *jettatura* to the Pope who passed over and under them. In course of time these scriptural allegories became confused with pagan devices. The Old Testament and Roman mythology intermarried and gave birth to designs absurd in sentiment and *barocco* in style,—Apollo, Moses, Minerva, the Virgin, Popes, donkeys, and heraldic animals, grouping amicably together, to illustrate texts from the Bible—somewhat after the fashion of

"Bould Homer, Venus, and Nicodemus" in the famous gardens of "the groves of Blarney." Some of these very tapestries, I doubt not, might even now be raked out of hidden chambers in the Ghetto, if any one had the will to purchase them.

At a later period Pius VII. (Chiaramonti), at the beginning of the present century, exempted the Jews from this tribute, and in place of it allowed them to present a book, bound in costly style, and with emblems exquisitely painted in miniature, which was dedicated with Latin verses to the Pope. One of these books was presented to Gregory XVI. It was painted by Pietro Paoletti of Belluno; that painter being selected in honour of the Pope, whose native town was Belluno; and was sent by his holiness to the cathedral there, where any one who is curious may examine it. To Pius IX. a similar book was presented, which cost no less than 500 *scudi*.

Let us now retrace our steps to the thirteenth century, when Innocent III., in the year 1215, re-enacted the decrees of the council ordering the Jews to wear badges of their degradation From this time forward, for more than two centuries, they were alternately favoured and oppressed, according to the character of the Pope—generally, however, being admitted to a certain position in case of eminent qualities and acquirements. Thus, John XXII. (1316), being averse to them, prohibited the use of the Talmud and ordered it to be publicly burned. Benedict XIII. (1394), on the contrary, being favourable to them, allowed a Jewish woman to take the care of his wardrobe, and a Jewish physician to take care of his body. This worthy leech, whose name was Joshua Halorki, was converted by him to the Christian faith, and, under the new title of Hieronymus de Sancta Fide, wrote certain works against the Talmud and on the perfidy of the Hebrew nation, for which service he received high honours from the Pope and as deep curses from the Jews.

Innocent VII. (1404) was also propitious to them, and among other privileges he granted to some of the Jewish physicians the freedom of the city, and exempted them from wearing the ignominious badge of their people. Martin V. (1417) showed a like graciousness, and did them the honour to select his favourite physician from among them.

But these sunny days now came to a close. The Papacy grew strong, and its enemies felt the weight of its hand. In Eugenius IV. (Condolmieri, 1431), the Jews found a cruel master. He banned them from the city, forbade them to hold any public office, and decreed that their testimony should not avail in a court of justice against that of a Christian. Besides loading them with taxes and tributes, he first conceived the happy thought of making their degradation subservient to the festivities of the Carnival. With this view he mulcted them of an annual fine of 1130 *scudi* in order to defray its expenses. This seed of sorrow took root at once and bore bitter fruit. From this time forward, one of the principal amusements of the Carnival was to maltreat the Jews; and the sport proved so excellent that cardinals and *monsignori* freely took part in it. It was Paul II. (Pietro Barbo), however, who in 1468 first ordained the races of this wretched people in the Corso, and gave form and law to the cruelty of the mob. The programme of ignominy was this:—First, a body of Jewish elders, clothed in a shirt or doublet, preceded the cavalcade of the senators who opened the Carnival. They were then obliged to run races every day; and it was the custom to give them a rich dinner beforehand so as to enable their bodies and spirits to sustain the trials they were to undergo. There were two classes of races; the one comprising old men, young men, and children, without reference to their nation; and the other being of horses, asses, buffaloes, and Jews. While it was optional with the former to race or not, it was compulsory with the latter—Jews and asses being treated as belonging to the same category. The racing by the Romans was soon abandoned, but the Jews had not the privilege of refusal, and the sport was too good to be foregone.

The course was from the tomb of Domitian, close by the Porta del Popolo, to the church of St. Marco, in the Piazza di Venezia; and amid the howls and shrieks of the delighted bystanders, who showered upon them as they passed the most insulting and disgraceful epithets, the poor old Jews, a little drunk with their repast and the liquor with which they tried to drown the sense of their ignominy, stumbled along the crowded Corso. Noble ladies and purple-robed cardinals and *monsignori* applauded this degrading spectacle, while the Pope himself looked down from his decorated balcony, and smiled his approval or shook his holy sides with laughter. If, after the dragoons have cleared a path for the horse races of the Carnival in the present day, you have ever seen an unfortunate dog endeavour to make his way down the Corso through the opening, and heard the screams and laughter, the scoffs and shouts of derision which urge him on in his affrighted course, you may have an inkling of the horror of that race of old Jews. But this spectacle, as we have described it, bad as it was, did not satisfy the greedy demands of the populace or the Pope, and a piquancy was afterwards added to it by forcing the Jews to run with a rope round their necks and entirely naked, save where a narrow band was girt round their loins. This brutal exhibition, more disgraceful to the Pope than to the Jews, was annually repeated during every day of the Carnival for more than 200 years; and it was not until the year 1668 that Clement IX. (Rospigliosi) absolved the Jews from its performance on condition of their paying a tax of 300 *scudi*, and also relieved them from accompanying the cavalcade of senators, they agreeing in compensation to furnish the prizes for the races.

Besides this, on the first Sunday of Carnival, a deputation from the Ghetto, composed of the chiefs of the Jews, were forced to go bareheaded to the palace of the Capitol, where were the *conservators* of the Roman senate. Here they threw themselves on their knees, presenting to the *conservators* bouquets of flowers and twenty *scudi*, which they prayed him to apply to the decoration of the balcony of the Roman Senate in the Piazza del Popolo. They then proceeded to the *senator*, and kneeling, besought his permission to reside in the Ghetto during the ensuing year. The *senator* placed his foot upon their brows and commanded them to rise, saying, after an appointed formula, that although they were not acceptable in Rome, yet out of pity they would be allowed to remain. This humiliation is not now required; but the Jews are still obliged to come to the Capitol, do homage, and pay tribute to purchase the prizes for the races, but (thank God!) it is horses and not Jews that are compelled to run in them.

In the mean time, between the institution of these races and their discontinuance, this much-abused colony was destined to be trodden down by one of the most bigoted, fanatical, and cruel princes who ever sat in the chair of St. Peter—the Neapolitan Caraffa, who in 1555 was made Pope under the title of Paul IV. To him the Christians owed the establishment of the Censorship and the Inquisition at Rome, and the Jews the revocation of all their privileges by the bull "*cum nimis absurdum.*" Hitherto the better class had preserved certain privileges in the midst of their disabilities and degradation. But this bigot, with one blow, sheared them all away. He prohibited Jewish physicians from practising among Christians; he disabled them from carrying on any trade or handicraft, and from the purchase and sale of merchandize; he imposed upon them heavy tributes, and prohibited them from all commerce with Christians. Even the title of Don, to which some of the highest Spanish Jews were entitled, he disallowed. Perfectly to separate them from all other classes, he ordered that they should not enter the city without bearing a badge of Hebraism; the men a yellow hat and the women a yellow veil; for, he says, "it is truly too shameless and unseemly that Jews, whose guilt has precipitated them into eternal slavery, under the pretext of receiving Christian compassion, should insolently assume to dwell among Christians and take Christian servants, and even to purchase houses, without bearing a badge."

Hitherto, certain Jews had for a long period been silently permitted to reside within the walls of the city, despite all the laws to the contrary, though for the most part they congregated together on the further side of the Tiber to avoid close contact with a people who hated and despised them; but Caraffa now imprisoned them within the narrow limits between the Ponte Quattro Capi and the Piazza del Pianto, now known as the Ghetto, though it formerly bore the name of the Vicus Judæorum. But Ghetto is its true name—the place of ban—the place for outcasts—as deeply they must have felt when, on the 26th of July, 1556, they were driven sorrowing into this pen and walled up there like beasts. From that time forward to the present day, more than three centuries, they have lived crowded together in its narrow confines, overflowed by every rise of the Tiber, and only by the utmost economy of room making space for the necessary separations into families and individuals. On one occasion, when the quarter was overflowed, they begged permission to come out of it temporarily, until the waters should abate, but it was answered that water would not hurt them.

But now that they were segregated in the Ghetto certain questions arose. The fourth part of the houses belonged to Romans, and there were even distinguished families residing there, among whom may be mentioned the Boccapaduli and the Cenci. It was impossible for the Jews to live in the houses without the consent of the proprietors, who might keep them roofless and houseless, either by refusing to let their houses at all, or by demanding exorbitant rents from a people who had no choice of place. To guard against this a law was passed, called the "*Jus Gazzaga*," which was to this effect—the Roman proprietors should retain the title to their houses, but should be required to make a perpetual lease of them to the Jews for a small annual rent, which by the terms of the contract should never be increased. The tenant was to be entitled to make such repairs and changes in the house as should seem to him proper, and was also permitted to sell and even to devise his interest; the landlord having no power to dispossess his grantees or devisees. This "*Jus Gazzaga*" is still in force, and the old leases made three centuries ago are still sold and devised as they then were with the same limited rents.

Banishment into the Ghetto was not the only evil the Jews suffered under Caraffa. The Inquisition did its holy office unto them, and many a one was burnt in the Campo dei Fiori and the

Piazza di Minerva. But the reign of Caraffa was short. Four years had scarcely elapsed when he died; and, when the Inquisition was plundered and the church of the Dominicans stormed, the Jews obtained a temporary relief. At least they had the satisfaction of pelting the monument of the Pope with mud and his memory with curses, and one of them even drew over its hand a yellow glove. At this the people laughed, fortunately for the audacious individual, considering the joke a good one, and Jews and Christians for once united in tumbling down the statue, and dragging through the mud its head with the papal crown upon it.

Their relief was, however, short; for in 1566, Paul V. (Ghislieri) confirmed the bull of Caraffa, and ordained that the gates of the Ghetto should be closed at Ave Maria, after which hour no one should be allowed to pass out or in. Any poor wretch of a Jew belated in Rome was therefore obliged to pass his night under the open sky beside his prison walls, unless he could make interest to open the gate with a silver key.

Foot-ball still to the Popes, their fate again changed when Sixtus V. (Felice Peretti), who has inscribed his name on so many of the public monuments and pedestals of Rome, issued in 1586 his bull, "*Christiana pietas infelicem Hebræorum statum commiserans,*" a monument itself to his humanity and truly Christian spirit. This bull threw open the doors of the prison built by Caraffa, and enabled the Jews not only to reside at their pleasure within any walled city or castle in the Roman territory, but also reinstated them in their privileges of carrying on all trades, except the retailing of wine and the sale of grain and meat. Through its provisions their intercourse and commerce with Christians was renewed, and they were allowed to become their servants, though not their masters. It even went so far in its humanity as to improve their habitations, to establish schools and synagogues among them, and to permit them to form a Hebrew library. It prohibited the summons of Jews to Court on their Sabbath, forbade their baptism by force, the imposition of improper and extraordinary expenses on such of them as were travelling, and reduced their tribute money to a reasonable poll-tax. Sunshine for once streamed in upon them. Their lot had never been so easy. But fortune is a wheel, and to the Jews for the most part a torturing one. In less than ten years it gave a violent turn. Clement VIII. (Aldobrandini) came to the throne, and they were again remanded to their prison and shorn of all their privileges.

In this wretched state of impotence and disgrace the Jews remained for two centuries, now and then experiencing a slight relief, as when Clement IX. abolished the law requiring them to run races in the Corso at Carnival, but still occupying a wretched and ignominious position. In the beginning of the 18th century, Clement XI. and Innocent XIII. (the names somehow terribly jar with the facts) renewed Caraffa's bull, forbidding the exercise of all trades to them, with the exception of the traffic in old iron and old clothes, "*stracci, ferracci.*" But it was not till 1740, under Benedict XIV., that they were allowed to sell cloth that was new.

How strangely their fate had changed since they were the chosen people! Then, by the law of Moses, agriculture was their occupation, and traffic was given over to strangers. Now they were only too happy to be allowed to exercise the humblest trades, and were not allowed to own or hire an inch of land, nor to cultivate an inch belonging to a Christian.

Thus driven to the wall by the Christians, what, then, was the occupation of this people during these long centuries of disabilities? Somehow they must live. The exceptions, as we have seen, distinguished themselves by the practice of medicine, and were received at intervals into the household of the Pope. But the masses earned a miserable livelihood by the most disreputable means, glad enough to earn it in any way. They continued to do what they had done in the time of Juvenal. They told fortunes, they dealt in magic, they made potions, they went about among the people professing mysterious powers, and extorting money from the fears of the superstitious. Here you have the two sides—the science of medicine, and its obverse, the practice of witchcraft. Besides this, they lent the money they scraped together at usurious interest. Their forefathers had invented bills of exchange; and they certainly took advantage of this invention, revenging themselves on the Christians for the shabby way in which they were forced to accumulate their golden heaps, by exacting an exorbitant interest on every loan which the necessities of the Christians forced them to demand. But in these cases—

> "We still have judgment *here* ; that we but teach
> (Cruel) instructions, which being taught, return
> To plague the inventor. This even-handed justice
> Commends the ingredients of our poisoned chalice
> To our own lips."

The Church by its edicts had demoralized the Jews to the utmost. It had left them no reputable means of acquiring property. The curse reacted. They took to disreputable methods of securing their livelihoods, and in turn demoralized their persecutors. The remarkable bull of his holiness Pius V., issued in 1569, "*Hebræorum gens sola quondam a Domino electa,*" gives us a curious glimpse into the habits of the Roman colony of Jews in his day. By the provisions of this bull they were banned from every spot in the Roman States with the exception of Rome and Ancona, and as a reason for this harshness the following statements, among others, are therein made: "For not to mention the various methods of usury, by which the Jews entirely consume the means of needy Christians, we also believe it to be clearly established that they are the protectors of robbers and thieves, whom they conceal, as well as receivers of stolen goods, not only of a profane class, but also appertaining to our holy worship, either for the purpose of hiding them awhile, or of carrying them to other places to change their form so that they may not be recognised. Very many of them also steal, under the pretence of carrying on a proper business, into the houses of honest women, precipitate them into the abyss of shameless indecency, and, what is most corrupt of all, they lead astray imprudent and weak persons, with Satanic practices, fortune-telling, wonderful remedies, and the practice of magic arts and witchcraft, into the belief that they can predict future events, and discover treasures, stolen and lost articles, and pretend to powers of divination in other ways which it is given to no mortal to possess."

There is little doubt that these same practices are continued to a certain extent even to the present day; and it is said that the Jewish women still go about the city secretly selling love potions, interpreting dreams, and lending their aid in most disreputable ways to the superstitious and lustful. For the most part, the women, however, exercise the art of the needle, and if there be a carpet to be sewn together, or a rent in one's coat to be repaired, their efficient aid is invoked by all. Their speciality is sewing and mending old and new clothes. The men go about the streets by day buying cast-off garments and rags, or any depreciated article on which the proprietor wishes to raise money. At every public auction their greasy faces, hooked noses, and black eyes are to be seen, and their thick voices to be heard bidding low sums, and appropriating every article which sells at a sacrifice. By night, with their basket on their back and a lantern in their hand, they rake over the refuse heaps in the streets, picking out from them bits of broken glass, rags, paper, and silver spoons if they have the luck to find them, and not till dawn breaks over the housetops do these night-birds return to their roost in the Ghetto.

Under the reign of the Cæsars, and at the age of Claudius, the number of Jews in Rome is stated at 8,000; but this number was diminished under the Popes to about one half, and has since but slightly varied. If we may trust the statements of a work published in Rome in the year 1667, under the title "Stato Vero degli Ebrei in Roma," there were then 4,500 Jews in the city, some 200 of which were respectable and well-to-do persons. At the present day they number 4,000. As they become rich, they generally change the Roman Ghetto for some city where they may live in a manner conformably to their wealth. For the most part they go into Tuscany, where they are entitled to equal rights with the other inhabitants, and chiefly congregate at Leghorn, where they form a large proportion of the population, and engage in commerce. At Genoa, there are, on the contrary, very few Jews; the cause of which is popularly attributed to the superior shrewdness of the Genoese in bargaining, according to the following equations:—

$$\text{Three Christians} = 1 \text{ Jew.}$$
$$\text{Three Jews} = 1 \text{ Genoese.}$$
$$\text{Three Genoese} = 1 \text{ Sciote.}$$

The same author also tells us that, despite the disabilities of the Jews in the Roman Ghetto, they had thriven and grown rich. After deducting all the tributes paid by them, which by his calculation amounted every five years to no less a sum than 19,470 *scudi*, he estimates their property at a million *scudi*. "235,000 *scudi* (he goes on to say) have the Jews extorted from the Christians by usury, and no evening passes that at least 800 *scudi* are not transferred from the pockets of the latter through the Ghetto doors into their houses." Indeed, these usurious practices became so excessive at last as to rouse the hatred of the Romans, and John of Capistrano once besought the Pope, Eugenius IV., to give him a fleet to carry away beyond sea the whole Jewish population. "Now he (the Pope) is dead," says our author, "it were to be wished that he would send from heaven a fleet to Clement IX. to transport all these thieves out of Rome." No love evidently was lost between the Christians and the Jews at this time.

When the French occupied Rome, the prison of the Ghetto was opened, and permission was given to its occupants to dwell in the city and to engage in trade. But on the return of Pius VII., in 1814, they were again imprisoned and afflicted with their old disabilities. Leo XII., however, was touched by an impulse of humanity, and gave them, besides their privileges under the "*Jus Gazzaga*," the right to purchase houses within the limits of the Ghetto, and hold them in fee. He also enlarged the boundaries of the Ghetto, so as to take in a portion of the Pescheria, and opened eight gates, which, however, were strictly guarded and closed at night.

When Pius IX. came to the papal throne in 1846, the Jews enjoyed the sunshine of his first liberal days. At the instance of Don Michele Caetani, Prince of Teano, always a sincere advocate of the cause of this unhappy colony, he confided to a commission the examination of its just claims, with authority to enforce them. The first step taken in these reforms was to exempt the Jews from the necessity of listening every Sunday to a sermon against their religion in the church of St. Angelo in Pescheria. The walls of the Ghetto were then levelled, no more to be raised, Ciceruacchio himself lending a hand to their destruction; and permission was given to the Jews to reside in the wards of the city adjacent to the Ghetto, and to exercise certain trades, before prohibited. Some of them gladly availed themselves of this privilege, and hired houses and opened shops beyond the limits of the Ghetto. But upon the return of the Pope from Gaeta, escorted by French bayonets, all the liberal decrees were at one blow struck away from the people, and the old tyrannous *régime* reinstated. Though the rights and privileges conceded to the Jews were not formally repealed, they were silently withdrawn, or so obstructed as to become inoperative. While those who had hired houses and opened shops in the city, and exchanged the squalid Ghetto for better dwellings outside its limits, were suffered to remain, a stop was put to further emigration.* The method adopted to secure this end was truly papal. The liberal decrees in their favour had delegated to the cardinal vicar the power to grant permissions to fix their domicile within the city. These permissions, granted freely at first upon petition, were now so obstructed by delays and difficulties of every kind, that the petitioner, wearied out by a long and fruitless struggle, at last abandoned the attempt. Many of the richest Jews then left Rome, and betook themselves to Leghorn, where they are affected by no legal disabilities of caste, diminishing thus the taxable property of Rome to the full extent of their fortunes, which in many cases were large. The ties of old habit bound some of them still to Rome, and they sought a compromise with the government, petitioning to be allowed to invest one-third of their property in the city. This was denied them. The result will be seen by the census. In 1842 there were 12,700

---

* Within a few weeks of the present time (Feb. 1860), a signal instance of the policy of the government towards the Jews has come to my knowledge. One of them having opened a shop just beyond the Ghetto limits, the *carabinieri* came and forced him to close it, under pretence of informality in the licence. In vain the Jew protested, having the misfortune to belong to his caste. The only reply to his expostulations was an order to shut up his shop.

Jews within the Pontifical States, and in 1853 this number was reduced to 9,237; 3,463, or more than a fourth of the Jewish population, having withdrawn.

What then is the present condition of the Jews in Rome? It is shameful, intolerant, and unchristian. A ban is upon these poor children of Israel, which is demoralising to them and unworthy of the century and of the Church. They are branded with ignominy, oppressed by taxes, excluded from honourable professions and trades, and reduced to poverty by laws which belong to barbarous ages. Shut up in their Ghetto, and forced to earn a miserable livelihood by the meanest traffic, they are then scorned as a filthy and dishonest people. Forbidden to raise their head, the Church that has crushed them under its decrees points at them the finger of scorn because they creep and crawl beneath their burdens. The favours granted them are hypocritical and visionary—the injuries alone are real.

That this statement is within bounds a few facts will plainly show. They are prohibited from holding any civil, political, or military office, and from the exercise of any profession or trade of public credit, such as that of advocate, notary, attorney, librarian, goldsmith, manufacturer, smith, stone-cutter, and the like; though, by a capricious exception, they have of late years been enabled to become carpenters, cotton-weavers, and cabinet-makers. No trade, in fact, is permitted to them, without clear proof that it has already been allowed in the past and consecrated by usage. While they are excluded from the right of taking part in the public works, ordered for the sole purpose of giving bread to the poor of the city, and from the right of embracing any of the fine arts or liberal professions, an exception is made in favour of the professions of physician, surgeon, and pharmacist. But even to the exercise of these there are certain grave obstacles and limitations. The public schools and gymnasia are all closed to them, and they are forced to depend upon their private means for all the preparatory and incidental studies imposed as conditions for such a career—such as the course of philosophy, Latin, mathematics, and physics. Admission to the university is only to be obtained by a special authorization upon supplication to the cardinal vicar, and the graduates are bound to take oath that they will exercise their skill only on those of their own religious creed. This limitation is even stated on the attestation which is given them in place of a diploma. Once, in semi-barbarous times, Jewish physicians prescribed for the bodily ailments of the Pope and the chief princely houses, but in these civilised days they are only considered worthy to cure each other.

They are also allowed to exercise the art of the apothecary or druggist, provided they can furnish documentary evidence of their education and skill; but it is not easy to procure a permission from the government, and cases are not wanting where the patent for free practice has been refused to applicants who have fulfilled all the requirements and conditions of the law, and have educated themselves specially to this end—the government, with a bitter irony, granting, instead of the required permission, an attestation of complete capacity, and there stopping.

But in Rome the Jews are not only excluded from all colleges and foundations of public education, except in the above-named case, but also from all institutions of beneficence and charity, such as hospitals, and houses of refuge and protection for poor and invalid persons; and this notwithstanding they are founded and maintained by funds of the public exchequer or municipality, raised by taxes which weigh as heavily on the Jew as on any other citizen.

Again, the Jews in Rome are not even permitted to hire a farm or a foot of soil, or to cultivate it either for themselves or even as labourers for others. If any one hire or cultivate land it is under the name of some Catholic who is the ostensible tenant, and if he be discovered he is subjected at once to pillage and punishment.

Prohibited thus from the exercise of honourable professions and trades, excluded from the colleges and hospitals, to the support of which they are forced to contribute, and oppressed by the heavy weight of ignominy which is cast upon them, the moral and material results need not be stated. They are demoralized in character, and beggared in purse. If, despite the restrictions and obstacles which everywhere oppose them, a Jew, by force of talent and energy, succeed in raising himself above the condition of the majority of his caste, and accumulate a little fortune, the government, never weary of oppressing him, denies him the common privilege of investing it in other real estate than the miserable houses within the Ghetto itself; and as the chief portion of these belong to Catholics or religious confraternities even this slight concession is little more than a mockery. This law, recalled into vigour in 1825, is also extended to all mortgages upon real estate in the city.

In the courts of justice, too, they are placed under a special ban. Their moral dignity not being sufficiently dishonoured by the humiliations already stated, their testimony is not admitted in civil questions, and all notarial acts and papers signed by them as witnesses are declared null. Yet, with an extraordinary inconsistency, they are accepted as witnesses in criminal cases, with this proviso, that their testimony, however rich, able, educated, and honest the witness may be, cannot avail against that of the vilest Catholic.

The execution of all the restrictive laws against the Jews and the settlement of their religious questions are delegated to an exceptional tribunal under the jurisdiction of the Inquisition, and especially of the criminal tribunal of the cardinal vicar. What justice is measured out to them there may be easily imagined. It is all arbitrary, and according to the weight of the cardinal vicar's hand. In civil causes, not touching commerce, a decree was renewed in 1834, by which they were withdrawn from the jurisdiction of the ordinary civil tribunals and subjected to ecclesiastical tribunals, composed of a single judge in the first and second instance, who having rarely to do with civil causes was esteemed all the better for the settlement of Jewish questions.

Within the last year Pius IX. released them from the obligation of petitioning the cardinal vicar for a special licence, without which they had previously been denied the special passport enabling them to travel within the Roman States. But this alteration is unsubstantial, inasmuch as the bishop vicar or inquisitor of any place where they go may arbitrarily expel them at any moment, or limit their stay to one, two, or three days at his pleasure; or levy a tax upon their entrance, as is actually done in some cases; and may arrest or imprison any of them who may be induced by necessity or interest to overstay the licensed period for an hour.

Let us now see what is their burden of taxation. In 1554 Julius III. obliged the 115 Jewish universities which then existed in the Pontifical States to pay each an annual tribute of ten *scudi* to the "Casa dei Catecumeni." These universities being nearly all suppressed by Paul IV., and the Jews restricted to the three cities of Avignon, Ancona, and Rome, the community at this last city were forced to pay the tribute due from all the universities which were suppressed; and Clement VIII., having inflicted on them other burdens, fixed the annual contribution at 800 *scudi*, of which 300 went to the benefit of the Monastery of Converts. These 500 *scudi* destined to the Casa dei Catecumeni were afterwards increased to 1,100, in consequence of this singular fact:—an apostate Jew, named Massarano da Mantova, having written a book against the Hebrew religion, Urban VIII. ordered the Roman community of Jews to pay him an annual pension of 600 *scudi* as a reward for attacking their faith, and after his death this pension was decreed perpetually to the Casa dei Catecumeni as an appendix to the 500 *scudi* which it previously received. In addition to this it was decreed that, if a Jew of any country should present himself announcing his intention of embracing Christianity, and before his baptism should withdraw, the expenses of his maintenance should be charged to the community of Jews at Rome.

Besides this, they are forced to pay to the surrounding parishes, as a compensation for the Christian population which might otherwise occupy the area of the Ghetto, the sum of 113 *scudi* annually. Being under the supervision of Catholic officials, they must also pay 205 *scudi* for presents to them at Christmas and in August. 109·92 *scudi* are also exacted for apparatus and boxes for the use of the public deputations in the Carnival. A regular tax on industry and capital now paid by 113 individuals, and varying in amount from 4 *scudi* to 150, is also required. 360 *scudi* are levied on them as salaries for the attorney, accountant and tax-collector of the Hebrew university, who are required to be Christians and Catholics. They are taxed one *baiocco* on every pound of meat they buy. And what is more preposterous than all, the secretary of the vicariat, who has special jurisdiction over the Jews, receives from them an obligatory stipend of 73·60 *scudi*, paid even now as compensation for the duty which formerly belonged to him of accompanying with carabineers the Jews who were forced to listen to the preaching against their religion in St. Angelo in Pescheria.

These extraordinary taxes are levied from a population so poor that it is estimated by candid and competent persons that, of the 4,000 now included in the Ghetto, more than one-half are entirely without property, and are forced to live from day to day upon what chance and begging may bring. All colleges, hospitals, and institutions of charity being closed to them, the expenses of education and the support of their own poor and sick fall also on the Jewish community itself. A serious illness of any one among half of the population throws him at once on the public purse. But under all these exactions the Roman Jews have established a church, a university, and good schools of instruction and elementary education, and tax themselves with 300 *scudi* to support the poor, in addition to all private charities. The Roman government and the Roman institutions do not even contribute a *baiocco* to charity or education; on the contrary, the financial administration of the university is subjected to a commission, the members of which are all Catholics, presided over by the minister of finance, and paid there for by the Jews themselves. In a people thus oppressed there must be immense vitality and energy, or they would long ago have ceased to exist. But, despite their sufferings, there are in this community persons of admirable education, liberal views, and perfect probity. That a large portion is demoralized and degraded is not so much their fault as their misfortune.

The ordinance of Sixtus V., by which Jews are prohibited from employing Christians, is still in force, but it is permitted to Christians to make servants of them.

Not only as a class do the Jews suffer in Rome, but the Church, entering into their private households, violates the sacred rights of families. On a baptism effected either by force, or when the person is not of an age to be conscious of the value of the ceremony or to give an intelligent consent, they found a right to tear a Jewish child from his parents, and prohibit all future intercourse. The case of the Mortara child has justly moved the indignation of the world. It has been made public, but it is by no means an isolated case. Was there ever a sadder spectacle than that sorrowing mother following from town to town the child which had been ravished from her arms, and in anguish of heart praying at the feet of obdurate churchmen for her maternal rights—for the scant permission to see and embrace her child? There is nothing surely that steels the heart like bigotry. Yet the logic of the Church is terrible, and, granting its premises, its conclusion is inevitable. But suppose some fanatical Catholic should drive a watering-engine some summer day through the Ghetto, and, flinging the hose right and left, should scatter baptismal water on all sides, in the name of the Father, Son, and Holy Ghost—would it be any satisfaction to the poor Jews to be assured that, by irrefragable logic, the Church would then be bound to tear from every family their little children who had thus become Christians, and that it would be its duty to inflict sorrow and misery upon all those wretched families? Or is it completely satisfactory to know that the Church does not desire this, and would even punish the fanatic with the watering-engine who turned the hose of baptism on these unfortunates? Would it heal their wounds to know that the Inquisition had stretched him on the rack?

This unhappy logic strikes in another way. A Jewish father resolved on apostacy has the right to offer up to the Church his wife and children under age. Yet if he withdraw from his vows, he has no right longer to live with his family, in his first religion. Though the children and wife may refuse the apostacy, they cannot be given to the husband and father. Logic does its work. The canonical laws order every convert to Christianity to make an offer to the Church of his or her relations; and if in such cases, during the novitiate of forty days prescribed by law, the individuals thus offered resist all attempts at conversion, so that the priests are compelled to send them back to their relations, the latter are forced to pay their expenses of maintenauce during the forty days.

In the Pontificate of Leo XII., a fact somewhat similar to that of the Mortara child occurred. A servant was reported to have baptized a Jewish child who was dying; and thus by the sprinkling of a little water changed a condemned heretic into a redeemed Christian. The Pope therefore ordered splendid obsequies to be performed, and a long procession of priests, *frati*, and soldiers, entered the Ghetto, and with great solemnity bore the body to the near church of St. Angelo in Pescheria, where masses were sung for its soul. The next day the Jewish father received a bill of the whole expenses of this ceremony, which he was forced to pay.

During the past year, on the eve of Lent, a report was spread abroad among the common people of Rome that a little Catholic child, who was missing, had been seized and murdered by the Jews, in order, according to their alleged custom, to confection with his blood their unleavened bread. What was the action of the government? Did it attempt to allay the excitement of the ignorant classes, which was threatening violence and murder, by a public proclamation declaring such a report to be calumnious, and instructing the lower classes that the supposed custom was only a horrible superstition, and never existed? Oh no! Carabineers were sent into the Ghetto, violating the sanctuary of their temple, and hunting through the houses in search of the missing child. The honour of the Jews was left spotted, and their personal safety threatened, without a word to give the lie to this infamous calumny, which had its origin in the statement of an ignorant woman, who received it from a magnetic medium. The poor Jews, in fear of their lives, dared not for days walk in the city, and God knows where the affair might have ended had not the child at last been found, far away from Rome, in the Campagna.*

---

* I have taken pains in the above account not to exaggerate in any particular the burdens which weigh on this unhappy people in Rome. The facts are sufficiently strong in themselves to awaken pity on the one side and contempt on the other. But that the reader may assure himself of the truth of these statements, he is referred to the article "Ebrei" in the "Ecclesiastical Dictionary," compiled by Gaetano Moroni, under the Pontificate of Gregory XVI., who was his patron; to the admirable pamphlet, "Sull Emancipazione Civile degli Israeliti," by the Marchese Massimo D'Azeglio; to an elaborate article on the same subject, published in the journal "L'Educatore" in 1857, from the pen of the Abbé Zanelli; another, in the ",Cimento," by Michele Mannucci; and still another, very carefully and candidly written, which lately appeared in the "Nazione," at Florence, on the 26th November, 1859. These among

But the air is thick and full of bad odours in this Roman Ghetto. Let us pass through it. A few steps lead us out of its precincts, and we stand on the banks of the Tiber, whose yellow waters, swinging round a curve, whirl turbidly along, and turn the slow wheels of great mills. The air breathes freshly on our faces,—and picturesque in the soft Italian light rise the towers, domes, columns, bridges, grey lichen-covered roofs, and crumbling ruins of Rome. The sun turns all to gold as it drops to the horizon. The round, broken, ivy-covered walls of the Golden Palace of Nero, that lift themselves before us, it regilds; the tall dark cypresses are hung with golden balls; the mediæval tower of Sta. Maria in Cosmedin is sheathed with flashing plates of gold; the yellow molten river of Midas sweeps along under our feet. Even in the windows of the Ghetto that look out upon it there are golden panes that dazzle the eye. Nature is as prodigal to their humble, wretched houses as to St. Peter's dome that towers against the evening sky. It gilds their roofs, and paints the flowers at their rickety lattice windows with dyes richer than Popes' tiaras and Cardinals' robes. It recognises no difference between Christian and Jew.

Look round. There, trembling behind its opal veil of air, rises the Alban Hill, and blushes soft and rosy as a dream. Villas and towns gleam out on those dim exquisite slopes, and a soft delicate air comes breathing over the Campagna and rustles through the trees that cluster at our feet, and bears its blessing, too, up to the Ghetto streets, where the breath of Christian charity is too dainty to enter.

---

others have been my sources of information, which I have carefully verified by conversation with well-educated Jews, who themselves are members of the Roman community, and suffer under their disabilities.

CHAPTER XVI.

FIELD SPORTS AND RACES.

THE Roman Campagna abounds with all varieties of game, and offers a rich field for the sportsman as well as the ornithologist. Here fly birds of every size and plumage, from the tall stalking heron, who lifts himself from the banks of the Tiber and heavily drifts away as you approach, to the invisible lark that, far up in the blue, pours "his full heart in profuse strains of unpremeditated art"—from the long lines of wild geese, that wing their way in wedge-like ranks towards the Pontine marshes, to the smallest *beccafico* that fattens on the luscious figs of autumn. Wherever you go there are birds, twittering from the hedges, singing in the groves, or wheeling above to spy afar off their prey upon the earth. One English traveller has stated his surprise in passing through Italy to see so few birds, and to hear none of that warbling and twittering with which the English lanes are alive. To him the Campagna was silent—he saw and heard nothing. None are so blind as those who won't see, and none so deaf as those who won't hear. Of all the extraordinary statements made by travellers, this seems to me the most amazing. One has only to visit the market of Rome, and see the immense numbers of birds of every kind, to satisfy himself of its entire untruth. Where thrushes, nightingales, and larks are so common as to be an ordinary article of food, it is quite impossible to believe that Rome is deficient in singing birds. Perhaps this traveller was not aware of the fact that birds do not select the middle of the summer or the middle of the day to sing in hot climates.

In the marshy plains around Ostia are miles upon miles of half-submerged country where not a dwelling is seen. Here vast fields of tall *canne*, with their flags half-mast high, rustle in the wind—here long, exquisitely tufted grasses wave their plumes, and heavy bulrushes nod, and slender reeds wave in the wind,—on their crests sings many a little bird, and from beneath their covert start into sudden arrowy flight hundreds of snipes with a shrill wailing whistle. Through the openings sportsmen may wade for a long autumn day and meet no living person; and if they do not fill their bags with marsh birds and snipes it is their own fault.

All along the coast, where the blue Mediterranean washes a low sandy country from Ardea round to Fumicino, there is excellent quail-shooting. These birds differ entirely from the American quail; they are smaller, have a uniform grey plumage, and their meat is brown. They migrate in the spring from Africa to Italy, flying by night across the sea in companies of thousands, and dropping all along the shore in the early morning. On the very skirts of the sea the *contadini* spread lines of nets upon poles, and the quails, exhausted by their long flight, and eager to gain an immediate resting-place, fly lower and lower as they approach land, and alighting on the first strip of the shore are at once caught in the nets. They are thus taken in great numbers, and it is not uncommon for tens of thousands to be brought into the Roman market in the course of a single day. There they are sold for a trifle, and are excellent eating. Those which have strength to fly over the nets seek refuge under the bushes and trees in the country around, where they are flushed by sportsmen and shot on the wing.

Woodcocks and various kinds of partridges are also to be found in the woods along the coast as well as in the interior. The woodcocks are remarkably large, and during the winter season the market is full of them. Ducks, too, are found plentifully in the lower marshes and pools towards the Pontine marshes, and there also alight flocks of wild geese on their way across Italy.

The season for quails is the spring. In May vast flights of these birds come over, and the sport is at its height. Then the inns at Fiumicino, Ostia, and all along the coast, are thronged with sportsmen. Everywhere you will see them in their long boots and rough homespun clothes, striding out on foot, their double-barrelled gun on their shoulder, and a couple of half-bred dogs leashed together and following at their heels. If the ground over which they are to hunt is distant, you will meet them rattling along in a low two-wheeled *carretta* with a rope bottom, their provisions and dogs lying under their feet, and one of the tough little Campagna horses harnessed into the shafts. All the summer long there is no shooting, except of little birds; but with October the sporting season again commences. Many a sportsman who has spent the summer in the city then makes an excursion into the country. The hunting *villeggiatura* commences, the villas are filled, and the crack of guns is everywhere to be heard. From the city the little *carrette* set off early in the morning for the distant sport, and by sunrise they are at the huts of Norcini. Here sportsmen often spend weeks, hunting and shooting all day long, and gathering in companies around their rude tables at night to recount the day's sport, to boast of their skill, or lament their bad luck.

Some of these hunters seek the wild boars that frequent the thick forests of Cisterna and Nettuno, and most exciting and dangerous sport it is; others pursue the wild deer or *capriuole*; and others, the ducks, hares, rabbits, woodcock, and smaller game which abound. Most of them are ready to shoot anything and everything they see. Their bags when they return are motley enough, and mingled with game birds is many a one which an Englishman or American would disdain to shoot, as beneath the dignity of a sportsman. Sportsmen and sailors are equally given to long yarns, and the wonderful stories which are told around the board at these nightly gatherings exceed sometimes those of Falstaff and "the misbegotten knaves in Lincoln green." If "confirmation strong" is not to be found in their bags, there is always an admirable reason at hand.

The foreigner who berates the Italians as a weak, cowardly set, with no love for manly sports, should take a trip with them for a week's hunting of the wild boar, and he will find the work quite as tough as deer-stalking in the Highlands, or even as shooting tame birds in an English preserve, with trained dogs to point game and his sisters to look on and applaud his skill.

Much of the game, however, which supplies the market is taken by the ignominious means of the net. Everywhere on the Campagna you will see them spread to snare the little birds. There is even a less manly way of securing them which deserves mention. A sort of green labyrinth of trees is planted in a circle on some height; through this are little alleys and openings, and in the centre is a leaf-covered hut. Here the sportsman carries scores of cages containing singing-birds of every description. Some of these he places in the hut, and some he hangs on the shrubby trees, the branches of which are smeared with bird-lime. The singing and twittering of the little prisoners attract the free birds flying over the trees, and down they drop into the green and inviting arbour. Here they are caught in the bird-lime, from which they cannot extricate themselves, and the guard, who keeps watch in his hut like a spider in the centre of his web, takes them by scores; sometimes even by hundreds in the course of a single day.

Another curious method of decoying birds common among the Romans is by the *civetta* and a bit of mirror. The sportsman purchases one of the owls which are always to be found in the market by the Pantheon, and taking it out into the Campagna, plants a pole, and ties it securely to the top; on the ground he places his mirror, and then hides himself behind a bush, or tree, or rock near by. The owl fluttering on the pole, and the glitter of the mirror, attract scores of larks, for these are very curious birds, and they gather around over him to investigate matters. From his hiding-place the sportsman shoots one after another of them without scaring the rest, for their curiosity entirely overcomes their fear, and they return again and again, despite the direful experience of their companions.

There is no place in the world more admirably adapted to hunting than the Campagna. It abounds in foxes, and there are no fences and few hedges to stop the hunter or risk his neck. Of late years a subscription pack of hounds has been kept in Rome, to which most of the Roman nobility and many foreigners are subscribers. The annual subscription is 30 *scudi*, but those who follow the hounds, and are not subscribers, are expected to send in a donation at the end of the season towards the maintenance of the pack. They meet twice a week during the winter and early spring, at an appointed place on the Campagna. On these occasions the scene is very gay. For days before the hunt the talk of all the English is about the "meet," and the Italians, aping the English, call it the "*mita.*" Scores of carriages thronged with foreigners and Romans, and multitudes on horseback, are then seen gathered together on one of the rolling heights; mingled with them are the red coats of the hunters. Horses are galloping over the green slopes; companies on foot are exploring the vicinity—lying in the shade of the ruins— talking and laughing round the carriages. It is a picnic of foreigners. Some bring out their hampers and spend the day in the ruins, and Spillmann has always a store of eatables for those who have not thought to supply themselves beforehand. Meantime the hounds arrive, and the group of hunters begin to straggle after them. Carriages follow as well as they can. Brown, Jones, and Robinson make little leaps over runnels and any impediments they can find, sometimes getting a tumble on the green sward for their pains, but always intent on showing to their admiring sisters what gallant horsemen they are. Wonderful riders and wonderful steeds make their appearance. Some turn out their feet as if they were dancing, and show the air between them and their saddle at every step in the most gallant way. At last the fox is found, and away stream the hunters, their red coats topping the knolls. The hunt sweeps off in the distance—now lost to sight, and now emerging from the hollows.

The volunteers soon begin to return, and are seen everywhere straggling about over the slopes. The carriages move on, accompanying as they can the hunt by the road, till it strikes across the country and is lost. The sunshine beats on the mountains, that quiver in soft purple; larks sing in the air; Brown, Jones, and Robinson ride by the side of the carriages as they return, and Count Silinini smiles, talks beautiful Italian, and says "Yas." He is a *guardia nobile*, and comes to the house twice a week, if there are no balls, and dances with Marianne at all the little hops. Signor Somarino pays his court meanwhile to Maria, who calls him prince —emphasizing the title when she meets her friends the Goony Browns. And so the hunting picnic comes back to Rome.

The last year we had no hunt, for, unfortunately, a young Roman was thrown and either seriously injured or killed; and the Pope declared hunting to be a dangerous amusement, which he could not permit. This broke up the whole sport. The hounds were obliged to be sold, and the English might grumble as much as they chose, and have reason on their side too, but *that* did not mend the matter. The hunt was over, and with it one of the pleasantest amusements for the foreigner in Rome.

The papal court had not always this objection to hunting. In the old times the hunt was joined in by cardinals and Popes themselves, and conducted with lavish luxury and expense. The Venetian ambassadors sent by the government to Rome at the time of Leo X. give some wonderful accounts of these gaieties in the "good old times." One of them describes a hunting-party given by Cardinal Cornelio, which is amusing, and shows the vast difference between the papal court then and now.

"Matthew Dandolo," says he, "went to hunt with the cardinal on Saturday, and they took a stag, a wild goat, and a hare. The cardinal was mounted on a dapple-grey Spanish jennet of great beauty and nobleness, admirably well paced and ornamented with black housings. He was dressed in a plaited priest's vestment, shirt of scarlet colour, and without lining. On his head, above his skullcap, he wore a Spanish hat, dark-coloured and ornamented with tassels of black silk and velvet. They went twelve miles out of Rome to hunt. The company comprised about one hundred horsemen; for when the cardinal goes a-hunting many Roman nobles and gentlemen of other countries, that take pleasure in the sports, accompany him. There was Messer Serapica among others, sad, and very much out of spirits. The cardinal sent on eight mules loaded with nets, which were immediately stretched in a little valley shut in by hills, not very high, but difficult to ascend. Through this valley the stags and boars were to pass. The huntsmen, whose business it is to know the haunts of the stags and other animals and their lairs, had not yet come up, having gone to lie in ambush for the game. When they arrived the cardinal dismounted, and took off his upper clothing, remaining in a jacket of brown Flemish cloth, cut close and tight to the body. The rest of the company also dismounted. Then the cardinal having remounted, and assigned to every one his place, they proceeded to a lovely meadow by which the stags were obliged to pass. A small river, deep and swift of stream, ran through it, and it was crossed by several little bridges. This meadow was guarded by dogs, of which there were a great number present. The cardinal then mounted on a jennet of great value, which his brother Don Francisco had brought him from Spain, and all set about driving the stag from his cover. Three or four were very shortly put up. Two of them ran into the net and entangled themselves; one was caught, but the other escaped. Then three exceedingly fierce boars were driven out from the valley, and the whole hunt, horsemen and runners on foot, hounds and mastiffs, followed them a good hour, teazing them incessantly, as they at one moment rushed into the cover, and then again were driven out by the hounds. A fine sight it was to see, and the cardinal was exceedingly delighted and exhilarated. After that, in another beautiful meadow where there was only one small shrub, was prepared the *buffet* of the cardinal, and a table for fourteen persons, and at the head of it a chair of state for his lordship. And thus, some sitting on stools, and others standing, they ate, while the dogs howled at the sight of the food. The hunting-horns were then sounded, and those who had followed the hunt on foot strolled about with their bread and cup of wine in their hands. But in the midst of the dinner down came a heavy shower of rain, which washed all the company well, and watered their wine for them in their cups. They continued their dinner, however, only ordering felt hats to be distributed among the guests.

"The repast consisted of the finest fish, both sea and fresh-water, of which the *laccia** from the Tiber is the best fish in the world. We have it in the Po, and know it under the name of *chieppe*; but in truth with us the fish is comparatively worthless. There were exquisite wines of ten sorts: sweet oranges peeled, and prepared with fine sugar, were served at the beginning of the dinner with the first dish, as is the custom in Rome. There were three hundred mouths to feed. Then all mounted again, and came to a coppice of under-

* This excellent fish, which is common in the market of Rome, is the same as the American shad; but it is not much valued here now.

wood, into which some hounds were sent. The huntsmen started a very beautiful wild goat, which the dogs at last caught and killed. Then they chased a hare and took her. After that another stag was found, but was not caught. An hour before sundown they returned to Rome.

"The next morning the cardinal sent the produce of the chase on a mule as a present to the ambassadors. He sent also three other mules, each carrying a very fine calf, and twenty very long poles, carried by forty porters, from which hung capons, pigeons, partridges, pheasants, peacocks, quantities of salted meats of various sorts, and most delicate buffalo-cheeses, besides three pipes of wine loaded on twelve mules, carrying two barrels each; and for every four of these mule loads there was another mule carrying an empty tun, well seasoned, for holding the wine in the cellar. The wines were of three sorts, and most exquisite. Besides all this, there were forty loads of corn for our horses. And Messer Evangelista dei Pellegrini da Verrocchio, house-steward of the cardinal, a man of worship and reputation, addressed the ambassadors, inviting them to dine with the most reverend cardinal on the following Tuesday. The presents, which were estimated at 200 ducats, were accepted, as also the invitation to dinner." *

This was the way in which the cardinals of the time of Leo X. gave hunting parties.

Of the old *palio* races of the Carnival, in which buffaloes, horses, asses, and Jews, used formerly to run, the horse-races alone remain. These still, as of old, close at Ave Maria every evening the sports of the day. In the midst of the mad pelting of bonbons and bouquets, the jabbering of *Pagliacci* and *Pulcinelli*, the grimaces of buffoons, the obsequious pompousness of the Carnival doctors, the thrumming of guitars, the cataracts of lime-pellets showered from windows and balconies, the clattering of carriages and bells, and the wild din of laughter and merriment, when all the riot is at its height, boom! goes the cannon. It is the signal that the races are about to begin. The carriages at once turn into the by-streets, the crowd flocks closer together, and there is a suspension of hostilities between parties who have been pelting each other all day with flowers, and abandoning themselves to the wild gaiety of the saturnalia of the nineteenth century. We lean over the rails of the balcony and watch the motley crowd below. Suddenly there is a movement, and down come the papal dragoons, their swords clattering and their horses galloping, while the crowd opens before them its living waves, and

* Relazioni Venete, Second Series, vol. iii. p. 94.

closes behind them like the waters after the Leviathan's keel. Arrived at the Venetian Palace, they wheel about, and again come clattering down the Corso. All now expect the race, and thin out from the centre of the street. Around the starting-place in the Piazza del Popolo is built an open square of wooden *palchi*, where the magistrates of the city and their invited guests are seated. A rope is drawn across, and in the open space beyond the horses which are to run come plunging and rearing. They are covered with spangles and crackling tinsel, and balls armed with sharp points that swing loosely over their backs. Starting, rearing, kicking, and with difficulty held back by their grooms, they press against the rope and strive madly to escape. The signal is given, the rope is loosed, and away they go—the tinsel flashes and crackles, the sharp-pointed balls prick and goad them on, and full speed they rush up the Corso. Wild cries salute them as they pass, that madden them more. The crowd in the street opens before them as they plunge along, cleaving the roaring mass. Sometimes, frightened by the din, and irritated by the goads, they start aside into the crowd and leave the wounded and killed behind them. There is almost no Carnival race without its victims. The magistrates and umpires await them at the barriers drawn across the street at the upper end of the Piazza di Venezia, and cries of triumph salute the winning horse.

The owner of the horse then makes his appearance, and receives the *palio* or prize. This is purchased by a tax levied upon the Jews; who, when they murmur at it, are told to thank God and the Pope that they are no longer obliged to run the races themselves. Accompanied by a band of music, with the *palio* raised on a spear over him, the horse then makes the tour of the Corso and principal streets, and receives the applause of the people. After this a crowd generally escorts him to the house of the owner, who makes his appearance at the window, and showers *baiocchi* and *mezzi-baiocchi* among them as *largesse*.

Palio races are not confined to Rome, but exist in other parts of Italy. Among the most remarkable are those to be seen at Florence on the day of San Giovanni, when races are run in the Piazza in four-wheeled *cocchi* invented by Cosmo I. in imitation of the antique chariot races.

Equally remarkable are the *palio* races of Siena. This interesting old place retains more of its mediæval features than any of the Tuscan cities; and ancient forms and customs which elsewhere have worn out are still exhibited here in the picturesque festivals which take place on the 2nd of July and the 15th of August. On these occasions there are *palio* races in the famous Campo di Siena, as the principal piazza is still called, where the different *contrade* or wards of the city contend for a prize. There are seventeen of these *contrade;* ten of which, selected by lot, are allowed to run their horses at each *palio.* Each *contrada* has its protector, and on its festal day two pages, dressed in mediæval costume, may be seen carrying him a great basket of artificial flowers. Between the various *contrade* there is a deep-rooted jealousy, which has outlived the old divisions of party. The ancient fanaticism which once led to fearful scenes of violence and bloodshed still breaks out occasionally, and is specially manifested in the races of July and August. For weeks before they take place the *gonfaloniere* and the representatives of the *contrade* are in session in the Palazzo Pubblico; and this subject is eagerly discussed everywhere. In fact, it is almost the only topic of interest to break the uniform sluggishness, and almost death-like quiet, of this once agitated city.

For several days previous to the real *palio* there are trial races in the Piazza, where a greater or less crowd is assembled. The festival is a moveable one, not occurring on a fixed day, but always on a *festa,* and generally on Sunday. Each of the *contrade* furnishes a horse, which takes its name and wears its colours. There are the Tartaruga, Selva, Chiocciola, Pantera, and Aquila, forming the first division; the Valdemontone, Torre, Nicchio, Civetta, and Leocorno, forming the second; the Drago, Oca, Bruco, Giraffa, Lupa, and Istrice, forming the third.[*] The purse is only about 180 *Francesconi;* but party spirit runs very high, and there is private jockeying and betting to any extent—the means to obtain the prize not being always perfectly scrupulous. The race is run in the Piazza del Campo, which on these festivals is decorated with much taste. Around the semicircle fronting the great tower of the Palazzo Pubblico are erected stagings, with tier above tier of seats. From all the windows stream rich draperies of every fabric and colour; some of silk and satin, some of tapestry, and some embroidered in silver and gold. All the world is " abroad to see," and every nook and corner is crammed with people. The Piazza, which is in shape a vast shell, of which the hinge is the magnificent old Palazzo Pubblico, slopes upward, amphitheatre-like, to the outer edge of the semicircle, which is rich in palaces. The centre is so densely crowded by the population of Siena and of the country around, that one might almost run across it on the closely-packed heads. The pave-

[*] There were originally sixty *contrade,* but they were reduced by the Plague of 1348 to forty-two, and under the Medici to twenty-three. In 1675, six were suppressed for bad conduct; thus reducing the number to seventeen.

ment is strewn with yellow sand, and the corners of the diameter, where the Piazza slopes steeply down in front of the Palazzo that occupies the lowest place, are padded with mattresses, to save from broken heads and limbs the riders, who are not unfrequently flung from their horses with great violence at this dangerous turning.

The horses used for these races are the small, nervous, Sienese breed. They are ridden without saddles, and each of the jockeys is armed with a thick *nerbo*, with which, by the ancient rules of the race still in force, he is privileged, if he choose, to knock his companions from their horses, or in any way, by cutting them across the face, or beating back their horses, to overcome his opponents. To see the little horses and the small course, one would at first suppose these races to be mere child's play; but there is often a violence of struggle which makes them anything but that. It is not at all uncommon for fierce fights to take place during the race between the riders, in the course of which one or more are beaten violently from their horses; and this, added to the difficulty of rounding the steep slopes and sharp angles of the Piazza, where the horses, going at full speed, sometimes lose their balance, and fling their jockeys headlong against the padded mattresses, make this sport more exciting and dangerous than would be at first imagined. The course is thrice round the Piazza, and as the race draws near the close the losing parties often attack each other violently, and use every means in their power to drag and beat back the winning horse; so that the sport becomes at once a race and a fight.

At five o'clock in the afternoon the Piazza is open to carriages, which then make their entrance in long procession. The nobility and gentry bring out their richest equipages, the state hammer-cloths are on the boxes, the horses are decorated with plumes and flowers, the coachmen and footmen are dressed in quaint old liveries of the ancient times, and each vies with his neighbour in the splendour of his equipments. Towards seven o'clock the course is cleared; bands burst forth into music, making the whole place echo; and the grand procession of the races enters. First come the seven representatives of the seven *contrade* which do not join in the race, and after them follow the ten *contrade* which are to contest the prize. Each *contrada* is preceded by a drummer, who beats like mad on his drum. Then follow two flag-bearers or *alfieri*,* dressed in ancient costumes of rich colours, and bearing the flags of their con-

---

* The rank of *alfiere* was once held in high honour, and he was elected with great pomp and ceremony. After his election, the captain and *consiglieri*, accompanied by crowds from the *contrade*, visited his house with trumpets and drums, and presented him his flag on a silver tray.

trade, which they wave backward and forward—now flinging them high in the air, and catching them as they fall ; now twisting them round their bodies ; now whirling them under their legs, and over and under their arms and round their necks ; and executing with wonderful skill and grace all sorts of strange manœuvres. Then follow four officers, each attended by two pages, and all in mediæval costume. Then, accompanied by his groom, comes the running horse, gaily decorated with flowers, and his hoofs covered with gold leaf; and after these, two mounted *fanti*, each with a helmet on his head, from which nod three tall plumes of the colour of his *contrada*, and clothed in a parti-coloured dress with the arms of the *contrada* on his back. In this order, one after another of the *contrade* enter the Piazza ; and when they are all in the effect is wonderfully picturesque. The drums are all beating together, and the bands are all playing at once, till the din is almost deafening ; while the crowd salute their *contrada* as it passes with loud cries. The air seems to be full of rich flags that are whirling everywhere. Splendid hangings float from all the windows, and show brilliantly against the soft greys and yellows of the houses and palaces. The amphitheatre is paved with faces. The grand machicolated tower of the Palazzo seems to lean over against the blue sky, and, still beyond, peers into the Piazza the black and white striped campanile of the Duomo. And all this barbaric clash of music and pomp of costume carries one back out of the present century into the middle ages.

At last rolls in the great *carroccio*, drawn by six horses, with a tall pillar in the centre, surmounted by a bell, and from which wave the flags of the various *contrade*, while on its platform, in costume, stand pages, and the seven representatives of the *contrade* that do not run, and around it is a group of men that steady it with ropes as it slowly clatters along, covered with draperies and gaily gilded. In front of it, on the top of a pole, is the silver plate, which is the prize, tied about with black and white ribbons, these being the Sienese colours. This is perhaps the most peculiar feature of the festival. It is the relic of the old car or *carroccio*, invented by the Milanese in the middle ages to bear the flag in battle. The Italians then were in the habit of fighting desultorily ; and to reunite them and give solidity to their charges this *carroccio* was invented, which it was a point of honour to defend to the last. All the Italian cities adopted this custom ; and in war the *carroccio* always accompanied the army. It was drawn by two oxen, covered with red and white housings ; and wherever it stopped was the place of battle. From its centre rose a tall mast, from which floated the white standard with a red cross, and at each corner was a man who steadied it with a rope against the wind and the jarring of its motion. On the summit was a bell to give the signal for attack and retreat, or to call to council. The direction of this *carroccio* was allotted to the most expert in military tactics and the art of war, who became its captain; and, to give him greater authority, he received by public donation his helmet and sword. In the period immediately succeeding Federigo 1., the *podestà*, who had also the supreme command of the "*milizie*," commanded the *carroccio*. In Siena there was a special officer nominated for this duty, called "*capitano del popolo*," who was the head of the magistracy of twenty-four, and could not be a foreigner. His dress consisted of an under vest of red, over which was an ash-coloured tunic worked in scarlet and gold, a red velvet cap, red shoes and stockings trimmed with gold, and a red *toga* with a golden cord fastening it round his neck. The commander of the *carroccio* was accompanied by eight trumpeters, and a priest who said mass during the battle, and shrived the dying. The car itself was the *pratorium;* wherever it was posted were the head-quarters. Here signal for battle was given, and here was the refuge of those who were driven back or wounded, as the old rhyme says :—

> "È il carroccio nel campo un imago
> Della patria, una casa paterna,—
> È un' concilio che i Duci governa,
> È un' asilo, una meta, un' altar."

The *carroccio* originally used in these Sienese *palii* was taken from the Florentines in the famous battle of Monte Aperto, fought on the 4th of September, 1260; a battle, by-the-way, truly wonderful in its statistics, according to the Sienese. If we believe them, they numbered only 1,100 against 40,000 Florentines; and yet, with a loss of only 300 to 400, they killed 10,000 of their antagonists. We know of nothing like this save the slaughter in India by the English troops, as related by the English journals. When at last the old *carroccio* would no longer hold together, a new one was made after the old model; which is that at present in use, as I am told.*

While we have been talking of the *carroccio*, the procession has made the tour of the Piazza, and arrayed itself in front of the Palazzo Pubblico, glowing with many colours. The jockeys mount and make little runs, and then all together come to the starting-post, where a rope is stretched across. Let me now describe what took place at this race when I first saw it in 1857. As the horses

* See "Le Contrade di Siena, da Flaminio Rossi," MS., in the public library of Siena.

appeared there was an unusual agitation in the crowd, for the "Tartaruga" horse, which wore black and yellow for its colours, had proved in the trial races the best horse. Whispers and mutterings were heard all round, men shrugged their shoulders and said meaningly, "*La Tartaruga non vincerà,*"—the Tortoise shall not win,—"*davvero, non vincerà—per Dio, non vincerà.*"

"*Ma perchè?*" I asked innocently—"Why not?"

"*Eh! perchè!*" "Why indeed!" was the answer, with a significant shrug. "Don't you see his colours? they are Austrian."

"Well; but the *contrada?*" asked I. "What will they say? Will they agree that he shall not win?"

"Whether they agree or not, the Tartaruga shall not win. First, because the colours are Austrian; and then, because, *per Dio*, he shall not win. You do not know the jealousies of these *contrade*—the betting, the violence, the hatred—and it has been settled that the Tartaruga shall not win."

"We shall see—*Vedremo.*"

As we spoke the horses came up to the rope, the cannon pealed from the fountain, the rope dropped, and away the horses went. Three or four of them only passed the stand, for at once a struggle and confusion was seen among the riders. The Tartaruga jockey, despite his struggles, was dragged from his horse and forced out of the lists. The people swayed backwards and forwards, jumping up and shouting wildly in their excitement. Among the horses that started there was the same struggle, the jockeys striking each other fiercely in the face and breast, grappling together, and belabouring their adversaries' horses over the head to force them back. One of them was knocked clean off his horse, but he caught his antagonist's bridle and spoiled his race also. Only two now remained. These, as they passed the starting post, on the second round, were fiercely assailed by the others. Some screamed, some threw themselves into the lists with wide extended arms to stop them. One horse was stopped, but the other broke through and continued the race amid the wild shouts of his *contrade*, and the still more violent screaming and hissing of the others. Some cried, "Stop, stop! it is a false start!" Some cried, "Go on,"—and on he went. There was dire confusion. Two of the horses, maddened by the tumult, broke away and rushed through the excited crowd, which in turn became alarmed and began to scatter over the course. Meantime, the first horse continued his race, got over the third round without being stopped, and came up to the goal. The cannon fired—the race was over—he had won.

Then ensued the most excited scene. A crowd of persons of his *contrada* rushed to the winner, tore him from his horse, embraced him tumultuously, lifting him off his feet, and kissing him on both cheeks. The other jockeys and their *contrade* were equally fierce in their rage. They came along, now throwing their arms wildly in the air, now flinging their whips on the pavement, now seizing their own heads between their hands and literally tearing their hair, and breaking forth in mad vociferation. All over the Piazza the same scene was enacting. Here and there were disputant groups; some, in their excitement, straddling wide and half-sitting down, with both hands violently gesticulating in the air. Such a scene of excitement without evil consequences I never beheld, and no one could doubt the extraordinary excitability of the people after beholding it.

Everything, however, exploded in gestures and words. A mass of friends attended the winner to the post, where the prize, a silver dish surmounting a painted banner, was given, and he was borne away in triumph.

After the races in July, the winning horse is escorted by his *contrada* to the church, where he is carried in for a benediction; the people sometimes breaking through all bounds in their enthusiasm, and making the walls of the church ring with their cheers.

On the subsequent day the winning horse is paraded through the streets with music; then brought up-stairs to the second story of the Palazzo Chigi, and exhibited from the balcony to crowds of spectators below in the Piazza, who roar their applause.

These *palio* races were instituted in Siena in the year 1650. For fifty years previous to this period the races were run by buffaloes, ridden by *fanti*; that sport having taken the place of the old bull-fights in the year 1599. "*Perchè i costumi cominciarono di ingentilirsi.*" This, however, did not seem to have pleased the people, and on the occasion of the arrival in Siena of His Most Serene Highness the Grand Duke Ferdinand II. and his Grand Duchess Vittoria della Rovere, with their eldest son, Prince Cosimo, the present horse-races were substituted, and have ever since maintained their popularity. The first took place on November 6th, 1650, when the number of horses that ran was twenty. In 1655, the day set apart for the *palio* was changed to the 2nd of July, and remained so ever since. In 1719, the number of horses was restricted to ten by a civic decree, in consequence of an accident by which Osti Paci was killed. At the same time it was decreed that "*nerbi*" should be distributed by the police to the riders at the time of the race, in order to prevent the use of certain long, elastic whips (*fruste lunghe elastiche*) which it had previously been the custom for the *contrade* to provide, and by which the *fanti* could be easily knocked off from their horses and were in danger of their lives. On March 7th, 1721, all the rules of the *palio* now in force were laid down, and have never been altered, excepting in the substitution of the *nerbi*. These *palii*, therefore, are precisely the same that they were more than two hundred years ago.

In 1655, Alexander VII. visited Siena, his native town, and on this occasion he was received with great pomp and fêted for twelve days. Among other amusements, there were *palii* of horses, and the marble wolf of the public fountain in the Piazza for several days poured forth from his mouth abundant streams of wine. The Piazza and city were also illuminated with torches, lanterns, and artificial fireworks; and one hundred gentlemen paraded through the Piazza (as I learn from an old Sienese manuscript), making a splendid show of themselves—"*rendendo vaga mostra di se.*" Great cars also appeared on the Piazza in the evening. On one of these was represented the wolf and the river Ombrone, which held a flag with S. P. Q. S. on it; while Justice, Prudence, Force, and Temperance sat before with a great shield. The other car represented the city of Rome, under the form of a matron, with a wolf and a child, who stood on a pedestal holding a standard; while Religion was in front, with the Pontifical keys and the triple crown, and Peace, Charity, and Innocence at her side. These were accompanied by forty pages in white and red livery, carrying torches, and were moved along by men hidden beneath them. It is interesting to know that just for this occasion, and to gratify papal tastes, the bull-fights were revived, which had been abolished fifty years previously.*

In nothing does the kindliness of the Romans show itself more than in their treatment of the dumb beasts who serve them. It is very rare to see in the streets of Rome those reckless and brutal exhibitions of violence and cruelty to animals that are but too often seen in England and America. The French system of vivisection is here, thank God! unknown. This people is passionate, but not cruel in its nature. The Church, too, takes animals under its protection, and on the day dedicated to Sant' Antonio a celebration takes place which is most characteristic, and, to my mind, full of humanity and good feeling, and calculated to produce a good effect on the people. This is the annual blessing of animals which takes place on the 17th of January, when all the horses, mules, and donkeys in Rome are carried to the Church of Sant' An-

* Relazione delle Feste nella Terza Parte del MS. P. Ugurg.—Sienese Library.

tonio (which was once a Temple to Diana,—*Quantum mutata ab illa*) to receive a benediction. The doors are thrown wide open, and the church and altar are splendid with candles, and the crowd pours in and out to see the pictures and make the sign of the cross. The priest stands at the door, and with a broom dipped in holy water sprinkles the animals, as they pass in procession before him, and gives them his benediction. All the horses in Rome are there, from the common hack to the high-bred steed of the prince; some adorned with glittering trappings, some covered with scarlet cloth and tinsel, with red roses at each ear, and tufts and plumes of gay feathers nodding at their heads. The donkeys come too, and often bray back their thanks to the priest. Some of the riders also are gaily dressed; and those who are more superstitious, I mean reverent, receive beside the benediction a card with prayers and blessing, for which they pay according to their means. But see, there is a rustle in the crowd—who comes now? It is Gaetano, coachman of Prince Piombino, and prince of coachmen, mounted on an open car, and driving his magnificent team of fourteen horses with an easy skill which provokes the plaudits of the crowd. Up he comes, the people opening before him, and triumphantly receiving his benediction passes on gallantly and sweeps round into the great Piazza of Sta. Maria Maggiore, followed by the eyes of all. And here, too, are the great black horses of the cardinals, with their heavy trappings and scarlet crests, lumbering up with their luxuriant coaches all glittering with golden carving, to receive the blessing of Sant' Antonio. All honour to thee, good saint, who blessest in thy large charity not man alone, but that humbler race who do his work and bear his burdens, and murmur not under his tyrannical inflictions—that inarticulate race who suffer in patient silence "the slings and arrows of outrageous fortune!" Thy effigy shall be hung upon my stable-walls, as it is in every stable in Rome.

CHAPTER XVII.

FOUNTAINS AND AQUEDUCTS.

"Nobil onda,
　Chiara figlia d' alto monte,
　Più ch' è stretta e prigioniera,
　Più gioconda
　Scherza in fonte,
　Più leggiera
　All' aura va."—*Metastasio.*

ROME is the city of fountains. Wherever one goes he hears the pleasant sound of lapsing water. In every square it piles its columns in the sunshine, toppling over with the weight of myriad pearls and diamonds, and plashing back into the carven basin. From year to year the splendid fountains of St. Peter's toss their white waving veil of spray into the sky, embroidered with prismatic gems, to cool the sultry air, and lull the senses with their rustling murmur. From the Janiculum the Fontana Paolina rolls its silver cascade with a roar into its granite basin. Over artificial rocks, at the feet of Neptune and his Tritons, rush the many streams of the Fontana Trevi, and gathering in a broad and flashing fall, slide into the little quivering lake below, that keeps the blue of the sky in its troubled bosom. Seated in the Barberini Square, on his travertine shell, and supported by dolphins, the picturesque Triton of Bernini blows from his conch into the sky a stream of pearls. From mossy grottoes, where giant river gods are watching in stone, burst forth beneath a lofty obelisk the many streams of the Piazza Navona; and as if one fountain did not suffice for this great square, it is flanked at both ends by two others. In the Piazza di Spagna the lower waters gush out into a stone boat, and pour over its sides into a wide well. In oblong basins of Egyptian granite, that once were bathed in by the ancient Romans of the age of Caracalla, plash the fountains of the

Farnese Piazza; and on a circular basin of oriental granite from the Temple of Romulus, a massive column of water crumbles constantly in the sun beneath the colossal figures of Phidias and Praxiteles in the Quirinal. Everywhere there are fountains—on the heights of the Capitol, and in the valley of the Pantheon, that is overflowed yearly by the Tiber, when the mountain streams are swollen.

Not only in the piazzas, where elaborate vases, figures, and obelisks surround and embellish the fountains, is the sound of water heard—at every corner it pours its single streams from gaping mouths. In the court of every house it plashes and gurgles, as it fills the simple stone wells. In every garden it spirts its fine thread into the air. Under-foot, below the surface of the pavement, it glides, to cool the earth. From old Egyptian lions' mouths it pours solemnly. Vast receptacles for washing, it fills with its constant streams—in the open air, where scores of Roman women stand all day, and shake and beat their linen in the sun—or under the dark shadows of palaces in gloomy cellars, where no ray of sunshine ever penetrates.

Everywhere around these fountains are picturesque groups, who pause to chat while the stream fills their copper vases, before they bear it away on their heads. Here climb and scramble little boys, and sit astride the marble lions' backs, or lean over to drink from the gushing stream. Here the thirsty horses of the *carrettieri*, stop and plunge their noses into the basins, jingling their bells as they toss their heads. Here peasants fill their dried gourds on their way out on to the Campagna. Here, in the summer, orange and lemon stands are placed, each with its little jet drawn from the fountain through a *canna*, or slender tin canal; and here the melon-seller erects his booth, swashing his boards constantly with water.

As you walk the empty streets at midnight you hear the low bubbling sound of water everywhere. Shut your eyes near any one of the great squares, and especially in the neighbourhood of the Fontana Trevi, and you can scarcely believe that you are not far out in the country, where leaves whisper and torrents flow and tumble. In the morning the foreigner just arrived runs to the window, and opens the shutters, thinking that it is raining, but it is only the fountains, and the sun bursts in with a surprise.

Go out upon the Campagna, and all along the road at intervals you will meet wells and fountains, where the horses and oxen are drinking, and where the *carrettieri* fill anew the wine-casks on which they have levied a way-tax. In the noble old villas at Frascati you will find extraordinary water-works. Great fountains tower shivering with sunshine into the air, and fall into vast basins surrounded by balustrades, where carven masks, half hidden by exquisite festoons of maidenhair, pour their slender silver tribute. Down lofty steps, green with moss, the water comes bounding and flashing like a living thing, to widen below into a pool, where glance silver and goldfish. Through the green alleys, over which sombre ilexes twine their crooked branches, or down the vistas of clipped laurel hedges, you will see the silver lines of fountains sparkling against the green background. In ruined gardens the water dribbles over staggering leaden pipes into basins, on whose rim green lizards bask panting in the sun, and slowly drips into the mantling pool, greened over with decay.

Come with me to the massive ruins of Caracalla's Baths—climb its lofty arches, and creep along the broken roofs of its perilous terraces. Golden gorses and wall-flowers blaze there in the sun, out of reach; fig-trees, whose fruit no hand can pluck, root themselves in its clefts; pink sweet-peas, and every variety of creeping vetch here blooms in perfection; tall grasses wave their feathery plumes, out on dizzy and impracticable ledges, and nature seems to have delighted to twine this majestic ruin with its loveliest flowers. Sit here, where Shelley wrote the "Prometheus Unbound,"* and look out over the wide-stretching Campagna. There sleep in the sunshine the steep sides of Gennaro, with tender purple shadows nestling behind its cloven wedges. There, like a melody, rises from the long still level of the sea the varied and undulating line of Monte Albano, sweeping in exquisite curves to the crest of Monte Cavi. Far off a shining band flashes between the land and sky—there lies the Mediterranean. Below you, stretching off towards the mountains, amid broken towers, tombs and castled ruins, that everywhere strew its rolling surface, behold that long line of arches, with here and there great gaps opening between lofty, ivy-covered fragments that seem like portions of grand porticoes—that is the Claudian Aqueduct. It domineers over all other ruins that you see—stretching its arches out and out till, "fine by degrees and beautifully less," they run away into the mountains' bosom. There it lies, like the broken vertebræ of some giant plesiosaurus, a ruined relic of a mighty

---

* "This poem," says Shelley, in his preface to "Prometheus Unbound," "was chiefly written upon the mountainous ruins of the Baths of Caracalla, among the flowery glades and thickets of odoriferous blossoming trees, which are extended in ever-winding labyrinths upon its immense platforms and dizzy arches suspended in the air. The bright-blue sky of Rome, and the effect of the vigorous awakening of spring in that divinest climate, and the new life with which it drenches the spirits, even to intoxication, were the inspiration of this drama."

age and a distant time. From the "heart of the purple mountain," the shadow of trees and the song of birds, it drew its waters to supply the baths of the Romans in this very ruin on whose heights we stand; and the sylvan stream that listened on the hill-tops to the nightingale, and was brushed by the wavering butterfly, here leaping at last to light from its dark and narrow prison heard suddenly the clash of gladiators' swords and the murmur of a Roman populace.

Look down there from your dizzy height. Sunken in the ground are monstrous, inform blocks, the fragments of the ceiling that roofed with mosaics these spacious halls. When these great pieces fell Rome shook with their thunder, and the people said, "There is an earthquake!" Of the giant columns of granite which once bore them up, nothing now remains save shattered fragments strewn upon the ground. But one of them still stands in the Piazza di Trinità at Florence, holding on its top the figure of Justice—"out of reach," as the Florentines say. The statues and precious marbles of antiquity are all gone, save a few broken bits and relics, kept in a fenced-in chamber below. The Farnese family and their successors, the Frati, swept the place of everything. Its ancient marble guests, the Flora, the Farnese Bull, the Hercules, and the Venus Callipyge, are now in the museum of Naples; and in the Villa Borghese and the museum of San Giovanni in Laterano you may see portions of the mosaics of athletes which once adorned these walls. The sloping pavement of black and white mosaic crumbles away daily under the tooth of time, and the reckless destructiveness of travellers. Sheep and goats nibble under the shadow of the massive walls, that still stand firm as ever. Once in a while a spasmodic and idle effort is made at excavation, when a few old broken-down beggars are let in to make believe dig, at a few *baiocchi* a day. But, except at such times, nothing could be more peaceful, grand and beautiful than these "mountainous ruins of the Baths of Caracalla."

Let us reconstruct them as we stand here, and imagine them as they were in the days of their perfection.

They were commenced by Caracalla in the year 212, continued by Heliogabalus, and finished by Alexander Severus. The baths themselves covered an oblong rectangular space of 720 feet in length by 375 feet in width; at both ends was a large hall with a semicircular tribune, all paved in the richest mosaic. These were devoted probably to gladiatorial exercises, to recitations of poets, and to lectures by philosophers and rhetoricians. Connecting them was an immense oblong apartment, called the *pinacotheca*, or *cella caldaria*, where were the hot baths. On one side of these and on a lower level, was another chamber similar in shape, containing the cold baths, and called *cella frigidaria*. On the other side was a vast circular edifice, called the *laconicum*, which was composed of a large central hall surrounded by chambers, and containing the vapour baths. The modern staircase by which we ascend to the platforms of the ruins occupies one of the pillars of the *cella caldaria*; so that, looking down over the side towards the city, we see the *cella frigidaria*, and opposite, the long hall of the *cella caldaria*; while still beyond rise the giant towers and arches of the *laconicum*, through whose open spaces gleams the western sky. The *cella caldaria*, which was surrounded by columns of granite, were probably the most magnificent of all the halls.

Outside the central building was an open space, surrounded by porticoes and gardens, and containing a gymnasium, stadium, arena and theatre, where games, sports, plays, and races took place; and beyond the porticoes on the westerly side was a great reservoir to supply the baths; the water being brought to it by the Antonine Aqueduct, which was fed by the Claudian Aqueduct, and brought over the Arch of Drusus. The circuit of this magnificent inclosure is nearly a mile, and within its baths could be accommodated 1600 bathers at a time.

But these were not the only public baths of Ancient Rome, not even the largest. The Baths of Diocletian, which according to Barouius were built by 40,000 Christians at the command of their great persecutor, covered an area of 150,000 square yards, and afforded baths to no less than 3,200 persons, or double those of the Thermæ of Caracalla. The remains of this magnificent structure are scattered over the Piazza di Termini; some portions are built into studios, some into granaries for the French troops, some embodied into the church of San Bernardo, and some into the Termini prisons. In its very centre stands the noble church of Sta. Maria degli Angeli, built by Michael Angelo, and shapen out of the *cella caldaria*. Here one still sees the massive columns of Egyptian granite in their old places, and from the vaulted roof still hang the metal rings on which the ancient lamps were hung. Behind, where once was the swimming bath, stretches the beautiful cloister of the convent of the Certosa; and there, wandering among its silent and peaceful arcades, or lingering round the central fountain over which wave the grand cypresses planted by Michael Angelo, one may ponder the wonderful changes which have taken place on this spot. Now and then you may see a monk moving solemnly along, but he will not speak unless he passes another of his order, and then he will only say, "*Fratello, dobbiamo morire*," (Brother, we must die). To which a hollow answer will come, "*Fratello, morire dobbiamo.*" So, breathing the orange blossoms, you may dream there over the past, and in its silence summon up the loud murmurs, the noisy games, the bloody sports that once it knew.

Besides these, there were the Baths of Agrippa, to which some antiquaries have considered the Pantheon to be the hall of entrance; the Baths of Constantine, which covered the summit of the Quirinal, and occupied the present site of the Consulta, the Palazzo Rospigliosi, and the Villa Aldobrandini; the Baths of Nero and Severus, which occupied a portion of the Piazza Navona, and extended thence nearly to the Pantheon; and the Baths of Titus on the Esquiline. To these the people flocked in crowds. Here they lounged and bathed, looked upon the games, betted on the gladiators, struggled in the gymnasium, and listened to the recitations of poets and rhetoricians.

The extraordinary number of *thermæ* shows how universal among the ancient Romans was the daily use of the bath. It was not confined to the rich classes, but extended to all, and was usually taken after exercise, and before the principal meal of the day, then *cœna*, which in the time of Augustus was made at about three o'clock. Before these vast imperial *thermæ* were built, none of the Roman baths were free. The price of a bath was, however, only a *quadrant*, which was the smallest coin in use, and this was paid to the *balneator* or keeper of the establishment. Children, however, below a certain age paid nothing. It was then the custom for those who wished to court the favour of the populace to throw open the baths to the public on certain days free of expense. But after the emperors built their *thermæ* no charge was ever made, and every one who chose might have a bath.

The bathing in the *thermæ* was without individual privacy. Originally, men and women bathed in separate chambers; but in the licentious days of the empire both sexes bathed indiscriminately together. Later, this practice, which naturally led to the grossest immorality and indecency, was forbidden by Hadrian and afterwards by Marcus Aurelius; but it none the less existed as late as the time of Alexander Severus, who prohibited, under severe penalties, any baths to be open in Rome for promiscuous use by both sexes. One has only to read Suetonius to acquaint one's self with certain shameless and disgustingly dissolute practices of the emperors in their private baths that almost surpass belief. Nothing, indeed, shows the low condition of public morals among the ancient Romans, and their open licentiousness, more plainly than the manner in which their public baths were conducted.

The modern Romans are not the children of their ancestors in this matter of bathing. In proportion to the number of inhabitants, there is less accommodation for public bathing in Rome than in any other city I know. The common people are not a bathing people. "*Dio mio*," cried one of them to whom I recommended a bath, "What? wash me from head to foot in *cold* water! I shouldn't dare to do it! I never did it in all my life. *Avrei paura davvero.*" Those Anglo-Saxons who take a cold bath every morning are looked upon here as little less than mad; and even the physicians shake their heads and say, That may do in your country, but it won't do here; and in this I am inclined to think they are right. Not that I mean to indicate that the Romans are, on the whole, a dirtier people than any other. By no means. The lower classes in no country are given to over-cleanliness, but in the middle and upper classes, their habits, I take from observation, to be quite as cleanly as the average. They wash themselves, but they do not take baths. They use the wash-bowl, but the bathing-tub and the shower bath frighten them. In the summer only do they indulge in the full luxury of water, and then they throng the shores of Civita Vecchia and crowd the esplanade of Leghorn to bathe. From morning to night the bathing-houses are besieged and the screams of bathers are to be heard. Oddly enough, however, it is a common custom for the whole family to take one bathing-house together and bathe all at once, without a notion of indelicacy. "All things are as they seem to all;" but I confess to certain old-fashioned notions—prejudices of education, perhaps, which I cannot overcome.

Mastro Egidio, the Solomon of the Longaretta, is a serious personage of great influence, and who has by no means a humble idea of his own importance. For forty years he was the Fontanaio of the Acqua Paolo at San Pietro in Montorio, and always wears the true Roman dress of his order—short-clothes with buckles on his shoes, a shirt without plaits, a blue sash round his waist, a *beretta* with a purple tassel on his head, and a double chain to his watch dangling from the fob. His memory runs back to the time of Pius VI., and at the election of Papa Gregorio XVI. he led the Trastevere squadrons to put down the seditious *carbonari* who agitated Rome. One day in those troublous times, seeing that the Pope was taking an airing in his carriage, Mastro Egidio summoned his band, and, going forth to meet him, presented himself at the carriage door, and assured the holy Father that he had nothing to fear, for the Trastevere was with him. The holy Father, putting forth his fat fingers, amiably patted the great Egidio on the cheek, saying "The Trastevere is always faithful."

"Holy Father," solemnly responded Egidio, "the spot where those holy fingers have touched me shall not be washed till Lent."*

Was not that a compliment?

But there are Mastri Egidii in other countries besides Rome. It is related that one of the gentlemen who received George IV. on his landing in Ireland preserved unwashed to the day of his death the hand which had been allowed to touch the palm of royalty.

It is the usual belief entertained by the English that they are the only clean people in the world. The Americans agree to this statement, with one exception in favour of themselves. But ready as I am to concede that the higher classes in England and America are scrupulous in this respect, I cannot agree that this is a characteristic of the lower classes; nor do I believe the middle classes, on the whole, are cleanlier in their habits there than in Italy. At all events, it must be admitted that the daily use of the bath is of comparatively late introduction into Anglo-Saxondom. Fifty years have made great differences in this respect. The ordinary notion of an Italian being a dirty fellow is derived, I suspect, in great measure, from the fact that he wears a beard, which till within the last five years was in England considered as proof positive of a dirty fellow. The same characteristic has been alleged by the English against every nation which wears a beard; and it is not ten years ago that a gentleman, in whose well-being I have an extraordinary interest, and of whose most private affairs I have an intimate knowledge, was told on a visit to London that, if he wished to go into society, he *must* shave off his beard, for that the prejudice against wearing a beard as being a dirty habit was so deep rooted, that it could not be braved with impunity. With the Crimean war the custom of wearing the beard was introduced into England, and now the English not only wear the longest beards in Europe, but find them excellent and admirable.

An Englishman, however, whether he be clean or not, looks clean. His fresh rosy face and light blonde hair give an immediate impression of cleanliness, that no Italian could possibly present, even were his *epidermis* scrubbed off by washing. But if any one, without prejudice, will take the trouble to walk through the Corso or over the Pincio on any day when the people are out, and examine them one by one, I think he will be persuaded that their linen is scrupulously white, their dress nice, and their hands and necks perfectly clean, to an extent rarely met with elsewhere in the same class, and

---

* Padre Bresciano tells this story in a paper published by him in the "Civiltà Cattolica."

certainly not to be seen in England. As for the lower classes, I never saw any who could be called clean, unless exceptionally. No, my good republican friend, not even in America, where you say there are no lower classes; and as for the lowest classes in England, nothing can exceed their filth and ragged wretchedness.

Apropos of washing, the learned Dr. Johannes di Mediolano, of the Academy of Salerno, gives us some very important information on this head. Washing after eating, he says, in his Latin verses, confers upon us a double gift; it not only sharpens the eyesight, but also cleanses the hands,—a fact which could scarcely have been known at his time, or he would not have mentioned it so gravely:—

> "Lotio post mensam tibi confert munera bina,
> *Mundificat palmas*, et lumina reddit acuta."

But I have somewhat strayed away from my subject. "Let us resume," as Byron says.

There were formerly no less than fourteen aqueducts, some authors say twenty, which supplied Rome with water. Of these, with the exception of three, the Acqua Virgo, the Acqua Claudia, the Acqua Alsietina, only the ruined arches, that form so picturesque and peculiar a feature of the Campagna, now remain.

Of all these ancient aqueducts, the Acqua Claudia and the Anio Novus were the most extensive and magnificent, and their ruins are the grandest of all that are seen about Rome. The Claudian Aqueduct was commenced by Caligula in the year 36 A.D. and finished by Claudius in 50 A.D. Its length was more than forty-six miles, and the source was near the thirty-eighth mile-stone on the Via Sublacensis. For ten miles it was carried above ground over those lofty arches, the remains of which, draped with ivy and blossoming with flowers, still stretch along the Campagna. Under its shadow sheep nibble, and between its sunny openings, or mounted on its broken ledges, herds of long-haired white goats crop the bushes and leaves that festoon it; while near by, leaning on his staff, the idle shepherd dreams the long day away in his quaint and picturesque costume. Wherever you go these arches are visible; and towards nightfall, glowing in the splendour of a Roman sunset, and printing their lengthening sun-looped shadows upon the illuminated slopes, they look as if the hand of Midas had touched them, and changed their massive blocks of cork-like travertine into crusty courses of matte gold.

Yet, magnificent as are these remains of the Claudian Aqueduct, they are surpassed by those of the Anio Novus, the highest and longest of all the aqueducts of ancient Rome. In length it was about sixty miles, and for the space of fourteen miles it bore its waters above ground over lofty arches, some of which were 109 feet in height. As they neared the walls these two great aqueducts, *par nobile fratrum*, joined together to pour their refreshing tribute into Rome.

But grand as is the effect of these colossal aqueducts upon the Campo Romano, still grander glimpses of them may be caught in the mountains. Hire a horse at Tivoli, and, taking a bridle-path through the quaint and picturesque olive forest, ride on for seven miles into the heart of the country. You will find no lack of wild beauty all along the road to delight you. The forest itself is filled with aged olives, that twist their hollow mossy trunks into every sort of fantastic shape, and stretch out their grim and withered arms across the path, with a wizard-like resemblance to enchanted human forms. Here and there you will see the woodcutters or guardians of the forest, and come across the rude *capanne* in which they dwell, and once in a while will meet with wandering flocks of sheep or goats. But for the most part it is a solitary ride, so lonely and secluded that, if the shape of Pan should start from behind a tree, you would scarcely be surprised; and the pipe you hear in the distance may well be his. At last you will come to a deep valley cloven down between two lofty hills. At its base babbles a torrent through tangled bushes and trees, and over it stride the gigantic arches of the Claudian Aqueduct. The tall poplars which grow beside the stream are dwarfed to bushes as you look down on them, and from below, as you gaze up at the colossal aqueduct, it seems like the work of the Titans.

All around Tivoli wherever you go are massive remains of these Roman works; and at a mile beyond the town, in the direction of Subiaco, the road passes beneath one of the arches, the top of which is crowned by an old mediæval tower. Most travellers who go to Tivoli content themselves with making the tour of the falls and *cascatelle*, visiting the villa of Mæcenas, and the romantic villa D'Este, and lunching in the Temple of Vesta; but few ever see the grand old castle, and fewer still explore the adjacent country, so rich in picturesque ruins of the ancient time. Yet here an artist might fill his portfolio with new and characteristic sketches of great beauty, and the antiquarian might spend weeks of purest pleasure.

In the ancient aqueducts the water was carried in channels of brick, or stone, lined with cement, and covered with an arched coping. Sometimes along the bottom of this channel were laid pipes of lead, *terra-cotta*, and even of leather for the water; but generally it flowed in a stream through the trough of the channel. At intervals along the course of the aqueduct were constructed reservoirs, called *piscinæ*, in which any sediment might be deposited; and near the city was a vast reservoir, called *castellum*, which formed the head of the water and served as a *meter*. From this the water was distributed into other smaller reservoirs, from which, again, the city was supplied by pipes. Why these aqueducts were built above ground seems never to have been satisfactorily answered; but as the fact that water was distributed in pipes through the city, and jetted in fountains, shows that the ancient Romans could not have been ignorant of the simple law that water will find its level, the giant arches would seem to have been constructed purely for architectural beauty.

Of the Claudian Aqueduct, only a portion was used by Sixtus V. in building the present aqueduct, which is called, after the conventual name of its founder Fra Felice, the Acqua Felice. It is not even an established fact, however, that any portion of this aqueduct was used; some writers declaring that only the remains of the Acqua Alexandrina were employed. These waters are drawn from a spot near the Osteria de' Pantani, on the road to Palestrina, and supply the loftier part of the city, from the Piazza de' Termini, where are the Baths of Diocletian, to the Piazza Barberini. They also feed twenty-seven fountains, among which the principal are the Fontana di Monte Cavallo, the Fontana dei Termini, and the Tritone de' Barberini. The water is clear and pellucid, but heavy, and is not highly esteemed for drinking.

Of all the fountains in Rome, the Triton, in the Piazza Barberini, that blows from his conch shell a stream of glittering pearls, is the most original, and, though *barocco* in style, the most harmonious in composition. On the other hand, the Fontana dei Termini, with its basalt lions, is the ugliest and most ludicrous. Over it in a great niche stands a colossal figure, with outstretched hand, swaddled in oppressive draperies, which is intended to represent Moses; but, in fact, the figure is that of a hideous dwarf, with a ferocious face covered by a massive beard, and with two great horns on its forehead. It is quite impossible to determine whether this dwarf has no legs or no body—both it cannot have. You cannot help smiling as you look at this monstrous abortion, and yet there is a tragedy connected with it. As the story goes, it was the work of a young and ambitious sculptor, who boasted loudly that, if the commission to make this statue were given him, he would model a Moses which should, to use his phrase, beat that of Michael Angelo all to rags. The government, impressed by his enthusiasm, gave him the commission. He locked himself into his studio, shut out the world, and gave himself up, body and soul, to his great work. At last it was completed, and the doors were thrown open to the public. Such a roar of scornful laughter then saluted his ears, that the poor artist, driven mad by his disgrace, threw himself in despair into the Tiber, and was drowned. Nevertheless, the government completed the statue, and there it stands in the Piazza di Termini, a warning to all ignorant and ambitious young sculptors.

The ancient Acqua Alsietina was restored by Paul V., and now supplies the Trastevere quarter, under the name of the Acqua Paolo. It was originally built by Augustus to supply water for his *naumachiæ* and it still subserves one of its old uses in turning the flour-mills on the slopes of the Janiculum, and feeds the massive Fontana Paolina and the exquisite fountains in the Piazza of St. Peter.

But by far the most esteemed of all the waters of Rome are those of the ancient Acqua Virgo, which still retains its name of Acqua Virgine. The name of this aqueduct was derived from a tradition that its source was discovered by a young girl, who pointed it out to some soldiers who were perishing of thirst. It was restored by Nicholas V., and for purity, lightness and absence of all sediment, its waters are unequalled by any in Rome or elsewhere. It enters the city on the Pincian Hill near the Porta Pinciana, spreads over all the central portions of the town, supplies the magnificent fountain of Trevi, the fountains in the Piazza di Spagna, the Piazza Farnese, and the Piazza Navona, and pours daily into Rome no less than 66,000 cubic *mètres* of water.

There is still another water, called the Acqua Sallustiana, which supplies a very small district in the neighbourhood of the Palazzo Barberini and the Porta Pinciana, and is highly esteemed. I shall not easily forget the solemn and majestic articulation of one of the *padroni di casa* in this vicinity, who, in recounting the various advantages of his house, always wound up with this climax: "*E poi, abbiamo qua l' Ac-qua Sal-lus-ti-a-na, l' ac-qua la piu buona che si trova a Ro-ma, l' Ac-qua Sal-lus-ti-a-na.*" It was impossible not to be impressed with this solemnity, and the *padrone* was to a certain extent right; the *Ac-qua Sal-lus-ti-a-na* is an excellent water, but it does not compare with the Acqua di Trevi.

Besides, the Acqua Virgine still subserves some of its ancient purposes, and though the days of the *naumachiæ* are gone, yet Rome cherishes the old traditions, and still exhibits vestiges of the ancient games. The grand and picturesque old Piazza Navona, once the Circus Agonalis of Alexander Severus, and now the vegetable market of Rome, offers in the month of August a spectacle which plainly recalls the old *fontali*. On Saturday evening all the benches and booths are removed, and the great drain which carries away the water spilled by the three fountains is closed. The basins then fill and pour over into the square till in a few hours it is transformed into a shallow shining lake, out of which, like islands, emerge the fountains with their obelisks and figures, and in whose clear mirror are reflected the cupola of St. Agnese and St. Giacomo, the ornate façades of the Doria, Pamfili and Braschi Palaces, and all the picturesque houses by which it is inclosed.

From the surrounding streets crowds of *carrettieri, vetturini*, and grooms now pour into the Piazza, mounted on every kind of horse, mule, and donkey; some riding double and even treble; and all laughing and shouting at the top of their voices. Then, with the clang of trumpets, come galloping in the horses of the dragoons and artillery, accompanied by hundreds of little scamps with their trousers rolled up to the crotch,—and splash they all go into the water. The horses neigh, the donkeys bray, the people scream, the little boys are up to all sorts of mischief, pelting each other with rotten oranges, squeezed lemons, and green melon rinds, till the Piazza echoes with the riot of voices and the splashing of water.

The next evening the sport is better. The populace crowd the outer rim of the Piazza, where numbers of booths are erected. The windows of the houses are thronged with gay faces, brilliant floating draperies, and waving handkerchiefs. Not only horses, mules, and donkeys are now driven into the artificial lake, but carriages welter nave-deep in the water, and spatter recklessly about; whips crack madly on all sides like the going off of a thousand sharp India crackers; and horses plunge and snort with excitement, sometimes overturning their carriages and giving the passengers an improvised bath.

After the sun has gone down lights are sprinkled about everywhere, and curiously-decorated cars come forth bearing a motley bevy of Naiads, Tritons, and other watery personages, who play carnival tricks and blow hoarse conches. At one end of the Piazza, towards the *Apollinare*, where the water is very shallow, sloping shelves are erected by the *cocomerari*, where amid glittering little lamps are set forth in long rows tempting wedges of water-melons. Around these are benches for the customers, and in a stentorian voice they invite purchasers with cries of "*Belli cocomeri! an'am, an'am. Qui si magna, si beve, e si lava er grugno.*" "Beautiful water-melons! come on, come on. Here you eat, and drink, and wash your chops with the beautiful water-melons." There is an illumination in every window, torches flare around the streets and flash in the water, the people dance, sing, and devour figs and watermelons, and the whole Piazza is a perfect saturnalia of noise and nonsense.

Every house in Rome, has a great stone trough or *pozzo*, into which a stream of water is constantly pouring with a hollow gurgle. The method of drawing water from these troughs is peculiar. From the kitchen windows which look down into the courts a stout iron wire leads to a spot above the trough. Upon this is suspended, by an iron ring and pulley, a tin or copper pail that is run down and drawn up upon this suspension bridge by a stout rope. All day long you will hear the rattling of this apparatus, as the stout *donna di faccende* souses the pail down into the fountain with a sudden slide, and then slowly drags it back dripping and creaking to her high window. Often there are little wooden balconies built out from the kitchen window which opens to the floor, with a sloping roof of tiles to shed the rain, and in such cases they serve as the platform to which the water is drawn. They are generally very picturesque, with their pots of flowers, their brilliant carnations, their large *terra-cotta* vases, their spiring weeds that grow out of the caves under the curved and moss-stained tiles, and the primitive shapes of the wooden railings. Here, by the half-hour together, the Roman women will lean and talk to each other across the court, and a charming picture they sometimes make, as they stand there in the sun, with a background of delicate grey walls stained by the hand of time with exquisite gradations of colour.

There is in many of the courts a large stone basin below for the washing of clothes, and all day long you will hear the song and incessant chatter and laugh of the washers. When their clothes are thoroughly washed, they are brought up-stairs, and swung out on long iron wires that stretch across the court, or from angle to angle of the houses. Each article is fixed to little rings, and a rope running through a ring at the opposite end enables them to be drawn out one after another over the court, where they hang and flap in the air until they are dry.

On these little platforms and balconies sturdy Juliets of the kitchen carry on mysterious communications with Romeos of the stable or garden below, and when no eye is looking they let down a cord to draw up—not a bouquet of roses, but a good stout cabbage or cauliflower, which their lover ties to it. Here in the winter the old *padrone*, in his faded dressing-gown and velvet skull-cap, often shuffles out and seats himself in the sun, and mumbles to himself, as he warms "his five wits;" and shall I not confess that here also I have often stood for an indefinite space of time, charmed by the varying and homely picture and watching the fun that goes on? Nothing can be more picturesque than these views from the back windows. Here a terrace with rows of flower-pots—there a quaint balcony broken into exquisite light and shade—above, perhaps, a tall tower looking down into the court, or an arbour of grapes, dappling the grey floor or wall with quaint shadows; and oftentimes a garden close by, with its little dripping fountain and its orange-trees, "making a golden light in a green shade," while above is the deep delicate blue of the Roman sky, against which are cut out the crimped edges of tiled roofs. Screams of wild Campagna songs, with their monotonous drawl, pierce the air, as the self-forgetful *donna di faccende* remembers her Campagna home and rattles out on their wires her files of snowy clothes.

Tidy American housekeepers will, I doubt not, differ from me. They will object that the place does not look clean, and that things have a careless and ruined look that they do not like. They would paint and whitewash it all over, for the demon that besets them is cleanliness. But, my good friends, we cannot have everything; we must choose; and when all is arranged according to your ideas, all that charms the eye of the artist is gone. Besides, what is dirt?—it is only a good thing in a wrong place, as has been well said,—and I am afraid it will never be agreed between us where the wrong place is.

My friend Count Cignale is a painter—he has a wonderful eye for colour and an exquisite taste. He was making me a visit the other day, and in strolling about in the neighbourhood we were charmed with an old stone wall of as many colours as Joseph's coat—tender greys, dashed with creamy yellows and golden greens, and rich subdued reds, were mingled together in its plastered stone-work; above towered a row of glowing oleanders covered with clusters of roseate blossoms. Nothing would do but that he must paint it, and so secure it at once for his portfolio; for who knows, said he, that the owner will not take it into his head to whitewash it next week, and ruin it? So he painted it, and a beautiful picture it made. Within a week the owner made a call on us. He had seen Cignale painting his wall with surprise, and deemed an apology necessary. "I am truly sorry," he said, "that the wall is left in such a condition. It ought to be painted all over with a uniform tint, and I will do it at once. I have long had this intention, and I will no longer omit to carry it into effect."

"Let us beseech you," we both cried at once, "*caro conte mio*, to do no such thing, for you will ruin your wall. What! whitewash it over! it is profanation, sacrilege, murder, and arson."

He opened his eyes. "Ah! I did not mean to whitewash it, but to wash it over with a pearl colour," he answered.

"Whatever you do to it you will spoil it. Pray let it alone. It is beautiful now."

"Is it, indeed?" he cried. "Well, I hadn't the least idea of that. But, if you say so, I will let it alone."

And thus we saved a wall.

CHAPTER XVIII.

BIRTHS BAPTISMS, MARRIAGES, AND BURIALS.

N the purely Roman quarters of the city of Rome, where old customs still exist, and the influence of the stranger is little felt, may be frequently seen a large card hung against the window or at the entrance of the grocer's shop, on which are printed or scrawled in large letters the words, "*Bacili per le Partorienti.*" You naturally apply to your courier for an interpretation and an explanation of this sign. But a courier has generally the same surly unwillingness to give full information on any subject that a sea-captain has to tell you how the wind is and how many knots you are making; and as your courier is no exception to the general rule, he contemptuously shrugs his shoulders at your ignorance, and, speaking in a language he calls English, but which has the same confused resemblance to it as the reverse of worsted-work with all the straggling ends to the finished pattern on the right side, he ungraciously growls out, "*Bacili per le partorienti*—Dat is wash-bowl for vooman *en couches.*" Now you are quite as much at sea as you were before, but you are afraid of your courier (all Americans are), and would rather rot in ignorance than be bullied, and as you know he will bully you if you ask another question, you make a note of the words with the intention of asking what they mean.

Will you allow me to tell you? They mean, literally, "bowls for lying-in women;" and that you may understand what these are, you must know, that it is an old custom, "of which the memory of man runneth not to the contrary," among the middle classes in Rome, as soon as a mother has given birth to a child, for the *comare,* who is the English cummer, gammer, or, in polite phrase, god-mother, to present her with a large *bacile* or bowl, heaped full of such articles of food as are fitting for her during her confinement. The contents of the *bacile* are generally *paste* of all forms and patterns, such as *maccaroni*, *vermicelli*, *stelletti*, *anelletti*, and *capelletti*, which are built up into grotesque shapes—the favourite design being of a ship with *maccaroni* masts sailing in a sea of *semolino*, where imbedded eggs show, dolphin-like, their backs — delicate young chickens, not Mother Carey's, swim breast upward—and savoury herbs vegetate luxuriantly round the smooth rim of the bowl. This *bacile*, built so curiously, and looking for all the world like the bowl the wise men of Gotham went to sea in, is formally presented to the mother with a gracious ceremony of congratulation, and she lives upon its contents during the period of her lying-in.

Before the birth of the child, and during the confinement of the mother, nothing is so much guarded against by all who surround her as odours. Visitors are enjoined to put aside every kind of perfume before entering her chamber. Flowers are strictly prohibited, and any husband who should dare to bring a cigar into the room would be looked upon as a mere brute. Though ordinarily obtuse in the sense of smell, the Italians think that perfumes are poisons during the season of child-bearing; and though they will keep the windows and doors closely shut until the air is foul with over-breathing, and leave the long wicks of their lamps to pour a poisonous smoke into the already stale atmosphere, yet at the same time, in order to guard against the evil effects of a chance perfume, they will cover the bed, and stick into the nostrils of the mother the leaves of the *matricario*, which is used as a sedative to prevent spasms and nervousness. Nor is this custom confined to the sick chamber of the *partoriente*. I have seen stout hearty women, when near their confinement, walking about the streets with two great sprigs of this plant (centaury) thrust into their nostrils, and presenting a most ludicrous appearance.

Long before the birth of the child the *comare* and *compare* have been chosen among the most important acquaintances of the parents, and, the moment the happy result takes place, the husband hastens to inform them of it, and to make preparations for the ceremony of baptism, which usually is performed within forty-eight hours. In the mean time the "wise women" of the neighbourhood, who are thought to be skilled in divination, are admitted to the chamber of the mother, and then, after examining carefully the infant, even *ad unguem*, they prophesy his fortune, and wish him all sorts of luck. The husband meanwhile makes all the arrangements for the baptism, which it is the ambition of every Roman should take place either at St. Peter's or at St. John Lateran's, and prepares presents for the *levatrice*, the sacristan, the bell-ringer, the coachmen who are to drive the company to the church, the *chierico* and the *curato*—for no ceremony of importance is ever performed in Rome without *mancie* to all the parties concerned.

If the child be a girl the baptism is not much of an affair; but if it be a boy great preparations are made. He is dressed in a gala dress, covered with an embroidered cloth, and carried in the arms of the *comare*, who has on her holiday bodice and satin skirts, and all her jewels and rings, and her great *filograne* pin stuck into her hair. The seat of honour in the first carriage is given to her and the child, and they are accompanied by the midwife and the nearest female relations. In the second carriage is the *compare*, with his brother or brother-in-law on his left. If you meet this convoy you may know at once the sex of the child by the colour of the ribbon pinned to its dress, which the *comare* takes special heed shall flutter out of the carriage window. A red ribbon indicates a boy, and a blue ribbon a girl—blue being the colour of the Virgin, to whom all female children are dedicated.

Arrived at the church, the priest receives it near the font, accompanied by a little boy who carries a candle, a box of salt, and a vase of oil. He mumbles an indistinct hum of Latin, looking carelessly round him the while; rubs the oil behind the child's ears; makes the sign of the cross on its forehead, mouth, and breast; thrusts his soiled finger covered with dirty salt into its mouth, till it spits, grimaces, and screams with disgust; then, lifting the *stola* from his own neck, he places it over that of the child, ladles out some holy water from the font and pours it over his head, and the ceremony is over. It is a superstition that the child screams because the devil goes out of it, and the priest with his dirty finger and nauseous salt is pretty sure to secure this good omen, and thus to content the soul of every true Catholic present. If it did not scream under such circumstances, "the devil must be in it."

In case, however, the child be very ill and not expected to live, it is competent not only for the priest, but for any Catholic to baptize it—for the salvation of a human soul is not to be hazarded; and priests do not always move rapidly; and in such cases no time is to be lost. But there is this inconvenience, that being once baptized, the ceremony cannot be repeated. There is also another difficulty, in case the child be born of Jewish parents; for any pious Christian chambermaid or nurse may in her affright at some spasm of the infant's utter the words of baptism, and thus render it the duty of the Church at once to deprive the Jewish mother of her offspring, and forbid all intercourse between them,—a sad case, not so unfrequent as may be supposed, and of which the Mortara case furnishes a well-known example.

When, however, the child is well, and the baptism is performed by the priest in church, the day is one of great pomp, ceremony, and rejoicing. The father on these occasions is not of much importance, and, to confess the truth, has the air of an interloper, who is present on false pretences. You see him standing about on the outskirts of the group in a fatuous way, awkwardly twisting his hands, blushing and breaking into little spasmodic laughters when he is addressed, making sad efforts to appear quite at his ease, and venturing at times upon jests which, though well received by weak-minded persons of his own sex, are looked down upon scornfully by all the women. A truly pitiable figure he makes, and one cannot help wondering what under heavens he is doing "*dans cette galère.*" Meanwhile, all the petticoats revolve like satellites around the little red baby in the centre, keeping up a constant chorus of "*Quant' è bellino—oh Bimbo, Bimbino!*" sticking their fingers into its doughy cheeks, and examining its cap and ribbons, and coral, and fingers and nails, and wondering, and whispering, and whinnying round it. *La Gampina*, the nurse, is queenlike, lording it over all—radiant with pleasure and importance, frowning upon the husbands, chirruping to the baby, and patronizing the female gossips, who all feel in their secret bosoms a deep envy of her in these moments of her greatness. How grandly, surrounded by her satellites, she sweeps out of the church after the baptism is done, the black coats of the "poor male trash" scarcely daring to share her triumph, but following meekly, and in a melancholy way, after her, "bringing their tails behind them!" The crowd which has gathered round the font to see the ceremony from outside and inside the church gazes after her as she retires. Shaky old beggar-women, leaning on their crutches, send after the child their benediction, and then hobble away into the corners to talk it over among themselves, and prophesy and tell old stories, and croon away about it for hours.

The baptism over, the carriages, after making a long tour through the principal streets, return home, and then the friends sit down to a great supper or dinner, where all the varieties of the season are set out. There are great dishes heaped with golden fry, "*fritti misti*," among which are slices of cuttle-fish, liver, cauliflower, little fishes, brains, shreds of pumpkins, and artichokes, all mixed together—followed by *gelatine* and cold jellied meats, and boiled beef with mushrooms, and a great turkey, and a dessert of *ciambelle*, candied fruits, *pinocchiati*, and roasted chestnuts. The fare is uncommonly savoury, the red wine flows freely, *brindisi* are given to the whole family, always in rhyme, and there is great jollity—amidst which, perhaps, at times the piping voice of the young Roman citizen, in whose honour the *festa* is made, may be heard from the adjoining chamber.

As soon as the mother is well enough, she has a daily "reception," and, propped up in her bed, with both her nostrils stuffed with some sweet-scented herb, she smilingly receives the compliments and good wishes of all her friends who come to congratulate her, each bringing a present for her or her young Roman. Here, again, the husband plays a very inferior *rôle*; and if he venture to open his mouth, his ignorance of all the matters relating to the treatment of infants is openly jeered by the other sex, and he is recommended to apply his talents to the care of the shop.

The odour of tuberoses was formerly thought to be fatal to women "*en couches*." It is related that Madlle. de la Vallière, while she was lady of honour to the queen, having found herself unfortunately in this situation, and dreading an exposure, kept her room under a pretence of indisposition. But the queen suspecting the real state of the case, and curious to discover if her suspicions were justified, sent word that she would pay her a visit. The offer was received with a great show of gratitude, and the queen found, on entering the chamber, that Madlle. de la Vallière had filled it with tuberoses.

For those who are too poor to bear the expenses of lying-in, as well as for those who desire to conceal the fact, the hospital of S. Rocco offers a shelter and a hiding-place. This hospital was founded in the year of the jubilee in 1500, approved by Alexander VI., and confirmed by Pius IV. It stands near the Porta di Ripetta, has a large hall for the poor, and various chambers for those who can afford to pay and desire concealment, and is capable of supplying fifty beds. Each bed is separated from the rest by curtains and a screen. Any woman near her confinement who presents herself, whether married or unmarried, is at once received. Her name and condition are not asked, and she may also conceal her face if she desire, so as not to be recognized by any one. On the register of the hospital each inmate is distinguished by a numeral instead of a name. Entrance is forbidden to all men and women to see the patient, whether they are parents, relations, or strangers, and no one is admitted save the physician, surgeon, midwife, and the women attendants. The hospital being exempt from all criminal and ecclesiastical jurisdiction, the women who enter it are secured from molestation of every kind; and when they choose to leave it, provision is made to enable them to depart in the most secret way and at the most opportune time; the gate of the hospital not opening on any public street, but in a court which has two issues, one of which opens on an uninhabited lane which joins with other little frequented streets.

Women who cannot allow their condition to be known without loss of character are received in S. Rocco a considerable time previous to their confinement, and thus the honour of many families, says Morichini, is saved, and infanticide is avoided. Those who are not poor pay a small sum of about three *scudi* a month, which is increased if better care, attendance, and living than the ordinary affords be required. When they are near their confinement, however, all pay ceases. Women of this class are called, like the others, "*depositate*," and do not divulge their name and condition in life.

As soon as the children are born they are sent with all due precaution to the "*Pia Casa degli esposti in Santo Spirito*," those mothers who wish to receive them again placing on them a mark by which they may be recognized, and every one can at pleasure reclaim them from Santo Spirito at any time by a proper identification.

The average number of women who have here sought refuge between the years 1831 and 1840 is stated by Morichini to be 165 each year, which is very small in proportion to the population, compared with the number received in a similar manner in Paris, where from 2,000 to 3,000 are annually taken in.

In ordinary cases the hospital maintains these inmates free of expense for eight days previous to their confinement and eight days subsequent; but, if there be any special reasons, this time is enlarged. Many, however, only remain there two or three days, and some only a few hours. The medium period of their stay is from four to five days.*

The infants in Rome are not clothed in the long loose dresses used in England and America, but are wrapped in swaddling-clothes, wound closely about them from neck to foot, so that they look like little white mummies. This is a custom which has come down from the ancient Romans; and in an antique *basso-rilievo* at Rome may be seen a nurse presenting to the mother her infant child, girdled in "*incunabula*," or swaddling-clothes, precisely similar to those now in use, and having on its head the same close cap which is still worn. I hope my friends of the other

* The revenue of this hospital is 2,490 *scudi* a year, of which 690 are contributed by the public treasury. It is administered by *confraternità*, and presided over by a partial deputation. See Morichini, Instituti di Pubblica Carità, vol. i. ch. 7.

sex will bear with me, when I confess that to my mind there are advantages as well as disadvantages in this method of dressing infants. Though the child is more restricted in the use of its legs when thus swaddled, yet this is in measure compensated by the fact that it is less liable to injuries of the spine from being held across the arm of a negligent nurse, is preserved from danger of rupture, and is supported equally at all points at a period when the organs and muscles are undeveloped and weak. Straight legs and a straight spine are certainly desirable; though it is so charming to the nurse and the mother to force a "wee toddling thing" to stand on its bandy legs before they are equal to their burden, and though it does not look "so cunning" as it would in its long dresses, with its little bare arms and bare chest, it is really much less likely to catch cold, fever and croup; and, besides, a swaddled baby is much more out of the way of danger and disease. I have always found the infants themselves very well content in their swaddling bands, and my experience is that Roman infants do not certainly cry more, if even as much as ours. Among the poor families who cannot attend to their babes as the rich can, and who are all day at work, this custom of swaddling is most convenient. The child is so well supported that it can be safely carried anyhow without breaking its back, or distorting its limbs— it may be laid down anywhere, and even be borne on the head in its little basket without danger of its wriggling out.

But whether swaddled or not, the children, in spite of damp rooms, bad food, and little care, grow up into stalwart maids and men, develop early, ripen into beauty, and fall in love, like all the offspring of Adam and Eve. The *contadini* almost invariably marry young, and as soon as the youth and maid can rake and scrape enough money together to buy the *trousseau* for the bride, and to purchase a few gold ornaments, they invoke the aid of the priest to help them into the holy bonds of matrimony. After the *sposalizio*, or betrothing, the *promessi sposi* go everywhere hand in hand together, and call each other *sposo* and *sposa*, for it is a sort of half-marriage, and is celebrated as such by dancing, singing, and eating, in company with their friends.

Among the peasantry the parents generally give half the dowry in money, and half in clothes. All the former is spent in jewellery for the bride; and, as it is never enough, the *sposo* adds to it all he can raise. He also buys the bed, and furnishes the chamber. The expense of the wedding is divided. The dowry is not so much measured by the means of the particular *contadini*, as by the custom of the neighbourhood; and in order to come up to the standard much hard work and pinching is often necessary. For months the maid and her family are employing every spare hour in weaving cloth for the bride, and in the winter evenings the hand-loom, which is everywhere to be seen in the *contadino's* house, is rattling and clattering, to make into home-spun linen the flaxen thread, which all summer long, at every interval of leisure, or while tending the cattle, they are spinning on their distaff. No *contadina* will marry until she has her jewels and ornaments, and upon them is generally expended every *baiocco* of solid money which she and her *sposo* have. They are young, and careless of the future. They are strong, and can live on the daily labour of their hands. The marriage is the great event of their life, and then, at least, for once, they will have their way and be happy, without consulting the cost. So all the money goes into the necklace of coral or golden beads, the long, dangling earrings, the wheatsheaf of gold which shakes from the dagger that holds up the shining braids of blue-black lustrous hair, and the broad rings that cover half her fingers. These ornaments are always of the purest gold, stamped with the government stamp, and, having a real solid value, are looked upon as a permanent investment. On holidays they are all put on, and when want comes, and hunger knocks at the door, they are pawned at the Monte di Pietà (the government pawnbrokery establishment) for nearly their value, to be redeemed when better days come back. It would be thought a disgrace to be married without these ornaments, and no one is so poor as not to have them.

At last the marriage takes place. The bride is dressed in her new costume, and with her golden chains and earrings gleaming on her neck, and her snowy white *tovaglia* folded over her head, she goes with her *sposo* to hear mass, take the communion, and be married. The communion is always given before marriage; and, as this cannot be taken after eating, the marriage naturally takes place in the morning. The whole party then return to the house of the bride, and there is a great *festa*, and laughter and joking, and a dinner, where all sit down together; and gifts are brought by the friends, who vie with each other in bringing the most expensive things they can afford to buy.

Among the ancient Romans, when the bride was conducted to the bridegroom's house it was customary to shower sweetmeats upon them as emblems of plenty and prosperity, and then began the nuptial feast (*gamos*). This custom, "with a difference," still exists, though it is wearing out; but, instead of receiving the sweetmeats on her head, the bride now carries round to the assembled guests a tray covered with them, and each guest takes a sweetmeat with one hand, and with the other places a gift on the tray. Among the noble families this same usage obtains. Besides the sherbets and cakes and refreshments of every kind, which are carried round to the company, each friend is presented with an elegant box of *bonbons*, on one side of which are stamped the arms of the bride, and on the other the arms of the family.

Even after the marriage has taken place, the mother, if she be over-scrupulous and bigoted, sometimes refuses to give up her daughter for a day, thinking in this way to approve herself to the Church, and bring good luck to the young couple. But this is rare. Ordinarily the bride accompanies her husband home, and there remains shut up, and seeing no one for two or three days—sometimes for a week. She then makes a formal entry into the world. Dressed in her betrothal costume, with all her rings on her fingers, and accompanied by her husband and an escort of friends and relations, she passes through the principal streets to show herself, and her gold ornaments and dress, and to receive congratulations. The promenade over, all return to the house, and again there is a dinner or supper, and all sorts of gaiety. Rhymed toasts are given, and all unite in wishing for her male children as the best of luck. The marriage festival is then complete, and thereafter she bends her neck to the every-day yoke of hard work.

A short time since, at Siena, I met one of these bridal processions, on its way to the public promenade of the Lizza, to show themselves to their friends. It was Sunday, and there they knew that the world of Siena would be congregated, and they would be for the time the "observed of all observers." The bride wore a broad Tuscan hat, under whose flapping brim glittered two long pendant earrings; her hands were covered with golden rings, on some of her fingers reaching above the first joint, and a handsome necklace of pearls was on her sunburnt neck. She was a stout, healthy *contadina*, evidently married with an eye to work rather than beauty; and as she strode along, looking smiling and happy, and veiling her face behind a large fan at each exquisite joke of her escort, she towered a full head in height above her little wiry husband. I hope for his sake that she is good-natured, for in case of a "difficulty" I would not give much for his chance.

On the *festa* of the marriage it is the bride who is the centre of interest, the *sposo* is of little account. All the gifts are for her, except one, and that is a basket of eggs, which his friends send him on the occasion. If he happen to be an old man, they pay him still another compliment in the way of a "*serenata alla Chiavari*," howling under his window madly, with an accompaniment of pots and pans.

One of the little ballads sung about the streets of Rome gives an idea of the jollity of the marriage *festa*, and of the sorrows that come after. It is entitled, "*Il pentimento dei Giovanotti dopo che hanno preso moglie*"—(The repentance of young men after they have taken a wife). The verses describing the joys of the day are as follows:—

> "Fù assai lieto il primo giorno
> Che stringeste la catena;
> Nobil pranzo e nobil cena
> Cuoco esperto preparò.
>
> "Mille amici a voi d'intorno
> Rimiraste allegri in viso,
> E taluno all' improviso
> Dolci brindisi cantò.
>
> "Poi sì mosse al ballo il piede
> Per seguir l' antica usanza,
> E più d' una contradanza
> Lietamente si ballò.
>
> "Otteneste inde in mercede
> Delle danze e degli fiaschi—
> Buona notte e figli maschi—
> E ciascuno se n' andò."

Among the families of wealth and rank at Rome the *capitoli*, or betrothal, is a much more important and festal ceremony than that of marriage. Marriage must always take place in the morning, but the betrothal is celebrated in the evening. Elaborate cards of invitation are issued, setting forth the titles and parentage of the parties to be betrothed, and all the friends and relations are prayed to be present and assist at the ceremony. The palace is flung open, splendidly lighted and decorated with flowers, and the guests wear their richest dresses and ornaments. When all are assembled, the marriage contract and papers conferring the dowry and making the marriage settlements are read aloud by the notary, and formally signed by the parties and witnesses. Then comes the glad hum of congratulations, the bride and bridegroom are kissed by their friends, and all is gaiety and rejoicing. The marriage after this is more of a religious ceremony, often performed in travelling dress, and the bride and bridegroom, after a morning reception of friends, go off in their carriages to journey.

Not many years ago a curious incident occurred in one of the noblest palaces of Rome, at a betrothal where the bride represented one of the eldest and most famous of the princely houses, and the bridegroom was the head of one of the wealthiest. The guests were all assembled and the contract was read. At the side of the bride, who there, in the perfect flower of her remarkable beauty, attracted the eyes of all, stood the figure of a poor, decrepit, imbecile man, in whose face you read the sad history of insanity degraded almost into idiocy. It was her father—the head of the house—the prince. By dint of cajolement and persuasion he had been induced to take part in the ceremony, his presence being absolutely required. There, gazing vacantly around him, he heard the words of the contract, though they conveyed to him no meaning. When, however, the reading was concluded, and he was conducted to the table to affix his signature, he stopped, and seeing that all eyes were fixed on him, a vague fear seemed to come across him that he was to be circumvented in some way, unintelligible to him; and to the painful surprise of all, he absolutely refused to sign the contract. Vainly they endeavoured to persuade him. Steadily, and with an imbecile obstinacy, he continued to repeat his refusal.

"What would induce you to sign it?" at last cried one of the family, in despair.

"I will tell you," whispered the old man, drawing him aside. "Give me a *scudo*, and I will sign it."

Instantly a *scudo* was given him. He slipped it eagerly into his pocket, and then with a horrible smile of cunning went forward to the table and scrawled his name under the contract.

"*Grazie a Dio!*" said the whole company, and came forward to congratulate and smile and compliment, while the old man crept into a corner of his magnificent halls, and turning his back on the company, took out his *scudo* to examine it, chuckling all the while to himself.

From life to death is but a step. Marriage finishes, sooner or later, with a funeral. Before the very altar where the ceremony of marriage is performed the coffin is hereafter to lie; and returning with the bridal procession through the aisles of the church the eye will be caught by sad inscriptions of death on many a marble slab and monument. Imagine, then, that after accompanying the bride to the altar, we have lingered to look at the monuments, and to talk of "worms, and graves, and epitaphs."

Whenever death is imminent, the priest is at once called in to hear final confession, and give final absolution; and from this moment it is his duty to stay with the dying man until he has drawn his last breath. The candles are lighted, the friends leave the chamber, and priest and penitent are left alone together. After extreme unction has been given, the friends may return; and in such case, as the soul passes away, it is accompanied by the prayers of all around to "San Giuseppe, Maria, Jesu," to intercede for it above. It often happens, however, that the friends never return, but leave the dying man in the hands of the priest, who sometimes, through ignorance and bigotry, scares away his last breath by terrible intimations of divine wrath; and who, at best, can never supply the need of the kind and affectionate faces of friends in those last moments.

After death the body is entirely abandoned to the priests, who take possession of it, watch over it, and prepare it for burial; while the family, if they can find refuge anywhere else, abandon the house and remain away a week. During their absence the house is purgated; the bed on which their friend or parent has died is burnt; the chamber walls are rasped, and new papered or coloured, and oftentimes the whole furniture of the room is destroyed and replaced with new articles. This is specially the case where the death is by consumption, which is generally believed by the lower classes in Rome to be contagious. It is common for the friends of the bereaved family to offer them a villa, or house, for their retirement at such a season; and when they return to their own house a dinner is also sent them on their arrival. But such is the horror the Italians have of death, that they do not willingly return to a place where one of the family has died; and in case the house is not their own, they will often throw up their lease to avoid the necessity of so doing. "Così ho fatto Io quando morì la mia madre," said my coachman the other night to me. "E così farei ancora. Dio mio! non ci tornerei, davvero—non, davvero."

The body is not ordinarily allowed to remain in the house more than twelve hours, except on condition that it is sealed up in lead or zinc. At nightfall a sad procession of *becchini* and *frati* may be seen coming down the street, and stopping before the house of the dead. The *becchini* are taken from the lowest classes of the people, and hired to carry the corpse on the bier, and to accompany it to the church and cemetery. They are dressed in shabby black *cappe*, covering their head and face as well as their body, and having two large holes cut in front of the eyes to enable them to see. These *cappe* are girdled round the waist, and the dirty trousers and worn-out shoes are miserably manifest under the skirts of their dress —showing plainly that their duty is occasional. All the *frati* and *becchini*, except the four who carry the bier, are furnished with wax candles, for no one is buried in Rome without a candle. You may know the rank of the person to be buried by the lateness of the hour and the number of the *frati*. If it be the funeral of a person of wealth, or a noble, it takes place at a late hour, the procession of *frati* is long, and the bier elegant. If it be a state-funeral, as of a prince, carriages accompany it in mourning, the coachmen and lackeys are bedizened in their richest liveries, and the state hammer-cloths are spread on the boxes, with the family arms embossed on them in gold. Sometimes, also, on very special occasions, a band of music accompanies the procession. But if it be a pauper's funeral, there are only *becchini* enough to carry the bier to the grave, and two *frati*, each with a little candle; and the sunshine is yet in the streets when they come to take away the corpse. Ordinarily, if the person be of the middle class, the funeral takes place about an hour after Ave Maria.

You will see this procession stop before the house where the corpse is lying. Some of the *becchini* go up-stairs, and some keep guard below. The neighbours look out of the windows of all the adjacent houses. Scores of shabby men and boys are gathered round the *frati;* some attracted simply by curiosity, and some for the purpose of catching the wax, which gutters down from the candles as they are blown by the wind. The latter may be known by the great horns of paper they carry in their hands. While this crowd waits for the corpse, the *frati* light their candles, and talk, laugh, and take snuff together. Finally comes the body, borne down by four of the *becchini*. It is in a common rough deal coffin, more like an ill-made packing-case than anything else. No care or expense has been laid out upon it to make it elegant, for it is only to be seen for a moment. Then it is slid upon the bier, and over it is drawn the black velvet pall with golden trimmings, on which a cross, death's-head, and bones are embroidered. Four of the *becchini* hoist it upon their shoulders, the *frati* break forth into their hoarse chant, and the procession sets out for the church. Little and big boys and shabby men follow along, holding up their paper horns against the sloping candles to catch the dripping wax. Every one takes off his hat, or makes the sign of the cross, or mutters a prayer as the body passes; and with a dull, sad, monotonous chant, the candles gleaming and flaring, and casting around them a yellow flickering glow, the funeral winds along through the narrow streets, and under the sombre palaces and buildings, where the shadows of night are deepening every moment. The spectacle seen from a distance, and especially when looked down upon from a window, is very effective; but it loses much of its solemnity as you approach it; for the *frati* are so vulgar, dirty, and stupid, and seem so utterly indifferent and heartless, as they mechanically croak out their psalms, that all other emotions yield to a feeling of disgust. Death is solemn and sacred to all but those who deal with it as a means of living. The grave-digger knocks over a skull without remorse, and cracks a joke upon it. They " have no feeling for their business;" and so the *frate*, whose profession it is to mourn for hire, feels nothing—the edge of his feeling is blunted by custom—'tis "the hand of little employment hath the daintier sense." But while one cannot expect these hired mourners to feel any deep sense of sorrow, it would be but decent for them to "assume a grace if they have it not," instead of jesting and chattering, as they precede a corpse. The last funeral which I happened to see was in the street in which I live; and as I passed along the *becchini* had just brought down the body and slid it on to the bier. Two of the *frati*, who had been talking together, did not perceive this, and were scarcely ready when the procession started; however, they at once paused in their discourse at the signal to move, and one of them, with a deep bass voice, sang suddenly out, "*Miserere Domine*," then stopped short, turned his head aside, and stuffed into his bulbous, dirty nose a huge pinch of snuff, which in his earnestness of discourse he had omitted previously to dispose of. After this duty was performed, he resumed the argument with his friend, *sotto voce*, bursting now and then into a sudden strain of chanting. And this is the way in which the *frati* mourn for the dead in Rome.

A singular illustration of the carelessness and indifference, begotten by custom, is to be found in an incident connected with the conspiracy of the Pazzi in Florence. The design of the conspirators was to murder the two Medici in the cathedral, while they were engaged in performing their devotions. But it was difficult to induce any one to commit the crime there, on account of the sacredness of the place, and the natural repugnance to add sacrilege to murder. It was then suggested that a priest should be employed to decoy the princes into the church, and strike the first blow. And the reason given for the suggestion was, that his business and duty being in the church, and about the altar, the place had necessarily lost all special sacredness to him, and he would as quickly perform a crime there as elsewhere. The event proved the accuracy of this supposition. It was a priest who was employed by the conspirators, and who lent himself to the crime with utter indifference to the sanctity of the place.

Sometimes, on the occasion of the sudden death of a child or maiden, dying in the flower of her youth and beauty, the body is exposed to view on the top of the bier, dressed in white, with a wreath about the head and flowers strewn around it, and is thus borne along the streets. This, however, is rarer in Rome of late years than in Naples, where it is very common. One of the most touching spectacles of this kind that I ever saw was at S. Germano, a little town situated near the frontier of the Roman and Neapolitan territory, amid the most charming scenery of valley and mountain. As I was passing through the gate of the town, early one summer morning, I saw the dead body of a little child lying in its basket-cradle on the low parapet, close by the entrance. It was dressed in white, precisely as if it were still living. A little cap of coloured ribbons was on its head, while around its neck, and over its little hands, which were clasped upon its breast in the attitude of prayer, were strings of large beads. It looked so simple, lovely, and infantine, as it lay there in the open square, that I could scarcely believe it to be dead, save that its hands and face were too waxen in their beauty for life. The early morning light fell upon its face, and the faint fresh breeze played with the ribbons on its cap and dress; and there in its perfectness of peace it lay, while companies of country-folk, going by on their way to the market, paused, gazed on it respectfully, and, recommending it to the Madonna, passed on to the labour of life. It had been brought in from the Campagna, cradle and all, just as it lay, on the head of the peasant woman who sat beside it; and she was to bear it to its little grave, after it had lain in state, as it were, in the public square for all the people to see and bless.

In Siena it is the duty of the unmarried peasants in each parish to carry on their heads the dead bodies of the little children and infants, and deposit them in the church. This office they perform by rotation, or agreement. The corpse is adorned with ribbons, and such little scraps of finery as the poor family can afford; and as these become the perquisite of the *contadina* who has carried it to the church, there is no lack of readiness among them, to say the least, in offering their services. Around the body of the child is tied a long cord, which hangs out over the basket in which it lies; and it is the superstition that every one who ties a knot in that cord will receive for each knot an intercession for her soul by the little spirit above. Every one, therefore, ties a knot, and sometimes it happens that one of them steals a march upon the others by tying such a number of knots for herself as not to leave a chance for all the rest. In such cases it is not uncommon for the bigoted *contadina*, who has thus cheated the others out of their rights, to receive as a compensation therefor hard words and a slap in the face.

In Corsica also, says my friend L'Abbate, it is the custom to carry exposed on the bier, and crowned with flowers, the bodies of all young virgins. *Ma quando sono vecchie vergini, nò.* The fact is, however, that "old virgins" are very rare in Italy—almost unknown, out of the convents; for every woman must either get married or retire into a monastery and take the veil. "An old maid," in the English sense, is a *rarissima avis*, about as rare as the phœnix.

The funeral procession we have left has in the mean time borne the body to the church. There it is laid on a catafalque adorned with large placards, stamped each with a large skull and cross-bones, and standing before an altar in one of the chapels. Candles are then lighted around the bier and on the altar, and a mass is performed for the soul of the dead. This over, the corpse is left alone in the church in charge of a priest, whose duty it is to watch over it —a duty "more honoured in the breach than the observance." At midnight come the *becchini*, strip off the velvet pall, and, placing the naked coffin on the general *carretta*, carry it off with the rest to the Cemetery of San Lorenzo.

While they are carrying it off, let us give a glance at the expenses required for an ordinary funeral in Rome.

Every parish in Rome is furnished with a manual called "Statuta Cleri Romani," the greater portion of which is devoted to the enumeration of the taxes for the dead, and therein is prescribed minutely the kind of funeral required to be made by the family of the dead person, according to its rank and wealth. The different grades of persons are all classified, each with a distinct specification of the number of priests and *frati*, as well as of the candles, torches and other items; and unless all the requirements are punctually complied with, the family is cited before the tribunal "Della Vicaria"—"*pro funere non facto et pro supplemento*" (Court Latin, *Latino di Curia*, as it is called in Rome; corresponding to Chaucer's "French of Stratford atte Bowe")—where the condemnation is without appeal. The notary, before opening the inventory, is bound to summon the *parroco* to inform himself whether the funeral expenses have been paid; if they have not, they constitute the first charge against the estate. Open the "Decisiones Sacræ Rothæ," and you will find in every volume cases relating to funerals, under the titles of "*jus funerandi, jus sepeliendi, jus tumulandi.*"

One of these cases I will cite, as it is of a humble class, and will give some idea of the strict cost of a funeral,—and will then explain the items. The circumstances of this case were as follows: —In 1846, a person in the public employ died, leaving a widow and seven children, the eldest of whom was twelve years of age. His only fortune consisted of his salary of thirty *scudi* a month, and his illness having lasted many months, his wife was forced to pledge the clock, kitchen utensils and other articles belonging to the house. After the death of her husband she went to the *parroco* (the parish priest, who seems to have been a good man enough after his way), exposed to him in tears her misfortunes and her poverty, and prayed him to grant her the most economical funeral possible. The *parroco* promised, and the following is a strict copy of the list furnished by him under his own name and handwriting:—

	Scudi.	Baiocchi.
Curato, Compagno, e Croce (Curate, Companion, and Cross)	0	40
Emolumenti e Guida (Emoluments and Guide)	1	45
Preti No. 10 (10 Priests)	1	0
Frati No. 50 (50 Monks)	2	50
Cassa (Coffin)	1	50
Portatori e Incassatura (Porters and Boxing up)	1	10
Emolumenti alla Reverenda Camera Apostolica (Charge of the Reverend Apostolic Chamber)	1	50
Messa Cantata ed Uffizi (High Mass and Offices)	1	80
Preti per Uffizio (Priests for the Offices)	1	0
Guardia da Notte (Night Guardian)	1	0
Alzatura (Carriage of Body)	3	0
20 Messe Basse (20 Small Masses)	6	0
Accompagnatura al Cimitero (Accompaniment to Cemetery)	0	30
	22	55

CERA (WAX).

	Lib.	Oncie.
Torcie de 2 libbre, No. 10, lib. 20 oncie (Torches)	20	0
Fiaccoletti ,, No. 12, ,, (Tapers)	24	0
Altare Maggiore, No. 6, de lib. 1 (High Altar)	6	0
Guardia (Guard)	1	0
Marretto (Large Candle)	1	6
12 Candele per Preti (Candles for Priests)	3	0
50 ,, ,, Frati (Monks)	9	10
14 ,, ,, le Altari (Altars)	7	0
12 ,, ,, l'Assoluzione (Absolution)	3	0
	75	4

This wax, at 32 *baiocchi* a pound, makes 24 *scudi*, which, added to the 22·55 *scudi*, make in all 46·55.

This, then, was the account furnished to a poor widow without a *sou*, as one of the most discreet in its requirements that could be made.

Let me now explain some of these items. The first is the charge for the *parroco* or curate, with his companion. Now, in point of fact, neither of these personages ordinarily accompanies the funeral; but, whether he attend or not, he must be paid 40 *baiocchi* for himself and his companion, or the *vice-parroco* and *chiericchetto* who carries the cross in front of the procession.

The second item for "emoluments and guide" is for the head *becca-morto* or *vespillone*, who directs the funeral, and this fee is in place of the shoes and hat that formerly used to be given, five *baiocchi* being given for the bier.

Next come the priests who accompany the funeral train. These receive ten *baiocchi* each, and the *frati* five *baiocchi* each, and besides a candle, which they do not light. The *baiocchi* of the *frati* go to the convent, the candle becomes their own.

Next come the four masked porters in their black sack, who carry the body. These receive twenty *baiocchi* each, and thirty *baiocchi* additional are given to the *becchino* who places the body in the coffin.

The emoluments of the Reverenda Camera Apostolica are the tax levied by the government for permission to deposit the body in one of the wells or public tombs.

The one hundred and eighty *baiocchi* for masses is solely for the *parroco*, the priests being paid an additional fee of one *scudo*.

The night guardian is the priest whose duty it is to watch the body all night as it lies before the altar; and the charge of three *scudi* for *alzatura* goes to the *becca-morto* who places the bier on its catafalque in the church.

Now for the wax. The *torcie* are candles with four wicks; the *fiaccoletti* are large candles with one wick. The ten torches of two pounds, which form the first item, are lighted around the bier when it is carried from the house to the church; but no sooner have they arrived there than they are extinguished, and become the property of the *parroco*. Then twelve other *fiaccoletti* are lighted and placed round the catafalque while mass is performed, for the illumination in the church must be greater than that in the street. These, as well as the candles on the high altar, also go to the *parroco*, and he also receives, as his perquisite, the *marretto*, a large candle containing a pound and a half of wax, which is never lighted.

Finally, though there be only fifty *frati*, there must be fifty-five candles, because two of these go to the *padre guardiano* and three to the *sagristia*.

The *parroco*, therefore, receives as his portion of the funeral fees:—

In Money.

	Scudi.	Baiocchi.
For the Accompaniment	0	40
For the Mass	1	80
For the Guard	1	00

And in Wax.

	Pounds.		
Torches and Fiaccoletti	44		
Candles on the High Altar, Guard and Marretto	15½		
	59½		
Less consumption	9½		
	50		
Which at 32 baiocchi the pound make		16	00
		19	00

Or in all 19 scudi.

While we have been considering the expenses of burial in Rome, the *becchini* have carried the bodies from the church to the Cemetery of San Lorenzo beyond the walls. This cemetery, which is the only one in Rome, lies about a mile beyond the Porta San Lorenzo, close by the interesting and ancient basilica of the same name. It was founded by the French during the ravages of the cholera in the year 1831; there being, previous to that time, no decent cemetery for any person not wealthy enough to purchase a right of burial within the walls of a church or convent. You pass from the city through a long avenue of acacias and elms, between villa walls, to the curious old gate; thence, following along the road, you have a beautiful view of the Campagna and mountains; and as if in contradiction to the hope and promise of this beauty, you see about half way to the cemetery a little chapel, dedicated to the Madonna, over the portal of which is a not very encouraging picture, painted on a blue ground, representing the Virgin and Child in glory above, and below tormented spirits in hell-fire with extended arms imploring assistance. Under this is inscribed, "*Salve Maria, regina cœli, mater misericordiæ.*"

This Campo Santo was for many years a disgrace to Rome. It consisted of a large walled-in square, checkered over with great wells or underground tombs of stone-work, which are shut each by a block of travertine. Every day it was the custom to open two of these, into one of which were indiscriminately emptied all the male bodies brought by the *carrettone,* and into the other all the female bodies;—the two sexes being scrupulously kept apart.

Since the present Pope has occupied the chair of St. Peter's a new order of things has taken place. These well-like tombs are no longer the indiscriminate repository of all the bodies which are brought to the cemetery, but are reserved for the burial of respectable persons who are able to pay therefor, and thus the overcrowding of these receptacles is avoided, and the terrible orgy of their purgation is no more seen.

In order to compensate for this, a large tract of land, adjacent to the cemetery, has been inclosed by a wall and made a portion of it, and it is here that those are buried who cannot afford to purchase a separate grave or tomb. A chapel has been lately erected, in which services may be performed over the dead, and where they may be temporarily deposited for the few hours before they are buried. At present the depository for receiving the bodies is a sort of cave or cellar hollowed out of the *tufo*, on a ledge of land forming part of the cemetery. Many other improvements are also going on now, for the government at Rome is doing its best to remove the disgrace which attaches to a church that makes no decent provision for the burial of the dead. Truly, as one of the priests of San Lorenzo said to me while explaining the plan of the cemetery, "It is a shame for Rome not to have a holy cemetery" (*un cimitero sacrosanto*).

They are now building around three sides of the square of the old wells a handsome arcade, under which is to be excavated a continuous row of tombs, which can be purchased by families of wealth, and adorned as they choose with monuments and slabs. On the open side is erected the new chapel fronting the entrance gate, and on higher ground, on the right of which the ascent is by a flight of steps, an open ground has been laid out and planted with trees, where private lots may be purchased and monuments erected. A few have already been placed there, and on one of them, built by the family of Paulsen Thorwaldsen, I was glad to see, lately, that a wreath of flowers had been laid by affectionate hands. It was the only instance of the kind I ever saw in this cemetery, for the Romans have a vague notion that it savours of superstition and idolatry to adorn the graves of the dead. How or why I do not understand; but this was the reason given to me by a cultivated person to whom I was remarking that the utter indifference shown by the Romans to the dead struck a stranger painfully, and that we could not understand why they never even threw a flower upon the grave.

The portion of the cemetery I have thus far described is for the burial of the rich, or, at least, for those who have the means to pay for their tombs; the charges are not, however, high. Thirty *pauls* a *mètre* is charged for the ground within the upper inclosure, and six *mètres* afford sufficient space for a small monument. In front of the arcades are also lots for tombs, each of which costs twenty-four *scudi*, and with the monumental slab forty-five *scudi*. In addition to this expense, however, a tax of fifteen *pauls* is levied by the Reverenda Camera Apostolica for permission to deposit a body in one of the public tombs. If, however, the burial be in a private tomb or grave, the charge is ten *scudi*. Times have changed since San Gregorio administered so severe a rebuke to the Bishop of Cagliari and Messina for demanding a price for the ground of burial. *Ma che volete?* San Gregorio is dead long ago, and you remember the Italian proverb: *Un cane vivo è meglio di un dottore morto!*

Curiously enough, like everything else in Rome which is managed by the government, the right to build the tombs and lay the masonry in the cemetery is a monopoly farmed out by the government.

Beyond these inclosures in the Campo Santo is the large tract of land devoted to the burial of the *ignobile vulgus*—the poor and lower classes who cannot afford to pay for the tomb or to purchase a lot of land. Those who have no means are buried free of expense, but those who have small means are charged 15 *pauls* for the privilege of burial. This is a wide desolate field, where every day is opened a trench to receive the bodies of the poor. The *becchini* bury them late at night, and deposit them in the great *tufo* cave, and early in the morning the coffins are placed side by side as close as they will lie in the long trench, and covered over with earth. A wooden stake, painted black, with its number on it, alone marks the spot; and when this rots away, as it soon does, the spot where any one lies can only be determined by the register of the name and number. Over this large space not a slab, nor a tree, nor a flower, ever can be seen. It is dreary, sad, desolate, and depressing. Vainly as you stand here you look out over the lovely Campagna, and see the tremulous hues of the afternoon painting the mountains, and hear the larks singing in the blue heights out of sight—a heavy pain lies upon the heart, the earth smells of mortality, and nature seems to sorrow over humanity. The voices of the labourers digging the long trench for their dead companions partake of the general gloom hanging over all, and gladness seems to have vanished from the earth.

No greater contrast can be seen than that between this dreary, desolate, heartless place, and the exquisite Protestant cemetery under the shadow of the pyramid of Caius Cestius. Here tall cypresses nod in the breeze and point their shadowy finger over the grassy dial of death, whose hours are marked by tombs. Here love has planted many a flower and trained many a creeping plant—twilight lingers lovingly upon its slopes—birds sing in the waving branches—the old pyramid seems to watch over it sympathetically—lizards slip out of the crumbling towers and ancient ivy-mantled walls which rise over it, and violets, daisies, and roses here bloom all the winter long. Truly, as Shelley has said, " It might make one in love with death to think one should be buried in so sweet a place." A sort of sacred silence hovers over the spot. The peaceful blue sky above, the flowers and grass below, the soft air murmuring aloft in the swaying cypresses, all seem to sympathize with the pilgrim who comes here, to sorrow not as one without hope over the little space which holds what was dearest to him on earth,—to hang a wreath on the white marble over it, and with tender care to arrange the flowers and bushes, which send not forth so sweet an odour as did the little spirit whose empty shell lies in the earth below.

Burial within the precincts of a church is now not only very difficult to obtain since the establishment of this cemetery, but is also very expensive. So large a sum is required, that only the rich can purchase this privilege, and such difficulties are in the way that only persons of influence can hope to overcome them. Converts, and especially English converts, may lay their bones within the walls of a church, for the marble memorial is a lure to other converts; but, generally speaking, the world of the dead is transported to the cemetery of San Lorenzo.

There are, however, some striking exceptions. Popes, cardinals, and all the dignitaries of the Church, are buried within its walls; and so also all monks and nuns find burial-ground within the precincts of their own monastery or convent. In some of the principal *basiliche* there are also private chapels erected by some of the Popes for the use of the princely houses from which they sprang, which are still used as places of interment for the family. Of these, the two most remarkable are that belonging to the Corsini family in San Giovanni in Laterano, and that belonging to the Borghese family in Sta. Maria Maggiore. Nothing can exceed the costliness of the marbles with which these chapels are encased. The gilt ceilings, the lavish ornamentation, the gems, gold paintings, *bassi rilievi*, sculpture, columns of precious marbles, monumental statues, and sarcophagi which enrich them, though crowded together in the *barocco* style of the period when these chapels were built, produce a very imposing effect. In the Corsini Chapel, under the porphyry sarcophagus, which formerly stood in the portico of the Pantheon, lies the body of Clement XII.; and between four fluted columns of jasper in the Borghese Chapel is the miraculous painting of the Virgin and Child, pronounced by a papal bull to be the work of St. Luke, and the same which was carried in procession by St. Gregory the Great to stay the plague that desolated Rome in the year 590. In the sepulchral vaults below this last chapel are buried the bodies of the Borghese family. The last which was laid here was that of the celebrated Princess Guendoline Talbot Borghese, distinguished for her wide charities, loved for her many virtues, and remembered almost with veneration by all who ever knew her.

Of this beautiful and accomplished woman, a remarkable story is privately told, which shows that her charities did not end with her life. One summer evening, when the dusky shadows were deepening in the church, an aged woman was observed to enter and prostrate herself in a dim corner near the Borghese Chapel. There, as if overcome by some great emotion, she hid her face, and prayed and wept. As she looked up from her prayer, she saw beside her a female figure clothed in black, who, looking at her with a sad and sympathizing gaze, asked why she was weeping so bitterly? She answered that she was very poor and very wretched, that all her family were dead, and unless the Madonna took pity on her, she knew not what would become of her. Thereupon the figure in black said: "Be of good comfort, you shall be taken care of; silver and gold have I none, but such as I have I give unto you." As she said these words, she drew from her finger a ring with a large stone in it, gave it to the old woman, and disappeared. The next morning the poor creature carried the ring to a jeweller to sell it. The jeweller was struck with its peculiar appearance, and perceiving that the stone was a very large and valuable diamond, which he suspected must have come into her hands by some unfair means, assured her, in order to obtain time, that he could not trust his own judgment as to its value, and wished to consult some other jeweller before fixing the price he would pay for it. Meanwhile he advanced her a small sum on account, and told her to call again the next day. What was her surprise on returning to find some gendarmes in the shop, who at once arrested her on a charge of stealing, and carried her to prison. It seemed that one of the friends to whom the jeweller had shown the ring had recognized it as one belonging to the Borghese family, and insisted that the prince should at once be informed of the facts. This was accordingly done, and the prince, on seeing it, is said to have been greatly overcome. On recovering, he declared that it was an old family ring, which he himself had placed on the finger of his wife in her coffin, and that it was buried with her in the chapel of Sta. Maggiore; that it could have been stolen from the tomb was impossible, as the chapel is locked and guarded day and night; and not only that the tomb could not have been rifled without its being at once known, but that even the chapel could not have been entered. The only solution that remained was, that the figure in black was the princess herself. Under these circumstances the old woman was at once released, and provided for by the prince.

There is one other cemetery within the walls of the city which must not be passed over in silence, if only for its strange and somewhat revolting peculiarities, and this is the subterranean burial-place under the Church of the Capuchins. Any of the snuffy old monks who are ranging about the church will show it to you "for a consideration." You descend a dark staircase and find yourself in a long corridor, out of which open four grim chambers dedicated to the dead. High grated windows let in the light, and the odour is of the earth, earthy. This is the cemetery of the Capuchins, and the floor you stand upon is holy earth brought from Jerusalem. Underneath this each of the *frati* is deposited after his death, without a coffin, and dressed in his monkish robes; the oldest inhabitant of the cemetery yielding up his place to the new comer. By this time the holy earth has done its work, and nothing remains of the oldest inhabitant who is thus called to resurrection but the skeleton, and the dried fibre which still clings to the bones and resists decay. This wretched remnant of their dead brother the monks now robe in one of the dresses such as he wore in life, and he takes his place with others of his dead compeers, who are ranged in little alcoves along the walls, to grin with them a ghastly grin at all visitors, until he drops to pieces, or is removed to make way for another. Nothing can be more frightful to behold than these dead figures; some with their mouths agape, some peering horribly out, some with the remnants of their hair and beard still clinging to their mummied jaws and skulls, and all grinning fearfully.

The architecture of the room is builded up of fragments of the human skeleton. Row upon row are piled bare skulls, leaving alcoves between them for the terrible figures I have mentioned. Strange decorations are made of the thigh-bones, ribs, and vertebræ, which are arranged over the vaulted ceiling in arabesque figures. A candelabrum of vertebræ, strung together, hangs shaking from the ceiling; and pillars and capitals of bones give apparent support to the chambers. The monks who accompany you to this cemetery show it with considerable pride, and seem to enjoy the prospect of being buried here. They offer you snuff from a little dirty box, and beg you to observe that there is no odour from the bodies, although they are buried very superficially. It is the property of the holy earth, they say, to prevent all odour from the dead. I only wish it could do as much for the living.

As the shadows of night come on the effect is horrible. Everywhere these indiscriminate skulls are mocking at you, and under their brown hoods the seated and standing figures gaze out of hollow eye-sockets, and almost seem to move. Above the arches is a long row of skulls, and as some visitor was lingering there after the shadows had begun to darken, fascinated by the horror of the place, and indulging in ugly thoughts about the grave, suddenly he saw one of the skulls roll down from its shelf and move slowly across the floor towards him, clattering its jaws as it came staggering along. Horror-struck, he shrunk back involuntary with a gesture of disgust and dread.

"*Non abbia paura,*"—"Don't be afraid," said the consolatory monk at his side, taking a huge pinch of snuff. "There's only a rat in the skull—that's all," and he put it back on the shelf.

If the traveller from Florence to Rome by the Perugia road stop at the little town of S. Giovanni, the birthplace of Masaccio, and enter the cathedral, he will see a most ghastly spectacle. It is the dried-up figure of a corpse, which, in making some reparations in the church, was discovered built up into the wall. Nothing is known of its history, but, from its appearance, the wretched victim would seem to have been thus walled-up alive, and to have perished slowly in the agonies of starvation. The skin, though shrunken away, still covers the entire skeleton, and the despairing look of the withered dead face, with its gasping mouth and glaring eyes turned upwards, as if to some aperture from which it hoped for rescue or drew in air, once seen, will not be easily forgotten. This was one of the methods of burial adopted by the great houses in the middle ages to relieve them of troublesome persons, or to wreak a terrible revenge; and those who are fond of chanting the praises of the past should see this miserable figure.

When, a short time since, the Medici Chapel at Florence, which contains the tombs of the grand dukes, was undergoing repairs, and some changes were making, these tombs were opened, and the ducal corpses exposed to view. Some of these, which had lain in their coffin for hundreds of years, were, to the surprise of all, found perfectly fresh and undecayed, as if they had just died; while others had fallen to dust. The only satisfactory theory to explain this phenomena would seem to be, that at one period grand dukes were helped to their last resting-place by poisons, which, pervading the bodies, had thus preserved them for centuries.

The admirable institution of the *Misericordia*, which is to be found throughout Tuscany, does not exist in Rome; but several of the confraternities attend to the duty of burying their own dead, and one of them, called the *Arciconfraternità della morte e dell' orazione*, assumes the duty of burying the bodies of all poor persons found dead on the Campagna or in the city. This confraternity was founded in 1551 by a Sienese priest, Crescenzio Selva, and confirmed by Pius IV. in 1560. It first had its chapel in San Lorenzo in Damaso, from which it was transferred to S. Giovanni in Ayno, and now is stationed in the Strada Giulia. It is composed of most respectable persons, who wear a *sacco* of black coarse linen. Upon information being received that a dead body has been found on the Campagna, notice of the fact is at once given to a certain number of the brethren, who, without delay, meet at the oratory, where they assume the black sack, and set forth immediately in search of the corpse. Day or night, cold or heat, calm or storm, make no difference; the moment the news is received they set out on their pious expedition. Nor is this duty always a light one, for sometimes they are obliged to journey in search of the body more than twenty miles; and under the pontificate of Clement VIII., when there was a great inundation of the Tiber, they reclaimed bodies which had been borne down by the current as far as Ostia and Fiumicino. They carry with them the bier upon which they place the body when it is found, and bring it back on their shoulders to the city.

Besides this duty on the Campagna, they also, in common with certain other confraternities, bury the bodies of the dead found in the city whose families are without means. The messenger informs the brethren when their services are needed, and towards evening, dressed in their black sacks, their heads and faces covered, and with only two holes cut in the *cappuccio* to look through, they may be seen passing through the street, bearing the body on their bier to the church, preceded by a long narrow standard of black, on which are worked a cross, skull and bones, bearing torches and chanting the *Miserere* and other psalms.

This arch-confraternity has the right to bury those which it recovers from the Campagna in whatever place it thinks proper; and this generally takes place in the cemetery belonging to it, which is near their oratory. Here, in the *Ottavario de' Morti*, a strange exhibition and ceremony take place. The subterranean tombs are all hung about with bones disposed architecturally, as in the cemetery of the Capuchins, with candelabra made of similar relics; and at the end are placed figures of the size of life, with waxen faces and hands, cleverly modelled and coloured, and draped in appropriate robes, to represent some scriptural story. This same exhibition takes place in several other cemeteries, as in those of Santo Spirito, of the SSmo. Salvatore, Della Consolazione, and of Sta. Maria in Trastevere. To these places crowds of Romans flock during the eight days, and join in prayers for the dead.*

After giving a description of this custom in Rome, Padre Bresciani thus bursts forth in a rapture of Catholicism: "I do not deny, and I must say so, that Protestants have not, and cannot have, such great charity as this for their dead; for they do not believe in purgatory. * * * And can you pretend that any man, however pure and pious, does not remain soiled in his soul by the dust of human intercourse; so that, before he can enter into the purity of heaven, he does not need a sweeping entirely to purify him?" (*Una spazzolata che tutto il rimondi.*)

As you walk over the Campagna, here and there you will see a little rude black cross set up by the road-side, or in the open fields. This marks the spot where some sudden death has occurred, where one has fallen by accident, or died in an apoplexy, or been stabbed in a brawl; and here you may generally be sure that the archconfraternity of death has performed its pious task.

The ceremonies which take place on the death of a Pope are somewhat curious, and deserve mention. As soon as he has breathed his last, the cardinal chancellor, dressed in his *paonazzo* robes, with the *chierici* of the reverend chamber, clothed in black without lace, enter the room, and cover the face of the dead Pope with a white handkerchief. The cardinal, after making a brief prayer, rises, the face of the Pope is uncovered, and approaching the bed, he strikes three times with a silver hammer on the forehead of the corpse, calling him as many times by name to answer. As the corpse remains speechless, he turns to his companions, and formally announces that "*Il papa è realmente morto.*" The Psalm *De Profundis* is then chanted, and the corpse is sprinkled with blessed water. The *Monsignore Maestro di Camera* then consigns to the cardinal chancellor the fisherman's ring (*anello pescatorio*), and immediately the notary of the pontifical chambers reads an instrument setting forth the death of the Pope, and the transference of the ring. The cardinal, before leaving the chamber, also informs by

---

* See Degli Instituti di Pubblica Carità, &c., in Roma. Di D. Carlo Luigi Morichini, vol. i. ch. 15.

writing the Roman senate of the death of the Pope, and orders the great bell of the Campidoglio to toll. When the boom of this deep sound is heard over Rome the world knows that the Pope is no more; and as it tells its sad news, all the other bells in Rome take up the strain.

The *penitenzieri Vaticani* now wash the body with warm perfumed water; and after twenty-four hours have passed the operation of embalming takes place. This is done under the superintendence of the surgeon of the Pope, and of one of the apostolic chamber, in presence of a physician of the same chamber, of the *archiatro*, and of the *speziale palatino*. The *precordia* are separately embalmed, and placed in a sealed vase to be carried to the Church of S. Vincenzo and S. Anastasio, in case the Pope die at the Quirinal; and to the Basilica of St. Peter's if he die at the Vatican. Sixtus V. was the first Pope who died in the Quirinal, on the 27th August, 1590; and his *precordia* were the first to be placed in the Church of S. Anastasio.

Before the time of Julius II. the bodies of the dead Popes were not opened and embalmed. It was then the usage first to wash the body with water and sweet herbs, and to shave the beard and head; then all the apertures were closed up with cotton-wool saturated with myrrh, incense, and aloes.[*] The body was then again washed in white wine, heated up with odorous herbs, the throat filled with aromatic spices, and the nostrils with musk. Finally, the face and hands were rubbed and anointed with balsam.

The washing and embalming being over, the body is dressed in its usual robes of a white cassock, sash with golden tassels, surplice, bishop's gown, red papal cap and stole, and exposed to public view on a funeral couch, under a *baldacchino* covered with a red coverlet brocaded in gold, and stationed in one of the pontifical ante-chambers, generally in that where the consistory meet. Four wax candles are lighted around it, and there, guarded by the Swiss and the *penitenzieri Vaticani*, it remains until the third day after the death, when it is carried to the Sistine Chapel. The procession which bears it to this second resting-place is very imposing. It is led off by six dragoons, two mace-bearers with torches, two *battistrade*, four trumpeters, and a company of dragoons. Then follow two trumpeters of the *guardia nobile*, with a cadet and four mounted guards, and then the company of Swiss guards and their captain, with the banner folded. After these follows a master of ceremonies, also mounted, preceding the litter with the corpse, on

---

[*] See Mabillon. Museo Italico, tom. ii. pp. 526, 527.

the head of which a cap is placed as it issues from the hall. The litter is borne by two white mules, surrounded by numerous *palafrenieri* and *sediari*, with lighted torches of white wax, and followed by twelve penitentiaries of St. Peter's, clothed in white, with torches, who constantly recite prayers, and are accompanied on either side by the *guardia nobile* on foot, and two lines of Swiss. Then comes the commandant of the *guardia nobile*, with a portion of his guards on horseback, the chief officers, and the master of the pontifical stables. A train of artillery closes the funeral procession with seven pieces of cannon, and a company of carabineers with trumpeters.

The corpse is then conveyed up the Scala Regia, where it is removed from the litter to a costly bier, on which it is carried into the Capella Sistina. Here it is undressed and invested with the full pontifical robes of red, with shoes, sandals, amitto, camise, cincture, girdle, cross, stole, fanone, under tunic, dalmatica, gloves, cape, mantle, mitre of silver plates, and ring. Red is the colour of mourning in the Greek Church, and this has been supposed to be the reason why the dead Pope is dressed in this colour; but as the Latin church prescribes *paonazzo* for this object, the custom, says Moroni, is rather to be considered as a memorial of the many Popes who have suffered martyrdom.

Here prayers are recited until the following morning, when the sacred college of cardinals assemble, in violet robes and *cappe*, accompanied by the chapter of the Vatican and the pontifical choir, who chant the *Subvenite Sancti Dei*. The canon deacon of the chapter, in black *piviale*, then gives absolution to the corpse with the usual genuflections, and the body is placed on a bier and carried by eight chaplains through the Scala Regia into the Basilica of St. Peter's, surrounded by the noble and Swiss guard, the canons holding up the hem of the coverlet. The chapter itself precedes the train with lighted torches, and the cardinals follow reciting the *Miserere* and *De Profundis*. When it has arrived in the centre of the great nave the *feretro* is placed on a high bed, absolution is again given, and it is then transported into the chapel of the holy sacrament, where the cardinals leave it and return home.

For three days the corpse, in its full pontificals, with a crucifix on its breast and two papal hats at its feet, is exposed with its feet reaching beyond the grating, so that the faithful may kiss them; and on the evening of the third day the burial takes place. The cardinals created by the deceased Pope then meet in the sacristy, dressed in violet, with the train-bearers in purple surplice and black cloak, the cardinal chancellor, and the prelate-clerks of the chamber.

The chapter of the *basilica*, with the cardinal arch-priest (who is the sole cardinal who goes in the *cappa*), preceded by a cross on a staff, then proceed to the chapel of the holy sacrament, with the choir singing the *Miserere*. The chaplains or almoners, assisted by the brethren of the holy sacrament, then place the body on a bier, and, accompanied by the noble and the Swiss guard, bear it to the chapel of the choir. In this chapel then come the cardinals, with the major-domo, the chief-chamberlain, the persons attached to the private chamber of the Pope in purple, and the pontifical masters of ceremonies in their rochets. The *responsorium* "*In paradisum*" is then chanted, and the highest canon bishop of the *basilica* gives absolution and blessing, incenses the corpse and the cypress coffin with special prayers, while the choir sings the antiphony "*Ingrediar*," and the Psalm "*Quemadmodum desiderat*." The body is then lifted into the coffin, the face is covered with a white veil by the cardinal *nipote* or some near relation, or, in default of them, by the *maggiordomo*; and the hands are likewise covered by the *maestro di camera*. Three velvet bags, worked in gold, are then placed in the coffin, containing specimens of the gold, silver, and bronze coins struck by the Pope. The highest cardinal of his creation then covers the whole body with a red veil, and after placing beside it a tin tube, containing a parchment, on which all the acts of the Pope are registered, the coffin-lid is screwed down and sealed by the chancellor, the notaries of the chapter and the apostolic palace, and the coffin is formally consigned by the cardinals to the chapter. This is then inclosed in another coffin of lead, bearing the pontifical arms, and properly inscribed and sealed; and this second coffin is inclosed in a third of wood, also sealed with seven seals, and the ceremony is over.

On the preceding evening the coffin, containing the body of his predecessor, is taken down from the niche near the chapel of the choir, and after being identified is carried into the "Grotte Vaticane," or to its appointed place, and in the empty niche the new coffin is placed, there to remain until the death of the succeeding Pope.

Formerly the ceremonies of the death of the Pope only occupied one day; but Gregory X., in 1274, ordered that the obsequies should be celebrated for nine days, and on the tenth the conclave should meet to elect a new Pontifex. For nine days, therefore, the obsequies are performed in the chapel of the choir, unless an important festival intervene, in which case they are intermitted for the day, and the wax is given to the poor. During all these days there are a number of ceremonies too long to describe here; the architrave of the great door, and that of the *atrium*, is draped with black; a magnificent *tumulo* is placed in the choir of the *canonici*, which remains until the sixth day, when a great and richly-ornamented *catafalque* is erected in the middle of the church. Twenty torches of white wax surround it, and other torches are lighted in all the chapels, and before the bronze statue of St. Peter. The *catafalque* and *tumulo* are guarded by the noble guard, in mourning. On the fourth day after the death commence what are called the *novendiali*, when masses are performed by the cardinal deacon and the cardinal bishops for nine consecutive days; and on the last day a funeral oration in Latin is delivered in praise of the dead Pope by a prelate chosen by the sacred college. This ends the ceremonies.* During this time a thousand impressions of the arms of the Pope, with death's heads and skeletons printed on black, are plastered over the walls of all the patriarchal *basiliche*, and are not removed until the election of the new Pope. This same usage takes place also when any one of a distinguished rank or office dies, only the placards are confined to one church. The expenses attending the funeral of a Pope are very great, and Moroni states that the *novendiali* of Pius VIII. cost about 20,000 *scudi*.

The funeral of a prince or *marchese di baldacchino* is also a pompous ceremonial. Two or three chambers in the house are hung with black, yellow, and gold, with fringes of gold-lace; three or four altars are raised; the office of the dead is said, and masses for the repose of his soul are performed during all the days that the body is exposed in the palace. At 21 o'clock (three hours before Ave Maria), twelve *capuchins* recite the office; at 22 o'clock, twelve *minori* do the same; these are succeeded, at 23 o'clock, by twelve priests and the *parroco*. The body is dressed in the *abito di città*, with a sword at its side and a cap and plume on its head. It is then laid on the floor upon a rich coverlet, worked in gold, in one of the noblest halls, under a black pavilion; and a gentleman in black keeps guard over it day and night.

It is then carried to the church, in a black funeral carriage, hung with black, and drawn by two horses, with black trappings, the footmen and coachmen being dressed in the richest liveries, and the box covered with a splendid hammer-cloth, on which the arms of the deceased are blazoned in gold. A squadron of grenadiers precedes the convoy, then come two persons with torches, a servant with the insignia of the umbrella, other servants with lanterns, and

---

* The reader who wishes to know more fully all the ceremonies of these *novendiali* is referred to the Dizionario Storico Ecclesiastico di Gaetano Moroni, vol. viii. p. 194, vol. xxviii. p. 41.

the procession closes with a company of grenadiers. The family and friends all send their carriages, with the richest liveries, and accompanied by servants with torches. The body is borne in the carriage, and on one side sit the curate and the priest, and opposite the *dilatore della croce*. Arrived at the church, the body is placed on a bier, the clergy receive it at the door with lighted candles, the cross is raised on a spear, absolution is given by the superior of the church, and the body is then laid on the pavement in front of the altar upon a rich coverlet, with benches placed around it covered with black, and decorated with the arms of the deceased, and with death's heads and bones. Four *banderuole* of black taffets with the arms are placed on the ground near by. At the head and at the foot is one great lighted candle, on candelabra or silver columns, and all about are spread waxen torches, unlighted, and disposed in the shape of crosses. Benches covered with black are also placed on either side for those who are to perform the office, and for the persons of the ante-chamber who assist at the mass. This is generally celebrated by the superior or by a bishop, after which absolution is given round the body, the servants standing by and holding candles. Then the body is placed in the coffin, on a mattress or cushion, and a tube of tin is put at its side, on which is an inscription of his name, titles, &c. The coffin is then sealed up, placed in another of lead, which is sealed hermetically, and again into a third of cypress, and deposited in the family tomb.

Among the anecdotes relating to the death of some of the Popes, given by Moroni, two may not be without interest here. In the year 896, Stephanus VII. disinterred the body of the Pope Formosus, who had then only been dead forty-eight days, and dressing it in all the sacerdotal robes and ornaments, he placed it ceremoniously in the pontifical chair, and thus addressed it: "You Bishop of Porto, how, in your mad ambition, did you dare to usurp the universal Roman chair?" As the corpse did not reply, he ordered it to be thrown into the Tiber, which was immediately done. But Theodorus II., who succeeded Stephanus on Feb. 12th, 898, caused the body of Formosus to be fished up, and restored it to its place in the Vatican Basilica. And Novaes, in his Life of Pope Formosus, relates, on the authority of various writers, that when the body entered the church all the images bowed to it.

The fate of the Pope Innocent X., of the Pamfili family, was sad enough. After being in the agonies of death for nine days he expired, and his sister-in-law, the famous, or infamous Olimpia Maidalchini, savage to him as to her other lovers, rewarded his lavish generosity by refusing him even the boon of a coffin. So the body was carried coffinless to a chamber in the Vatican, used by the bricklayers to store their materials in, and one of them, out of compassion, lighted a tallow candle and placed it at his head to keep away the rats. Finally, however, a prelate paid for having the body placed in a coffin and buried in the cheapest way. And this was the end of the Pope Innocent X., who built the noble villa Pamfili Doria and gave it to the ungrateful Olimpia.

CHAPTER XIX.

SUMMER IN THE CITY.

THE tide of strangers which pours into Rome in the autumn and overflows the streets, the hotels, and the lodging-houses during the winter, ebbs gradually away as the spring deepens into summer, and before the last days of June have come the city is empty, silent, and Roman. The sun bakes all day on the lava pavement, and they who are in the street at noon creep slowly along in the shadows, clinging closely to the walls. The shops are all shut for two hours, and the city goes to sleep. The plash of fountains sounds loud and cool in the squares; a few carriages at intervals rattle along, but were it not for the burning sun and the dry air that beats up from the pavement, you might rather suppose it was midnight than mid-day.

This modern *siesta* at noon, which is common throughout Italy, is of ancient origin. Varro calls it his "*somnus insititius*," and declares that he "could not live" without it. Cicero, also, speaks of it under the name of "*meridiationis*." Augustus used to enjoy it; and Pliny the younger says that during the summer his custom was to sleep at noon. Seneca, Theodoric, the Emperor Julian, and many others, have also admitted that they had the same habit, or, as Mrs. Malaprop would say, "own the soft impeachment."

It was at this time, or a little after the noon, that the ancients supposed the gods and genii to walk about the earth and show themselves to man. "The Lord appeared unto Abraham in the plains of Mamre as he sat in the tent door in the heat of the day;" and David, in the 91st Psalm, also speaks of "the destruction (or demon) that walketh at mid-day." Indeed it was generally believed, as St. Jerome informs us, that certain demons, called μεσημβριαζοντες or *meridiani*, then haunted the earth; and the Hebrew root "*Keteb*" (קטב), which is translated "destruction" in the English version, signified, he says, one of the fiercest demons, who openly assailed mortals at noonday. Theocritus tells us that it is not proper for shepherds to play the pipe at noon, for Pan is then weary of the chase, is cross and in bad humour. Lucan declares that when "*Phœbus in axe est*" that the priest himself trembles lest the gods should appear; and Ovid represents Actæon as seen by Diana at mid-day. So, also, it was when Paul was "come nigh to Damascus *about noon*" that the great light shone about him, and he heard a voice saying, "Saul, Saul, why persecutest thou me?" And at the same time the Hippocentaur appeared to Sant' Antonio, as St. Jerome tells us: "*media dies, coquente desuper sole fervebat.*"

However this may be, it is quite certain that in southern countries the noonday sun has the evil eye, and is apt to afflict those who walk too much in it with violent sun-strokes. And this, taken in connexion with the belief that the gods visit us in dreams, may explain the superstition that the noon or early afternoon, when the ancients took their *siesta*, was the time when demons as well as gods haunted mortals.

I am not aware that this superstition now exists in Italy, though the noon *siesta* is almost universal. The churches are then closed for two hours; but whether, according to the old belief, recorded by Porphyrius among others, the gods then enter their temples, I cannot say—all I know is that the priests go out.

But as twilight comes on the world again wakes up. Doors are opened, and their netted curtains wave to and fro in the light breeze which breathes through the cooling streets; the shrill cries of vegetable-sellers pierce the ear; carriages begin to clatter over the pavement and take up their procession through the Corso; the sunset brazes with splendour the throbbing sky; great shadows fill up the streets, and the cool evening air draws in from the Campagna.

Round every *caffè* seats are then set in the streets, where crowds gather to take sherbet and ices and cooling *bibite*, to smoke, to sip coffee, to whisper mysterious cabala of politics, and to read the newspapers, which in Rome are ominously published at twilight and not in the morning. There the *habitués* can see in the columns of the "Giornale di Roma" and the "Osservatore Romano"—called popularly "Il Somarone"—what the Holy Father did yesterday, and what he will do to-day. There, too, they may read all his allocutions and apostolic letters of benediction, and advice and reproofs in "*issimi*;" the American news, only three months old, from Venezuela and Brazil; the conversions of the heathen in

Timbuctoo; the comparative height of the barometer and thermometer in Paris, Turin and Rome; the latest views of the "Armonia;" the evil deeds of the Piedmontese everywhere; the ceremonies of the churches; and lately, even the telegrams and the programmes of the theatres—all for the small sum of five *baiocchi*. This would not, perhaps, entirely content any other people in Europe; but public morals demand that this "city of the soul" should not be tainted with the garbage of a free press; and those revolutionary ideas which do so much harm to the world meet on the frontier of the Roman States an impassable barrier. The censorship in Rome is very severe, and few liberal books are permitted to pass the cordon. The arguments in favour of this censorship are very plain, but not very conclusive. The more compressed are the energies and desires of a people, the more danger of their bursting into revolution. There is no safety-valve to passions like the utterance of them; no better corrective to false notions than the free expression of them. Freedom of thought can never be suppressed; and ideas too long pent in the bosom, when heated by some crisis of passion, will explode into licence and fury. Let me put a column from Milton into my own weak plaster; the words are well known, but cannot be too well known: "Though all the winds of doctrine," he says, "were let loose to play upon the earth, so Truth be in the field, we do injuriously by licensing and prohibiting to misdoubt her strength. Let her and Falsehood grapple; who ever knew Truth put to the worse in a free and open encounter? Her confuting is the best and surest suppressing."

But while we are reading the newspapers and discussing the censorship in the *caffè*, others are sauntering outside the Porta Pia, to sit under the arbour of some *osteria*, and breathe the fresher air of the Campagna, and empty a flask of red wine; others are thronging the cool circle of the Mausoleum of Augustus, where they smoke as they listen to the plays that are there performed in the open air; and others are strolling on the Pincio, or the gardens of the French Academy, now that the sun has gone, and sitting on the benches under the shadows of the myrtles, acacias, ilexes, and elms, in the very gardens of Lucullus, where Messalina gave her voluptuous entertainments. As night comes on the Corso is crowded with promenaders, who stroll up and down laughing and talking. The moon rising over the city fills the open squares with its radiance, and flashes upon many a musical fountain. The shadows of dark palaces are cut out sharply upon its soft field of light, and on either side the streets their high, irregular caves are printed in black *silhouettes* against the luminous Italian sky. In the *osterias* and *caffès* are heard the twanging of mandolines, the lisp of flutes, and the burr of guitars. Now and then comes along a serenading party, singing and playing as they go; or you will see a group dancing the *salterello*, and surrounded by a circle of lookers-on. All the windows are open, and against the interior light of the room dark half figures lean out to watch the crowd below. In the chemists' shops, and gathered about the door, you see groups of physicians, sitting each with his gold or ivory headed cane, which he holds wisely to his chin or nose as if it contained, like that of Paracelsus, some familiar spirit which could whisper mysterious secrets. No physician in Rome is without his cane—it is his badge of office; and held stiffly up between his legs, as he sits in front of the chemist's shop, it has a very imposing effect. This medical habit of smelling the cane is of mediæval pedigree, and is celebrated in a romantic ballad well known to us all:—

> "The Doctor came; he smelt his cane;
> With face long as a Quaker:
> Quoth he, ' Young man, what is your pain ?'
> Quoth I, ' 'Tis Betsy Baker !' "

The object of the doctor in this case is not manifest. But in its origin this practice was founded on a very good and sufficient reason. The head of the cane was stuffed with aromatic herbs and spices, and the doctor held it to his nose to secure himself from evil consequences when visiting a patient with a contagious disease. But though the reason is gone, the cane holding no longer a perfume box, the usage of holding it to the nose still continues in Italy, as you may assure yourself by looking at any medical group in the chemists' shops.

In the time of the great plague at Florence the physicians wore a sort of Capuchin hood over their heads, which extended down over the shoulders and completely covered the face. Before the eyes two great glasses were set into it, and over the mouth and nose projected a huge beak like that of a bird, which was stuffed with all sorts of savoury herbs. Imagine the effect of such a terrible figure coming into a sick-room. No wonder many a nervous patient died—of the doctor, if not of the disease.

Besides the promenading and dancing, the serenading and sipping *bibite*, there are other and more peculiar festivities which take place in Rome during the summer season. One of these is the *Luna d' Agosto*, as it is called, when crowds of Romans pour down into the Colosseum, at the full of the moon, in August. Rising from behind Monte Albano, it then shows its amber shield between

Monte Porzio and Frascati; and climbing the sky, pours its tender splendour full into the ruined shell of this grand old amphitheatre. Night then is more like a softened day; only the planets and a few great stars are seen,—the "lesser people of the sky" hiding in the deep vast of blue air. The slopes of the Palatine are then thronged with people flocking to the Colosseum, and the crumbled walls and galleries resound with the confused hum of a murmurous crowd. No strangers' voices are then heard; the air is stirred only by the soft bastard Latin of modern Rome, the laugh of girls, the echoes of song, the murmur of admiration, as the crowd move through the moonlit arena and disappear under the shadowy arches. Nothing is rude or violent, but calm and subdued, as if all were touched by the beauty of the scene.

Another of these summer festivities is the game of *gatta cieca*, which is played at night in the Piazza del Popolo. This is one of the most imposing of all the piazzas of Rome, and seen by moonlight it is singularly impressive, as well from its beauty as from its associations and monuments. Above it rise abruptly the terraced slopes of the Pincio, lined with trees, and adorned with statues, trophies and columns covered with *rostra*. A row of Dacian captives, with their hands crossed before them, stand on the marble balustrades, in Phrygian cap and tunic, and gaze sadly down into the square; on either side, beneath the statues of Rome and Neptune, a shining veil of water falls over semicircular basins with a soft murmur. There, dark and frowning, rises the massive gate of Michael Angelo, which opens on to the ancient Via Flaminia; and fronting it, at the opposite end, are the three main streets of Rome—the Babuino, the Ripetta, and the Corso, separated by the twin churches of Sta. Maria di Miracoli, and radiating like spokes from the central circle of the piazza. Over the pine-fringed boundaries at the right towers in the distance the misty cupola of St. Peter's. Lofty palaces close in a portion of the area, and near the gate rise the dome and the quaint pyramidal tower of Sta. Maria del Popolo, rough with its scales of stone. On the site of this church, according to old tradition, were buried the ashes of Nero, and here long after his death flowers were scattered by unknown hands. But the phantoms of the dead could not rest in their sarcophagi, and nightly they came forth to haunt the spot and terrify the superstitious. Vainly they were exorcised, until finally the imperial ashes were taken from their last resting-place and strewn to the winds, and over them the church of Sta. Maria del Popolo was built by Paschal II., and the ghosts were laid for ever.

In the centre of the piazza rises the ancient obelisk which once stood before the Temple of the Sun at Heliopolis, and at its base four Egyptian lions lie *couchant*, pouring from their mouths a stream of water that gurgles into the basin below. Under this lofty obelisk, carven with still sharp hieroglyphs, if the date given to it by some antiquarians be correct, Moses may once have walked; and here in the moonlight its long shadow travels round the piazza, as if to mark upon its dial the silent and solemn passage of time. When Rome was only a morass, it pointed with its silent finger to the intense Egyptian sky. Egypt and Greece, Republican and Imperial Rome, Isis, Osiris, Zeus, and Jupiter, have all passed away, since it was hewn from the quarry. Eighteen cycles of Christianity have vanished since Augustus brought it to the "centre of the world"— but unworn and untarnished, its edges and inscriptions fresh as in the distant days of Rhamses, here still it stands, to mock with its permanence the fleeting generations that have come and gone beneath its shadow.

Sometimes, perhaps, it has a home-sickness for its ancient land, when the populace of modern Rome crowd around it to see the *girandola* fling up into the sky its burning sheaf of fire, for then the odour of garlic and onion ascends, and it may remember the days when the Egyptians offered these savoury vegetables as first-fruits upon the altars of their gods. Sometimes, too, when the sharp, explosive tones of the Romans, playing at *morra*, strike against its red granite, it may have reminiscences of the glorious days of the *Osirtasins*, when, two thousand years before the Christian era, the same game was played beneath it by its builders. The "processions of the shrines" must give it a pang, too, sometimes, if any heart still beat within it.

But, whatever the obelisk used to see in Egypt, it now looks down in summer evenings on the game of "*gatta cieca*"* which the modern Romans play in its august presence.

This game, as it is ordinarily played, consists in bandaging the eyes of one of the players, who, after being turned round two or three times, endeavours to go blindfold to an appointed goal, on which a prize is placed, and touch it with a stick given him to aid him in his progress and to enable him to avoid obstacles. The three whirls generally so confuse the notions of the blindfolded person as to his position, that he often makes the most amusing blunders as he goes groping along in a false direction, and exhibiting at times a self-confidence when he is wrong, and a timidity of purpose when he is right, that is exceedingly absurd.

The Italians, who in many respects are children in a good sense,

* Blind cat.

greatly enjoy this game; and when the full moonlight floods the Piazza del Popolo in August, crowds flock there to join in the play and to look on. The *garzoni* of the Monti, the Trastevere, the Oca, and the Borgo are there, with their sweethearts and their friends. The black-eyed little *monelli* are perched on the balustrades of the Pincio, and on the backs of the lions under the obelisks, and the half of the piazza towards the gate is thronged with a gay crowd. The other half of the piazza is kept comparatively clear; for here the game is played. The players, under the supervision of a president and umpire, chosen by acclaim, are blindfolded under the obelisk; and any one who likes may join. The money constituting the prize is levied on the spectators, and placed in the hands of the president; and whoever walks from the obelisk into the Corso is the winner.

At a signal the blindfolded players are all whirled round three times, and off they go. Each, confident in himself, sets bravely out at first, but scarcely have ten paces been made, when there are doubts and misgivings, hesitations and abrupt decisions, and, amid the jeers and loud laughter of the spectators, they all wander about in different directions. Loud and numerous bets are now screamed out, some in earnest and some in irony. The players, excited by these screams, and not knowing whether it is their friends who are endeavouring to encourage them in the path they have taken, or their adversaries who are making fun of them, exhibit a ludicrous vacillation of purpose or a strenuous obstinacy in the wrong which elicits new cries.

"I bet ten *pauls* to one on Nino in the red cap," shouts one. "Taken," cries another; and Nino, hearing the bets and assured that he is right, marches stedfastly on and butts his nose against that of the lion, two paces from where he set out, amidst the derisive howls of the people. "Five *fiaschi* of Orvieto on Paoluccio," cries another; and he is immediately trumped by a second, who cries, "Five *fiaschi?* per Bacco, twenty flasks to a half-*foglietta* on *caro* Paoluccio." And Paoluccio, who has already made half the distance straight towards the Corso, and really has the best chance of winning, stops when he hears these cries and debates with himself, and then deciding that all this betting is ironical, makes a right angle and marches towards the Pincio. Louder cries and jeers now resound, and "Bravo, bravo, Paoluccio!" He now loses his head entirely and turns to the right about; but at his side he hears whispers, and doubting again, he determines to take the original direction again, and in so doing he makes a mistake and turns his back on the Corso, and wanders aimlessly down towards the gate.

Lo Zoppo, meanwhile, who is rather irritable, has got into the middle of the piazza and marches for the Ripetta; somebody cries in his ear, "*A sinistro*," and another tickles his cheek with a straw; at which he strikes out right and left with his fists and loses his road, and, determined to keep his own way, marches straight up to one of the fountains and tumbles heels over head into it.

There are, however, all sorts of cheating, for the prize is generally worth taking; and oftentimes friends agree to give certain preconcerted signals to indicate to the player the true direction, on condition that he shares the money, or that they drink it all away in an *osteria* together. But the crowd is up to this, and whenever they hear a peculiar signal there are echoes of it repeated in all directions and at the wrong time; so that the player, unless he is very sharp, has a more than even chance of being misled.

The fun is very good-natured, and it not seldom occurs that various trials are made before the prize is won. At last, however, some lucky fellow hits the Corso, and the whole piazza shakes with cheers that announce to him his victory.

Do not, I beg, my most serious friend, sneer at this childish game, nor come too sternly to the conclusion that a people which can be thus amused are not fit for liberty. The greatest loss any person or any people can sustain is that of their childhood. So long as the child survives in the man he is living, but when this is gone he is no better than a mummy-case. And when a people has lost its susceptibility to fun and its enjoyment of sport, even though it be childish, it has lost what no gravity can ever make up for. The world now overworks its brain and grows severe in its wisdom and feeble on its legs, and a morbid irritability of temper follows as a necessary consequence. When we scorn the body it revenges itself on the mind; only a healthy, vigorous frame can hold a healthy, vigorous body. *Mens sana in corpore sano.* The rights of the body need preaching in America more than elsewhere. We need recreation, healthy sport, foolish games, and athletic exercise. Be sure the man will think and act more justly, broadly, and efficiently, whose brain is not overworked at the expense of the body. These boat-races on the bay and river—this carnival of skating on the frozen ponds—are better than the office, counting-house, and furnace-heated rooms; and it is with real joy that every well-constituted mind must see them growing up among us. I am, however, one of those who do not count strength by weight, nor will I yet agree that the slender and beautiful American girls have less native stamina than their rosier and stouter English cousins. If the English have more fullness and roundness of muscle, the Americans have more fibre and sinew; and I will test the latter against the former any day, if they are only well developed. But the English have twice as good training; they are braced by daily exercise and fresh air—the Americans are kiln-dried in over-heated rooms. Let us hear an end of this sermon, and improve it by bowling down ten strikes, cutting pigeons' wings on the ice, galloping over the country, and straining the cords by handling the oar—and then we exiles from home shall not have to greet on the Continent so many old broken-down men of twenty-five and thirty pursuing their lost health, and so many pale, fragile girls faded into premature parchment and racked with neuralgia and consumption. Whatever you think of it, I find the *gatta cieca* a capital thing, and believe the Romans all the better fitted for liberty and self-government by the enjoyment of it. A child-like man is far better than an old-manny boy.

Were I a law-giver and law-maker, I would ordain the training of the people to sports and games as an obligatory part of education. I would declare that no man should be eligible to office who could not prove that he had enjoyed a hearty laugh at least once a day for two months previous to his election. Bad legislation, cruel criticism, savage rejoinders in debate, and the frequent use of the bowie-knife, depend more on bad digestion than on any one other cause. If the senators and House of Representatives must fight, let the differing parties, instead of brawling on the floor of legislation, threatening with bowie-knives and revolvers, and knocking down with bludgeons, appoint a time and place and have it out once a week with gloves, or even with fists on the green. We should have better laws and less of the barbarism of Southern "chivalry."

But, as I unfortunately am not the American Lycurgus, I have only to beg pardon for these aberrations, and come back to my Roman text.

Everybody has seen the *girandola* on the Pincian, but few have seen the *fochetti* in the Mausoleum of Augustus; for the latter take place only in the summer when Rome is the city of the Romans. The *fochetti* are artificial fireworks, elaborately composed to represent famous historical incidents. One of the principal subjects is the burning of Troy. When this is given, the portion of the amphitheatre where the *proscenium* generally stands is built over with architectural frame-works representing the rock of Ilium, the temple of Minerva, and the palace of Priam, behind which are carried all sorts of fiery conductors. The moment these are fired the flame runs with a blaze and crackle over the whole architecture, bursting from column and architrave, roof, door, and window, showering its rain of fire, pealing its startling cannonades, and darting its rockets everywhere, until a wonderfully coloured conflagration wraps the whole and glares against the sky. Then issue on all sides warriors dressed as Greeks, followed by the Trojan populace, represented after the usual manner of a populace on the stage by a few men and boys, who shout enough for a hundred, and make up to the ear their defects to the eye. The warriors carry torches in their hands and set fire to the houses, which send forth whirling Catherine-wheels, fling up incessant Roman candles, and blaze with Bengal lights of every hue. In the midst of the racket, roar and fizz of these fireworks, crack go the beams, and through the rolling clouds of smoke the columns of the temples and roofs are seen tumbling to the ground. After the temple of Minerva has perished in flame and smoke, the palace of Priam is fired. When this splits apart showing the nuptial chamber and lofty hall blazing with fireworks, the spectators shout with delight, and thousands of hands clapping together mix with the constant explosion of mortars and the spasmodic sputter of dying Catherine-wheels, making noise enough almost to rouse the dead Cæsars from their tombs below.

Other favourite subjects are the burning of Saguntum, the conflagration of Rome by Nero, and the destruction of the Capitol in the time of Vespasian. Of all these spectacles, that most enjoyed by the Romans is perhaps the last, for then are represented the Temple of Jupiter Capitolinus, the Tabularia and the Tarpeian rock, which touches their pride and reminds them of their ancient glory.

In artificial fireworks the Romans are eminently skilful, and at the *fochetti* as well as the *girandola* surprising effects are often produced. But no illumination can surpass for beauty the *moccoletti* that end the Carnival. Thousands of little waxen tapers then flutter about like living things, dancing along balconies and open windows, quivering up and down the entire length of the Corso, flickering from carriage to carriage, flying backwards and forwards at the ends of long *canne,* and pursued by flapping handkerchiefs that seek to extinguish them. A soft yellow light glows over the brown palace façades, gleaming on the window panes, and illuminating below a sea of merry faces. Up the Corso, far as the eye can reach, the *moccoletti* sparkle like swarms of brilliant fire-flies. The street resounds with a tumultuous cry of " *Ecco il moccolo—moccolo,*" as the little tapers are brandished and shaken in the air, and the loud jeers of " *Senza moccolo—senza moccolo,*" as dexterous hands and lips suddenly extinguish them. The scene is always gay, but the wild, glad exultation of the spectacle in 1848, when news of Italian victories came in from Lombardy, and the people, waving their *moccoletti,* poured into the Corso, cheering and singing their national songs, surpassed for enthusiasm anything I ever saw. I have never seen it since without a painful memory of those happy days, when the faces of all were bright with triumphant, irrepressible joy—when all were brothers in a great common success, and bands met bands with enthusiastic embraces and cries of *Viva Italia!*

This scene I can never forget, nor one other of a similar kind which I saw at Genoa in the autumn of 1847. The King Carlo Alberto had just granted those reforms which drew after them the early successes and the final sad defeats of that ill-fated struggle for independence. The people were full of hope; and when the king first came from Turin to Genoa, after embracing the liberal cause, they went forth to meet him and escort him to their noble old city. Rose-leaves showering from the windows fell like snow-flakes on him and his suite as they rode to San Lorenzo in the morning to hear mass. In the evening he rode through the city with his sons and a few of his friends, the people following him in thousands, each carrying a torch. Windows were all open and illuminated, the balconies were thronged, and every crevice, from pavement to eaves, showed eager eyes. The torches flared and flashed upon the little group of horsemen round the king, and with a mighty chorus that shook the air, and resounded down the narrow lofty streets, ten thousand voices sang the national song—

> "Oh giovani ardenti d' Italico amore,
> Serbate il valore pel dì di pugnar;
> E viva Italia! e viva Pio Nono!
> E viva Italia! e viva il Rè!"

Another wondrous illumination, called the *Luminara*, is to be seen every third year at Pisa, on the day of St. Ranieri.* At this festival the whole city is illuminated. Go where you will, thousands of twinkling lights, arranged in every shape, gleam along the eaves, windows, doors, and walls. But the chief spectacle is along the Lungo L'Arno. On either side the whole length of this imposing promenade the buildings are cased in scaffoldings, representing temples, rich Tuscan façades, Gothic churches, arcades, and, in a word, every imaginable architectural shape. The long garden walls are decorated by arabesque patterns, mixed with crosses, stars, and foliated devices. To these the effect of reality is given by thousands of little lamps, closely set together, so as to draw their outlines against the dark background with dotted lines of fire. Seen at a short distance, it is impossible to distinguish the true from the false. The rich old church of Sta. Maria della Spina, with its

---
* 16th of June.

quaint spires; the stern mediæval tower guarding the upper bridge; the façades of some of the noble palaces, whose marbles are yellowed with age and enriched by historical associations, and some few other buildings, show their real faces. The Lungo L'Arno in itself, in ordinary daylight, with the yellow Arno flowing under the arches of curved bridges between these files of grand old palaces, churches, spires and towers, is very striking, but when flashing with the myriad lights of the *luminara* its effect is truly marvellous. As you look down upon it from the bridges, the city seems more like an enchanted place than a real city of this earth. Barges with coloured lanterns and bright banners glide up and down the river, that, flashing back the splendid illumination, quivers and shakes, and shimmers with its golden glory. On the parapets at intervals are erected stagings where bands are stationed, and brazen music sounds above the confused hum of the crowds that stream along the streets. Above is the deep-blue sky, with its still and steady stars waiting till this fleeting splendour is past; and wondrously deep and infinite it looks as we lift our eyes from the magical city below up to its serene peace.

CHAPTER XX.

THE GOOD OLD TIMES.

HE Past never wants for praisers and apologists. Every one ends by being a "*Laudator temporis acti, me puero,*" and all countries as well as persons, in their old age, are prone to cherish ancient usages with pious love. It is hard to break down a church-window pictured over with saints, heroes, and demons,—even to let in a little more pure light and fresh air to a stifled people.

My design in this trivial chapter is only to show, as in a magic lantern, one or two little slides on which are old Roman pictures. I have thus far endeavoured to show you a few sketches of Modern Life in Rome, and before we part let us give a glimpse, only a glimpse, into the Life of the Past.

Among the relics of mediæval Rome may still be seen some curious old truncated towers, which stand as landmarks of "auld lang syne," when every house was a fortress and society a system of rapine. In the middle ages every powerful family was the nucleus of a greater or smaller body of vassals and dependants, who gathered under its authority and aided in its defence. Individual liberty was unknown—law was according to the

> "Good old plan,
> That he shall take who has the power,
> And he shall keep who can."

Feudal authority begot feuds. Every important house then had its tower of defence, into which it retreated in the day of trouble, and from which it showered missiles on its assailants. Some of the great princely families took possession of the ancient tombs, villas, and temples, and there intrenched themselves. The Colosseum was the battle-ground for many years of the Frangipani and Annibaldi, and the refuge of the Popes Alexander III. and Innocent II. Church and Empire, Guelph and Ghibelline, fought in these fortresses for dear life, and the people, nursed in blood, were turbulent, violent, and barbaric. The Mausoleum of Augustus was the fortress of the Colonna; the tomb of Cecilia Metella was one of the strongholds of Boniface VIII.; near it are the ruins of the castle of the Caetani and Savelli. The Mausoleum of Hadrian was made the stronghold of Honorius, and still remains at once a fortress and a prison. The arch of Janus was fortified by the Frangipani. Everywhere the ancient buildings were converted into fortifications. The city itself then bristled with tall towers, and of these two still remain— the Tor de' Conti, a huge brick tower at the foot of the Quirinal, erected by Nicholas I. in 858, and rebuilt by Innocent III. in 1216, from whose family it takes its name; and the Torre delle Milizie, at the head of the Via Magnanapoli. All the others have perished.

In the Tuscan cities, however, many of these towers may be seen, though for the most part they have been shorn of their lofty proportions, and cut down to a level with the surrounding houses. In the little town of St. Geminiano, however, there are standing no less than fourteen, all of their original height, and a strange picturesque character they give to the place. If any one would form a notion of the mediæval appearance of an Italian town, he should visit St. Geminiano. It is but a few miles off the main road, contains some beautiful frescoes by Ghirlandaio, and closely resembles in itself the quaint old cities painted by the early Tuscan masters in their backgrounds.

The Tor de' Specchi at Rome is a curious representative of the days of the old barons. Here dwelt Santa Francesça Romana, the founder of the order of the Oblate nuns, and the house is scarcely changed from what it was in her time. Here is the cell in which she lived, with the very pavement on which she trod, the narrow gothic windows through which she looked, the old worm-eaten benches she sat upon, all carefully kept in their original condition. On the walls is painted the history of her life by one of the scholars of Giotto, where one may see the dresses of the 14th century in the foreground, and in the background views of mediæval Rome, with its turreted houses and castellated palaces in which the Roman barons intrenched themselves. Here you may catch a glimpse of the old times, and turning round may compare it with modern Rome, which lies before you. What a strange jumble it was of war and prayer, humility and licence, luxury and barbarism! In those days the cardinals lived in fortresses, guarding their doors with pikes, barring their windows with heavy iron gratings, and keeping in their employ large bodies of soldiers.* The Pope was the mere football of different parties—sharing their luck in battle—now fleeing for refuge, now returning to the chair of St. Peter, his feet red with conquest. The streets were filled with soldiers belonging to different houses, jealous of the rank of their masters, involved in endless fights, and employed to carry out the base designs of their irresponsible lords. There was but one law—the sword.

Throughout the fifteenth and sixteenth centuries the palace of every cardinal was a little court. Guards of soldiers, mounted and on foot, surrounded it; in the stables were great numbers of horses, and the family of servants of every grade was a little army. It is related that Cardinal Ippolito D'Este, when he was sent as legate to France, carried in his train more than four hundred horses; and it is mentioned, not as an indication of pomp and wealth, but, on the contrary, of humility, that Cardinal Bellarmino had in his house only thirty servants to wait upon him.

The palaces of the princes not only swarmed with armed retainers, but with assassins, or "*bravi*" as they were called, who did the "secret service" of their lord. Within their precincts, as well as in the churches, any one who had committed a crime in the streets could obtain refuge, and no one dared to pursue them there—not even the officers of justice. The criminal then entered the service of the prince into whose palace he had sought asylum, assumed his livery, received his protection, and thenceforward snapped his fingers in the face of the world. In this way the princes surrounded themselves with unscrupulous adherents who owed them their lives, and were ready at their bidding to commit any crime. Those were "good old times." There were none of those miserable police officers about, but a merry life of wine and women, no law, and stabbing of enemies *ad libitum*.

Take, for instance, a little incident related by an old chronicler which occurred in the time of Gregory XIII., as illustrating the general irresponsibility of the nobility. The "*Bargello*," who was the chief of the police, had in the exercise of his office arrested some outlaws, who having escaped from Naples had placed themselves under the protection of one of the great Roman barons. As he was conducting his prisoners through the streets he was met by a set of young nobles, among whom were Pietro Gaetani, Silla Savelli, and

---

* Le case dei cardinali tutte s'erano messe in fortezza con bertesche; e la casa del vice cancelliere avea due bastioni. (Diario del Notaio di Nantiporto alla morte de Sisto IV.) Infessura, in his diary, states that "Cardinalis S. Petri ad Vincula multos pedites ac milites stipendio acquisivit et domum suum mirabiliter fortificavit et fulcivit."

Raimondo Orsini, who stopped him and ordered him to surrender his prisoners. The *Bargello*, says the old chronicler, "spoke to them, cap in hand, with great respect, endeavouring to quiet them and to persuade them to allow him to do his duty. They, however, would not listen to him, but attacked him and his followers, killed several, took others into houses and flung them from the windows, to the great ignominy and contumely of public justice."

This, however, was not the worst—an unlucky shot had killed the noble Raimondo Orsini; and the *Bargello*, fearing the vengeance of the Orsini, against which the Pope himself was powerless to protect him, immediately fled the city as the only means to save his life. But the noble house were not thus to be balked; and the brother of Raimondo, not being able to find the *Bargello*, slew in his stead the lieutenant-general of police as he was coming down from the papal palace on the Quirinal.

During these delightful days there were much rejoicing and festivity, if not among the people, at least among the princes. While the former were starved to pay for these splendours, and forced to eat bread, which, says Infessura, "was black, stinking, and abominable, eaten only from necessity, and the cause of much disease,"* nothing could surpass the luxury of the papal dignitaries. There were costly ceremonies of all kinds, when "the Florentine ambassador washed the Pope's hands at the beginning of the sacred rites, Venetian ambassadors washing them in the middle, and the prefect of Rome at the end of the same;"† and entertainments where Leon Cobelli says that "it was charming to see the Lady Countess and all her damsels come forth in different magnificent dresses every day for a whole week, and the great buffets, ten feet high, in the banqueting-hall of the palace, loaded every day with a fresh service of silver and gold."

In the "Relazioni degli Ambasciatori Veneti," I find the record of a banquet given by Cardinal Andrea Cornaro at Rome, during the Pontificate of Leo X., which may perhaps afford a layman an idea of what constituted a cardinal's dinner in those days. "The repast," says the ambassador, "was most beautiful. There was an infinite quantity of viands, and no less than sixty-five courses, with three different dishes at each course, which were continually changed with great agility, so that scarcely had one been partaken of than another was brought on. All was served on beautiful silver plate, and in great quantity. The feast being finished, we all arose stuffed and stunned (*stuffi e storditi*), both by the abundance of viands, and

* Rer. Ital. Script., tom. iii. pp. 2, 1183.
† Ibid., tom. xxiii. p. 137.

because at the table of the cardinal there was every kind of musician that could be found in Rome." One hundred and ninety-five different dishes is truly an apostolic dinner!

At Cardinal Grimani's, a few days after, the ambassadors relate that, it being a fast day, they dined entirely on fish like good Catholics, and sat at the table for *six hours*, and they mention among other fishes a sturgeon, the head of which was "larger than that of an ox," and which had cost eighteen golden ducats, a sum equivalent to about forty *scudi*, or eight pounds sterling.

One cannot help in this connexion recalling Andrew Fairservice's notions about Romanism at Osbaldiston Hall : " We hae mense and discretion," says he, "and are moderate of our mouths; but here, frae the kitchen to the ha', it's fill and fetch mair frae the tae end of the four-and-twenty hours till the t'other. Even their fast days— they ca' it fasting when they hae the best of sea-fish frae Hartlepool and Sunderland by land carriage—forbye trouts, grilses, salmon, and a' the lave o't, and so they make their very fasting a kind of luxury and abomination,—and then the awfu' masses and matins o' the puir deceived souls."*

The convivial suppers of the Pope himself were as luxurious and costly as those of Vitellius. They were enlivened by the jesting of buffoons and all sweet instruments and singing, in which the Pope, who was an excellent musician, joined; and whenever any one sang with him so as to please his holiness he was rewarded by a gift of a hundred *scudi* and more.† After supper he sat down to cards, and often lost at *primiera*, a game of which he was very fond, enormous sums. Marino Giorgi, the Venetian ambassador, says that his losses at this game, together with his "gifts," amounted annually to more than 60,000 *scudi*, all of which he levied from *vacanze di benefizii*.‡ Besides this, there were constant hunting, and fishing and hawking parties, at Corneto, Viterbo, and Bolsena, on the most extravagant scale. One of these, which was given by Cardinal Cornelio during the Papacy of Leo, has already been cited, and from this an idea of a papal hunt may be derived.

On the walls of the great ante-chambers in some of the princely

---

* It is curious to compare with this a dinner, reported by Macrobius to have been given by Metellus, the Pontifex Maximus, in the days of ancient Rome, at which several distinguished guests were present, as well as four vestal virgins. The dinner was magnificent, and Macrobius gives the dishes in book iii. chap. xiii. of his Saturnaliorum.

† Relazione Venete, Rel. di Marino Giorgi, p. 56. "Sopra tutti musico eccellentissimo, e quando canta con qualcuno, gli fa donare cento e piu ducati."

‡ Ibid.

houses of Rome may be seen large paintings representing jousts and festivals held in old times by the nobility; and in the bookstalls of the Piazza Navona (which is a sort of literary Ghetto), amid the soiled and second-hand rubbish, now and then is to be found a volume with illustrations containing descriptions of some of the spectacles which were once celebrated in this very piazza.

One of these festivals took place here in the year 1634, on the occasion of the visit of Prince Alexander Charles, of Poland, which s fully described by Vitale Mascardi, in a pamphlet published by him at the time, and enriched with numerous engravings. Cardinal Barberini was the prime mover in this festival, and in the palace of the family may still be seen a huge picture in which it is represented. The prince was first received in the noble house of Signor Orazio Magalotti, when Fame made her entrance into the saloon in a triumphal car, richly carved and gilded. A cavalier accompanied it, a golden eagle drew it, and Fame, with a trumpet in her hand and splendidly dressed, sang a wonderful ode of welcome to the accompaniment of a band of music. As she ceased a herald advanced, and announced that the Mantenitore, who assumed the title of Tiamo di Menfi, challenged all the world to contend with him in a tournament, to be held in the Piazza Navona on the 15th of February, when he would keep the field against all comers. The tilting he declared to be against a wooden Saracen set up in the lists —he to be proclaimed victor who, under the rules hereafter to be published, should give the three best blows.

The cardinal, joining with him in this scheme, at once appointed a *squadriglia* of four gentlemen in his retinue, who were to represent four captive kings, to respond to this challenge.

The formal acceptance of it, however, was made at the palace of the Signore Falconieri, where a great ball was given in honour of the prince. After many divers scenes had taken place, all the company retired into a great hall, where seats were formally arranged around an open square. Here appeared two nymphs accompanied by six *pastori* and a herald. The nymphs, adorned with flowers and brandishing spears, sang songs and odes to the accompaniment of various instruments, after which the herald advanced and formally accepted the challenge on the part of the four captive kings, and the six *pastori* then went through with some curious pastoral dances.

At the appointed day the jousting took place in the Piazza Navona. The piazza was magnificently arranged and must have presented a most imposing appearance. It was completely surrounded by a double tier of boxes for spectators, the lower of which were sufficiently high to allow the horses of the tournament to find shelter beneath them. On one side was a third row of boxes for the noblest ladies; and here, occupying the post of honour, was the box of the Donna Anna Colonna and the Donna Costanza Barberini. This amphitheatre of boxes was decorated, according to the taste of the various parties who were to use them, in splendid hangings fringed with gold, silver, and velvets. All were covered in so as to protect the inmates from the sun as well as from the rain, in case the day should prove inauspicious. But everything smiled; the day was perfectly cloudless, and the vast circle was crowded with the most distinguished ladies of Rome, all richly dressed and adorned with jewels. From the palaces and houses of the piazza floated draperies of gold and silver, and superb pictured tapestries; and not only the windows were thronged, but the very roofs were covered with crowds.

In the centre of the piazza were the lists, consisting of a triple line of fence-work, through which the cavaliers were to joust. On the centre line, near one end, stood the wooden body of the Saracen, against which all were to tilt. The principal rules were, that whoever struck the figure above the brow should receive three marks, from the brow to the chin two marks, and from the mouth to the chin one mark. Below the chin a stroke of the lance counted nothing, while if any one struck the shield or body of the Saracen he lost one mark.

Opposite the Saracen stood a great covered staging for the judges, and at the head of the lists was erected a lofty pavilion, covered with the richest stuffs, where the Mantenitore and his suite held their camp.

The arrival of the Donna Anna Colonna and Donna Costanza Barberini was the signal that the games were to commence. At the sound of trumpets there entered the Mantenitore and the various squadrons which were to dispute with him the prizes, each making the round of the piazza and then taking the stand assigned to it. First came the Mantenitore and his suite. He was preceded by four trumpeters, after whom followed six horses led by grooms; then came twenty-eight *staffieri* on foot; then four pages on horseback, who carried great silver salvers filled with sonnets and boastful challenges, to be distributed among the ladies. Two mounted *padrini* then followed, accompanied by a single horseman, and last the Mantenitore made his appearance, dressed magnificently " *alla Egittiana.*" He wore a superb robe of *ormesino*, fastened at his neck with a jewel of extraordinary size with *rilievi* of gold and pearls, and embroidered all over with *alamari* of pearls and gold in the figure of palms, the fruit being of splendid rubies. The under dress was equally magnificent, the sleeves being covered with embroideries of little pearls and trimmed with exquisite lace; long outer sleeves lined with red, sewed over with gold, hung dangling down, and floated with the motion of the horse; a gleaming cuirass was on his breast; at his side was a scimitar sheathed in a green scabbard loaded with jewels; his stockings were of silk and gold, and jewelled shoes were on his feet, armed with golden spurs. But the most extraordinary feature of his dress was a rich turban, woven of alternate threads of wool and gold, and glittering all over with jewels; above this rose a gigantic plume, or forest of plumes, made of green and white feathers curiously arranged one above the other in tiers, and rising to the height of some six feet above his head. These were bound together with flowers and gold tinsel, and crowning all were groups of snowy peacocks' plumes. In the centre of this wonderful *pennacchio* was seen the escutcheon of the Mantenitore—a blazing sun, with the motto "*Non latet quod lucet.*" The spear which he bore in his hand was of silver tipped with gold.

His horse was equally splendid in his trappings. Magnificent housings fringed with rich lace, and fastened at the crupper and over the breast with great brooches of costly jewels, fell to his knees; and on his head was a lofty *pennacchio* which nodded as he advanced. The engraved portraits of this personage and his suite given by Mascardi show a marvellous richness of costumes and indicate a splendour equal to that displayed in the beautiful frescoes of Pinturicchio at Siena.

The next *squadriglia* was that of the gentlemen of the cardinal, representing the four captive kings. All eyes were fixed on them, the fame of their splendour having preceded them. Nor did they disappoint expectation; and as they made the circuit of the lists loud cries of applause saluted them. These four cavaliers were Count Fabrizio Ferretti, Francesco Battaglini, Girol. Martinozzi, and Dominico Cinquini. They were dressed in rose colour. Their breasts were covered with steel cuirasses over shirts of golden mail, below which hung superb vests, with fringes of gold and great drops of pearls. From their shoulders floated magnificent mantles, richly worked in gold and embroidered with flowers, and royal crowns of gold on their heads, surmounted by plumes of exquisite yellow feathers. The equipments of the horses were equally costly, and no expense had been spared in the costumes of the whole suite. At the head of the *squadriglia* rode the dwarf of the cardinal, mounted on a richly-caparisoned bull.

After these came the other squadrons, equally splendid in all their appointments, and each with its suite, all of which the worthy Mascardi elaborately describes. As they entered they distributed *cartelli*, accepting the challenge of the Mantenitore, and as soon as the inclosure was filled, signal was given by trumpets and the tilting commenced, and continued with great excitement and enthusiasm for five hours. The Donna Anna Colonna offered as a prize a rich *gioia* of diamonds, which, says the gallant Mascardi " did not more splendidly shine forth from the purple of its beautiful cluster of roses than did its charming donor." Twelve cavaliers showed equal grace in tilting for this, and at last it fell to Virginio Cenci by lot.

The Mantenitore showed great skill; and on one occasion tilted with two lances, one in each hand, guiding his horse by holding the reins in his teeth ; and afterwards he struck the Saracen with three lances tied together.

The cardinal gave as a prize a jewelled sword, *armacollo*, beaver cap, gloves, and, in a word, a sumptuous and complete suit; and this was taken by the Conte Ambrogio, one of the cavaliers of the *squadriglia Provenziana*.

Night now began to come on, and the shadows were deepening in the piazza when the sound of artillery was heard, and a new wonder appeared. This was no less than a great ship, which was seen to approach the theatre. The *mastro di campo* immediately sent forth to inquire what it was, when answer was returned that it belonged to one of the gods who had come to visit the tilting field. Orders were then given to admit it, and in the light of more than a thousand torches this splendid toy made the circuit of the piazza. The low wheels on which it moved were hidden under artificial waves. The sides were covered with arabesque brackets, between which were shields of silver, bearing alternately a sun, a column, and a bee, the emblems of the noble houses of the Mantenitore, the Colonna, and the Barberini ; over these was a cornice of laurels with silver brackets, between which were port-holes for four cannon. The prow was formed of the head of a strange and monstrous fish plated in gold, and on the end of its long snout was a golden bee; under this was the figure of a syren with a double tail curled up on either side, and carrying in one hand a sun and in the other a column.

On the poop was a raised platform surrounded by an open temple resting upon four pilasters richly ornamented, inclosed by a gilt balustrade, and bearing aloft a golden lantern. Round the prow also was a gilt balustrade. From the bowsprit swelled a sail, and from a tall mast in the centre, on the yards of which was a furled sail, floated a rich gonfalon with the arms of the three families emblazoned on it. At the mast-head was a flag of the same, and a sailor was constantly climbing up and down the rope ladders. Under the temple on the poop sat the god Bacchus, and near him were eight Bacchanti, who sang and played the harp, violin, and lute. These, with four satyrs, four shepherds, and three cannoneers, constituted the entire equipage on board; while at the side of the vessel ran sixteen fishermen in long robes of blue, covered with silver scales, and carrying torches in their hands. Accompanying this vessel was another with six sailors, a pilot, shepherds, and ten nymphs, who played on musical instruments. To the sound of music and the peal of their cannon these two vessels slowly moved round the amphitheatre, and paused before the boxes where were seated the Donna Anna and the Donna Costanza and their *cortège*, as well as under that occupied by the Marchesa di Castel Rodrigo, the wife of the Spanish ambassador. Then all was hushed, and the god Bacchus, accompanied by a chorus of the nymphs and shepherds, sang an ode, and the *riso*, as the concluding portion of the song was called, terminated the music, in the words of Mascardi, "with a superhuman grace."

After the ship had made the entire tour of the piazza, the *cavalieri* and their *padrini* were all graciously invited by the Donna Costanza to her palace, where they partook of a "*lautissima colatione*" at the expense of the cardinal.

The ship was afterwards, at the unanimous request of the people, carried through the principal streets of Rome by daylight, and gave universal delight.

And thus ended this splendid show for the day. A great dinner was afterwards given by the cardinal at the grand gallery of the Cancelleria; and such satisfaction did he get out of this, that again, on the subsequent Tuesday, he gave a reception at the Palazzo Colonna, which terminated the splendours of this carnival festival.

But these are fragments from the ecclesiastical and princely robes —let us look at a few rags which are taken from the people. In the fourteenth century it was the custom among the Romans, as well as throughout Italy, to celebrate Sundays and *festa*-days by sham battles, when the people were divided into two parties, each armed with wooden swords, spears and shields, and having on their heads wooden helmets called *cistas*. These games generally ended in bloodshed, which added greatly to the amusement. In some of the Italian cities the combat was with slings, the two parties issuing from separate gates and fighting fiercely together for hours. At Modena there was a "*pratum di battaglia*" expressly for these combats. Milan had also her "*brolium*," where the youths contended with arrows and spears. On these occasions not only the men of rank and dignity engaged in the contest, but the common people of both sexes.* St. Bernardine mentions these mortal games as common in Perugia. In Siena, where they flourished under the title of "*giuoco dell' elmora*," the battle was fought with spears and stones. St. Augustine reproves these games as unchristian. "Not only the people," he says, "but relations, brothers, parents and children divide themselves into two parties, and for continuous days at certain periods of the year fight together with stones and kill each other as they can. And I wish most sincerely that I were able to root out this cruel and inveterate evil from their hearts and manners."† Such was the loss of life during these battles that it became necessary to prohibit them, but it was impossible entirely to root them out. In Siena the inhabitants of the Borgo and the city had furious contests, called the "*giuoco della pugna*," in which numbers of dead were often left upon the ground. These combats with fists were instituted in place of the "*giuoco dell' elmora*," but they were always attended with similar fatal results; for though the battle began with fists it ended with weapons of every kind. In 1317 a terrible fight occurred, in which many were killed, and peace was with difficulty restored. In 1536 one of these battles took place in the presence of Charles V., who especially commended it; and such hold had they on the people that they survived even in the beginning of the present century.‡

In Rome these combats flourished until within a very few years under the name of "*Sassaiuole*." They usually took place in the Campo Vaccino, or at the Cerchi, or on the slopes of the Coelian Hill at the Navicella. All the little boys were taught the use of the sling, in which they became proficients. The Roman mothers used to hang their lunch on a tree, and they could not have it unless they brought it down with a stone. The statues of Donna Lucrezia, Marforio, and the Babuino were noted targets, and bear tremendous marks of "punishment." Pasquino also suffered terribly under their stones.

The great parties between which these battles were fought were the Montigiani who inhabit the Rione de' Monti on the Esquiline, and the Trasteverini. These two wards contain more of the old Roman blood than all the rest of the city. Each boasts its ancient

* Murat. Antiq. Ital., tom. ii. De Spectac. et Lud. Pub. Med. Æv., p. 833.
† De Doctrina Christiana, lib. iv. cap. 3.
‡ Gentile Sermini, Giuoco della Pugna, L'Assedio di Siena del Bulgarini, Part ii. p. 233.

Roman descent, and between them has always existed a profound jealousy. On festal days they fought terribly together with stones, forming into great companies with leaders, attacking each other furiously in their strong posts, and often leaving scores of dead and wounded on the ground. It is not until within a very short time that the government has succeeded in suppressing these bloody contests; and the old usage still shows itself in any row. The first thing an angry Roman seeks, if he have no knife to plunge into the breast of his adversary, is a paving stone to fling at his head.

Besides these games, the Romans had their bull-fights and horse and buffalo races. As late as the fifteenth century these races still took place before Lent in the Circus Agonalis, where the senator of Rome presided *en grande tenue* and adjudged the prizes, which were generally a ring of gold and a *pallium* of woollen and silk. There were also games in Monte Testaccio, where *charettes* of pigs were tumbled down the hill for the amusement of the people. The expenses of these games were defrayed by a tax of 1130 florins levied annually upon the Jews—the curious charge of the thirty additional florins being intended to represent the thirty pieces Judas received for betraying Christ.

Joustings, tournaments, and hunting parties were common in the old days. Some of these *caccie* took place in the arena after the manner of the ancient Romans, and some in the Campagna. The *caccie* of wild animals long survived in the Campo or Piazza in Siena, some of which were very remarkable. The hunters were clad in the various costumes of their guilds, and had great wooden cars, or *macchine* as they were called, very richly adorned. On these the victors used to hang the skins, and portions of the body and entrails of the animals they had slain, as trophies. This custom is alluded to in the following verses:—

> " Hic est ille locus Campus celeberrimus, hic est
> Quo fiunt ludi varii, et celebrantur honores
> Virginis, et curru tauri cervique trahuntur
> Viscera, et armatus sonipes pro munera certat."*

One very pompous spectacle of this kind was held on the 15th of August, 1516, on the festival of the Assumption—rather an odd way of celebrating it. In the buffalo races superb *macchine* were often constructed at great expense, which were carved and covered with paintings representing all sorts of allegorical figures, and sometimes adorned with gold, silver, and jewels. On one occasion, at the

* Vittorio Campanaticense De Ludo Pagne.

festival of the Madonna in 1546, the cost of the cars amounted to 100,000 florins.

Bull-baiting was once a favourite sport of the Italians. When Margaret of Austria entered Florence, previous to her nuptials with Alessandro de' Medici, called Il Moro, two bulls were baited and killed in the square for her delight, and for the delight of the young bride who accompanied her, Catherine de' Medici. This was one of the most popular amusements at Rome, and till within a very few years mounting a furious bull was one of the chief games in the Mausoleum of Augustus. Specially famous for this feat was Luigetto la Merla, called "Lo Zoppo," who is still living. After the dogs had worried the bull to desperation, Luigetto advanced, and flinging over his horns a noose, dragged him roaring with rage to a pillar in the centre of the arena. There, holding him down by an iron ring passed through his nose, he flung over him a heavy saddle, buckled it firmly, and sprang on his back. The moment the bull felt himself mounted he roared and foamed with rage. The noose was then suddenly loosed, and at the same moment fireworks placed under his belly were fired. The maddened bull then dashed wildly round the circus, struggling in every way to fling his rider; but Luigi, firmly planted in the saddle, was too much for him, and kept his seat, riding him round the ring amid the wild cheers of the spectators; after which the noose was again thrown over his horns, and he was dragged back and secured to the column, and the rider sprang to the ground.

This is all over now, and instead we have only the annual circus in the autumn, and the drama in the summer months. How tame these look compared with the bull-baiting, the *sassaiuole*, the tumult and riot of the good old times! But the "good old times" have not utterly gone,—we have still the *equuleus*, which has been revived by the most eminent Cardinal Antonelli, to be applied to prisoners who are obstinate and will not confess; and we have dungeons and prisons on the old pattern, where robbers and assassins and political prisoners are confined together in the same public hall; we also retain the insane hospitals on the good old plan, and in the country jails you may hear the ribald songs of the prisoners who crowd to the grating that opens on the street, and beg and curse; and we have still secret tribunals as in the past, and courts not open to the public, where all the pleadings are printed in Latin. The streets, too, at night are not altogether so safe as they might be; for, when driven to desperation by want, the Romans take to feudal customs; and in the ill-lighted alleys of the city, remote from the patrol, they demand in a somewhat imperious manner, at times, your purse and your watch. *Ma che volete?* Are not the rules of our fathers good enough for us? are we alone wise in our generation? Do not let us be in a hurry in our pretended reforms. *Festina lente* is a safe rule. Let us, as far as we can, conserve the principles and the practice of the past. All old customs are good in part, because they are old; and we must take care not to pluck up the grain with the tares: where there is honey there are flies. Nothing is perfect: seasoned wood does not crack. If a man will not testify the truth, we must make him; and the *cavalletto* is an excellent method that we had foolishly done away with. As for open tribunals and juries, that system is productive of the worst effects in England and France. The Church knows what is best for us; and while people are wicked, and do not have faith in it, the prisons must be full. Robbery and brigandage seem to have disappeared from the Romagna since that country wickedly abjured its allegiance; while they still exist within the Papal rule, and in the city of Rome. But irreligion is worse than robbery. The rebellious heart is the fiercest of brigands. There is much excuse to be made for a poor creature tempted by want to theft. The government is paternal so long as its subjects do all their religious duties. It shuts its eyes for seven years to the embezzlements of the Marchese Campana in the Monte di Pietà, and shall it not be equally generous to a poor devil, with not a crust to put in his mouth, who is driven by necessity to carry on the improper trade of robbery? But he who seeks to overthrow the government, and who insults the Church, or who nourishes secret desires against the temporal power of the Church, is wicked of heart, and should be punished severely, and placed among the worst of the prisoners.

Padre Bresciani, in the "Civiltà Cattolica," is certainly of this opinion. He bravely defends Cardinal Antonelli, and the introduction of the *equuleus* or *cavalletto*; and, *à propos* of thieves, he tells a story which illustrates the customs of certain classes in Rome, who levy taxes on travellers without reference to the Papal laws, after the old way of the middle ages. These persons, he says, are known to the police, and friends to the police, with whom they share their ill-gotten gains, and are therefore permitted to live and exercise their profession freely. If you want your watch which has been stolen, do not go to the police, or at least do not go without a good bribe. There is another and better way, that you may employ on occasions, as you will see by the following incident.

A short time since a gentleman wandering along by the ruins of the Palatine, passed by the arch of the old Cloaca Maxima, when he heard the cry of a woman calling for help. Hurrying down the bank, he saw a young woman in the flower of her age lying stretched on the ground. "Ah, *signore*," she said, "I have been waylaid here by three drunken soldiers while I was seeking for wild chicory; and as I was endeavouring to escape, one of them knocked me down with a stone which he threw at me."

The gentleman was preparing to give her all the help he could, when suddenly two men leaped out upon him, one of whom, menacing him with a knife, demanded his purse and the other his watch. Seeing the odds, he considered the better part of valour was discretion, and immediately surrendered both; and both men as well as the woman disappeared.

His purse, unfortunately for him, was well filled with gold; but he lamented more than this the loss of his watch. It was a gift from his dead brother, and for this rather than for its intrinsic value he regretted the loss.

Under these circumstances he went to a friend to consult with him what steps he should take to recover it.

"I don't object even to paying its full value," said he; "but I must have it again, if possible."

"It is unnecessary to offer its full value to the police," was the answer of his friend. "Offer twenty-five *scudi;* that will be more than the robbers can get for it in the Ghetto; and they will be glad to return it for that sum. Follow my directions, and I'll promise you shall have it in your pocket to-morrow evening. Go to-morrow at about eleven o'clock in the morning into the Campo Vaccino, where the excavations are making. That is the time when the workmen take their *siesta,* and make their second *colazione.* You will see them lying about under the walls of the Farnese Gardens and the Arch of Titus, and the slopes of the Palatine. Among them is a band which always keeps by itself, and with whom the other workmen will not mix. This is composed of a set of sad scamps, who are always watched, and yet who manage to carry on their thieves' trade despite the police. The chief of this band is called Beppone. He is a little fellow, with a pair of ash-grey whiskers, and his customary seat is on some old beams near the ancient *rostra.* He is their broker and treasurer, and through his hands all the articles stolen by the band must pass. Go straight to him, tell him your story, offer him twenty-five *scudi* for the watch, and it is yours."

When eleven o'clock struck the next day, the gentleman was in the Campo Vaccino. All happened as his friend had told him. The workmen at the striking of the hour abandoned their work, and sought the shadow of the walls to eat their lunch and take their *siesta.* There, too, was Beppone, whom he immediately recognised, sitting in his customary seat. He approached, told his story, and offered twenty-five *scudi* for the watch.

Beppone listened, and when this offer was made he turned round, and calling to a group sitting at a short distance, cried, "Eh, Nannetto, who was on the rounds of St. Giorgio and the Cerchi yesterday?"

"*Lo Schiaccia col Barbone,*" (The Smasher and Big Beard) was the answer.

"May an apoplexy take you!" cried, in return, Beppone. "The Smasher was at St. Andrea della Valle, and Big Beard was on guard at the Santi Apostoli."

"So they were—let me see. Ah, yes. The Sausage and Jessamine were there with the Pivetta. I remember now."

"Very well," said Beppone, turning to the gentleman. "Come back to-morrow and you shall have your watch; *ben inteso,* after the countersign and the twenty-five *scudi.*"

At the appointed hour the gentleman returned. There sat Beppone on his tribunal like a judge. "*Buon giorno,*" he said. "Now for the description of the watch—what was it?"

Its owner then gave a careful description. "All right," said Beppone; "there's your watch; and now for the twenty-five *scudi.*"

But the good old usages are, in most instances, dying out. Even the knife itself is not used as it once was. After the festivals fewer wounded are annually brought into the hospitals. Between Sunday and Monday it was common within the last quarter of a century to see six, seven, or eight wounded men brought in; but now this is rare. The customs are growing milder since the time of Leo XII., who introduced many salutary reforms.

"Eh! *giovinotti!*" cried an old Roman matron a short time since, leaning out of her window in the early morning, and calling to the *staffieri* who had gathered under the *portone* of the palace. "Eh! *giovinotti,* how many wounded did you carry last night to the 'Consolazione?'"

"Not one, *eccellenza.*"

"Eh!" said the old lady with a sigh, as she drew back her head. "The Romans are losing their manhood and growing to be old women. They are no longer the Romans of my time."

No! alas! they are not. The bull-fights, the jousting, the *sassaiuole* are over. The stabbing is diminishing; the firing of guns out of the windows on Sabbato Santo grows more and more feeble yearly; the shambles are no longer in every street. The women are beginning to wear the detestable French bonnets, and to lose their beautiful costumes. Sedan-chairs are almost never seen; everybody goes in a carriage, and only the sick are borne along in litters; and by and by, if things go on thus, we shall lose, Heaven help us, even the prisons and the bandits, and at last, who knows? the very Pope himself.

APPENDIX.

Song of the Pifferari.

Note.—"The Athenæum" (Jan. 24th, 1863), speaking of this notation, says, "The *pifferari* tune noted by Mr. Story is by no means one of the best to be found. A more characteristic one, of the same style, was wandering the streets of London some months ago." To this I have only to say, that though other and "more characteristic" tunes may be played by *pifferari* in London, this is the only air ever played by the *pifferari* at Christmas in Rome.

POPULATION OF ANCIENT ROME.

What was the population of Rome during the imperial days is a question which has been frequently discussed and never satisfactorily settled. Some modern authors place it as low as 700,000, and one estimates it as high as fourteen millions. The truth probably lies somewhere between these two extremes.

By the census of Servius Tullus (A.U.C. 180), which was the first regular registry of the population of Rome, there were 80,000 citizens capable of bearing arms. This number had soon increased to 110,000; and in the year following the expulsion of the Tarquins (245), the returns of the census make the number of Roman citizens between fifteen and sixty years of age to have been 130,000.* Ten years after this number had increased to 150,700. Dionysius, however, says that more than 133,000 registered their own names and fortunes, and the names of their sons who had arrived at manhood. And Pliny tells us that in the year of the city 364, the number of freedmen in Rome was 152,580.

In the middle of the fifth century (A.U.C.), the Romans were divided into thirty-three tribes, and the total number of citizens, including, besides those enrolled in the tribes, the Ærarians and the people of those foreign states which had been obliged to receive the *civitas sine suffragio*, amounted to 272,000. In 488, Eutropius (Lib. 2) gives the number of citizens at 292,334.

In 501 the census is stated at 297,797;† and in the first quarter of the sixth century, the whole number of Roman citizens able to bear arms is stated by Livy (xxii. 54) to have been 270,000. In 527 A.U.C., when preparations were made to repel the invasion of the Gauls, the returns of the population capable of bearing arms presented a total, according to Polybius‡ and Eutropius,§ of no less than 750,000 or 770,000. This included the entire population of Southern Italy, but excluded all the country north of the Rubicon and the Macra, as well as Bruttium and the Greek cities of Magna Grecia. It is questionable whether this number included or excluded 50,000 reserves for Rome; but taking it with this deduction, it shows the population to have been very large. Of this body the Umbrians furnished 20,000, the Cenonians and Venetians 20,000, the Sabines and Etruscans 50,000, and the Latins 84,000. The city of Capua, which was the second city of Italy in importance, was reckoned to be able to raise 30,000 foot and 4,000 horse.‖ Dr. Arnold estimates the proportion of Roman soldiers, as

---

* Plutarch, in Public., p. 103. † Liv. Epit: 18. Fast. capit.
‡ ii. 24. § iii. 5.
‖ Livy, xxiii. 5; Niebuhr, vol. ii. *note*, 145.

compared with those furnished by all the Latin and Italian allies, to be about two-fifths; which (if the total number were 700,000) would make the number furnished by Rome to be 280,000, or very nearly coincident with that mentioned by Livy. If, then, there were no less than 280,000 men able to bear arms in Rome, what must have been the population?

In the year 539, despite the terrible losses suffered in the campaign against Hannibal and the defeat of Cannæ, there were fourteen legions, or 140,000 men in arms, independent of the seamen and soldiers in the fleets, 70,000 of which are considered by Dr. Arnold to have been Romans. Now, forty years before, at the battle of Ecnomus, the Roman fleet of 330 ships contained, at the smallest reckoning, 140,000 ; each Roman ship having on board 300 rowers and 120 fighting men; and if we strike out all the rowers and treat them as galley slaves, there still remain 40,000 fighting men to add to the Roman army. These numbers are, however, only the numbers actually on the field, and afford no indication of the numbers capable of being called out in case of supreme necessity. It is to be observed, however, that the actual proportion of Romans to their allies in this army is not as two to five, but that the numbers were, as reckoned by Dr. Arnold, equal.

In the latter part of the sixth century of the city the number of Roman citizens given by the census was (in 589) 327,022; at about the middle of the seventh century they had risen to 400,000 ; and in 683, which is the last account remaining to us, though not the last account taken during the republic, the number of citizens was 450,000.

The numbers given by the census can of course only give a proximate idea of the actual population, for it must be remembered that the census included only Roman citizens, and excluded from its total sum of *capita*, every slave, *filius familias*, single woman, orphan, and foreigner, besides a large number who were struck from the register for unworthy conduct, and all freedmen who were not citizens. Dionysius, speaking of the census of the year 261, says that the number of citizens who were men grown amounted to above 110,000, and that the women, children, domestics, foreign merchants, and artificers, not enumerated, did not amount to less than treble the number of citizens (Book ix. c. 26). To these are to be added the slaves, who are generally estimated to have formed one-half of the population; and this estimate is moderate if we may trust the statements of some ancient authors. Pliny and Athenæus, for example, both speak of the immense numbers of slaves at Rome, and the latter says * that he knew very many (παμπολλοί) Romans, who had ten and even twenty thousand slaves and more. Pedanius Secundus, prefect of the city, having been murdered by one of his slaves in the year 814 (A.U.C.), all of his household slaves were executed in expiation of the crime; and of these, Caius Cassius tells us that there were 400 in his house. "At

* Deipnos, I. vi. p. 272.

present," he goes on to say, "we have in our service whole nations of slaves." We have a chance record, too, of one freedman in the reign of Augustus, who, though his fortune had been greatly diminished by the civil wars, left at his death no less than 4,116 slaves. Again, Plutarch, in his Life of Crassus, incidentally mentions some facts which show the enormous numbers of slaves owned by private persons. After the burning of Rome, perceiving that many houses in the city were falling, he purchased, additional to the slaves he then owned. five hundred more skilled in architecture and construction, and having bought a large number of houses, set them to work in rebuilding; and in this way, with his army of slaves, he acquired a great part of the city. But, apparently, from what Plutarch says, these 500 slaves formed a small part of the number he owned, among whom were writers, readers, silversmiths, stewards, builders, &c. Seneca also says, "The opinion has sometimes been put forth in the senate, that the slaves should be distinguished from the free. But it is manifest how dangerous it would be if our slaves should begin to number us;" thus plainly indicating the superior number of the slaves. Besides these come the freedmen not citizens, and Pliny tells us that in the year 364, the number of freedmen in Rome was 152,580. Then come foreigners, of whom the senate, in the year 565, by one decree, ordered no less than 12,000 who had settled in the city to return home.

If, therefore, we multiply the sum total of the census by three we shall approximate to the numbers of the free population, and by doubling the free population we shall get the total number of slaves and free persons.

Applying this rule to the last census of the republic that we possess, we shall have a population of 2,600,000 Romans. This number appears so enormous, that it is generally supposed not to apply strictly to the inhabitants of Rome, but to include at least the neighbouring people who were incorporated into the Roman people, and received the privileges of citizenship. That it did not include the total population of Italy is manifest from the statements of Polybius and Eutropius, who, as we have seen, give the population able to bear arms in Southern Italy alone, below the Rubicon and exclusive of Bruttium and the cities of Magna Grecia, at from 750,000 to 770,000, at the very time that Livy states the number of Roman citizens able to bear arms at 270,000. The census therefore given by Livy did not include this population, but at best only the Roman citizens living away from Rome in the south; and supposing this to be the case, and that three-fifths of the number stated in the census were not inhabitants of the city itself (this being the ratio of the census given by Livy to that given by Polybius), we have to reduce the population of the city of Rome at the end of the Republic from 2,600,000 to 1,440,000, which is still an enormous population.

Nor will this number even seem to us, perhaps, sufficient, if we take into account some facts which we have expressly stated by different authors. For instance, Athenæus tells us that he knew very many

Romans with from ten to twenty thousand slaves. How many are very many? Are they ten? Even at this low figure we have at once from 100,000 to 200,000 slaves. Yet ten persons can certainly not be called "very many." Again, take the statement of Pliny that, as early as the year 364, there were 152,000 freedmen in Rome. It is not a stretch of imagination to suppose that there were at least five persons to every freedman at the time. Yet this would give us as a population of Rome at that time 760,000, whereas the census of citizens is only about 130,000. Surely, then, this census did not enumerate any but the actual inhabitants of Rome.

Under the Cæsars the city was vastly increased by streams of people who poured into it as the centre of civilization. From the Monumentum Ancyranum we find that the *plebs urbana* was, at the time of Augustus, 320,000. This did not include the women, children, senators, or knights, so that the free population could not have been less than at least double that number, or 650,000. Adding the slaves as equal to the freemen, we have at once 1,300,000 as the least number at which the population could be reckoned; but, as Dr. Smith justly observes, it in all probability greatly exceeded that number. Indeed, this calculation is preposterous. The women alone would double the number of *plebs urbana*. The children again would treble it; the strangers, senators, knights, and others would quadruple it; so that at least we must reckon the free population at 1,280,000, and doubling this for the slaves, we have a total population of 2,500,000.

But, according to the learned Justus Lipsius, this calculation is far too small. Taking the number of 320,000 as the "*plebs urbana*," he makes an elaborate calculation, founded thereon, as to the probable population of the city of Rome, in which he cites many authorities, and brings much learning to bear on this subject. He considers that as the "*plebs urbana*" does not include the rich, the senators and knights, the "*plebs honestas*," nor the women and children, they could not fairly be reckoned as composing more than one-sixth of the free population. This would make the total free population about 2,000,000, which he asserts should be at least doubled for the slaves; so that, putting out of consideration the strangers resident in Rome, who were very numerous—so numerous indeed as, by the testimony of ancient writers, to form a very important portion of the inhabitants—we have about 4,000,000 as the total population. "Nor," says he, after examining all the authorities, "can I admit that there were less."

In respect to the number of the strangers, who are seldom considered in estimating the population of Rome, Lipsius cites some passages from Seneca, showing how large a proportion of the people they composed. "Look," he says, "at these crowds, for which the immense roofs (*immensa tecta*) scarcely suffice. The greater part of this crowd (*maxima pars*) are without a country: from the municipalities and the colonies, and indeed from the whole world, they have flocked here;" and again,

"The greater part of these have left their own homes and come to this greatest and most beautiful city, which is, nevertheless, not theirs" (*non tamen suam*). So also Lucan, speaking of the funeral of Julius Cæsar, says, "*In summo publico luctu exterarum gentium multitudo suo quæque more lamentata est.*" However these statements be reduced, it is plain that the strangers resident in Rome ("*populis rectisque frequentem gentibus,*" as Lucan says) were an exceedingly numerous body, not to be omitted in any calculation of the number of inhabitants.

But to take still another view of this question: Who were the "*plebs urbana?*" It is plain that they were not only "*plebs,*" but "*urbana;*" that is, they were that portion of the *plebs* which lived "*in urbe,*" that is, in the city proper, and within the walls; for the term "*urbs*" was solely applied to the city within the walls, and did not embrace that portion of the city without the walls: "*Urbs est Roma, quæ muro congeretur.*"* If, then, there were 320,000 "*plebs*" within the walls, how many were there outside the walls? Aristides Rhetor, who lived in the reign of Hadrian, says that Rome "*descendit et porrigitur ad mare ipsum*"—stretched down to the very sea; and in this statement he agrees with Pliny and Dionysius; the latter of whom says that the walls were so hidden by the masses of buildings that they could with difficulty be found. Suppose, then, that there were little more than half as many outside the walls as there were inside, we should have 500,000; and supposing that the *plebs* only constituted one-fourth of the total free population, we have 2,000,000, and, doubling these numbers for slaves and strangers, again we arrive at four millions.

But this was in the time of Augustus, when, according to the same Monumentum Ancyranum, the *capita* of Roman citizens were a little more than four millions. But when the census was taken in the subsequent reign of Claudius, the number of Roman citizens had increased to some six millions; and probably Rome itself had likewise increased its population proportionally.

These two statements of the census are, strictly speaking, of Roman citizens. It is, therefore, impossible that so enormous a population as this would indicate could have been included within the walls of the city proper, or within even the circuit about Rome; for, if we add to this number of citizens the free population not citizens, we shall have some twenty millions at least of free persons besides the slaves. The result clearly indicates one of two things, either that this was the number of persons having the rights of Roman citizenship wherever they were, or that it was the total of the inhabitants of Rome and its vicinity.

When the Emperor Claudius (says Gibbon) "exercised the office of censor, he took an account of 6,945,000 Roman citizens, who, with the proportion of women and children, must have amounted to about twenty millions of souls. The multitude of subjects of inferior rank was

* See *post*.

uncertain and fluctuating. But after weighing with attention every circumstance which could influence the balance, it seems probable that there existed, in the time of Claudius, about twice as many provincials as there were citizens, of either sex and of every age; and that the slaves were at least equal in number to the free inhabitants of the Roman world. The total amount of this imperfect calculation would rise to about 120,000,000 of persons, a degree of population which possibly exceeds that of modern Europe, and forms the most numerous society that has ever been united under the same system of government."*

In this calculation Gibbon states the census of Claudius as 6,945,000.† He also estimates the citizens represented by the census as only constituting one-sixth of the free population; for to this original number of citizens he adds thirteen millions as representing the women and children, and then doubles the result to include all other free persons. In the calculations, however, which have been made in this paper, the citizens have been taken as constituting one-fourth instead of one-sixth part of the one population; and this was assumed on the ground that Dionysius states of the census of the year 261, that women, children, domestics, foreign merchants and artificers not enumerated did not amount to less than treble the number of citizens. To avoid exaggeration of any kind this proportion was taken; but it would seem that both Gibbon and Lipsius considered it too small, and had reason to believe that the citizens were only one-sixth instead of one-fourth of the free population, and this they might well be.

But, taking them only at one-fourth, we shall have six millions as the citizens, eighteen millions as the remainder of the free people, making in all twenty-four millions; and doubling this for the slaves we have forty-eight millions as the whole population.

There still remains the question what portion of this population inhabited Rome and its suburbs, as the centralization of the Roman empire in Rome was far greater than that of the United Kingdom of Great Britain, Ireland, and Wales is in London. We may perhaps fairly assume that the ratio existing between the total population and the

* Decline and Fall, vol. i. 54.

† The exact numbers, as stated by Tacitus, appear differently in different manuscripts. In the Vatican MSS. they are 5,984,072, which seems generally to be thought the better reading. Other MSS. read 6,945,000, conformably to the statement of Eusebius, and this is adopted by Gibbon; and 6,964,000, which is adopted by Lipsius, and is borne out by Cassiodorus. The inscription on the Portico S. Gregorio (apud Gruterum, p. 301, n. 1), which stands in these terms: "Temporibus Claudii Tiberii Facta Hominum Armigerum ostensione in Roma Septies centena millia LXXXVI. mil X.," is not considered by the best authorities to be genuine. Brottier and Peguorius condemn it; and Oberlin, in his Notes to Tacitus (edit. 1819, Paris), says, "Parum vera aut fida mihi est. Et tamen cum de his saltem qui arma ferrent agat nihil nobis obstat."

inhabitants of the city will be equal in both cases ; and that, by applying this ratio of London to Rome, we shall not include a larger number than is probable. Now, in round numbers, the population of Great Britain, Ireland, and Wales is 30,000,000, and that of London may be said to be 3,000,000, or one-tenth. Taking then the population of the Roman empire as 48,000,000, one-tenth, or 4,800,000, will represent the inhabitants of Rome.

Or, assuming the estimate of Gibbon as just, we shall have one-tenth of 125 millions, or twelve millions, as the population of Rome and its suburbs. But as the centralization of London has been greatly increased since the network of railways has brought it so closely into connection with the country, let us rather take the population as it was in 1820, of twenty-five millions for the whole kingdom, and 1,500,000 for the city of London. This would give a ratio of about one seventeenth; and applying it to Rome, we should find that it contained about six millions.

Thus, as the calculation of Lipsius founded upon the Monumentum Ancyranum gives the number of the entire population of Rome as equivalent to the number of Roman citizens in the census of Augustus, so the calculation of Gibbon gives the same result in respect to the census of Claudius. And it would seem, therefore, to be doubtful whether the term " *civium Romanorum* " be used in its strict sense of citizen or in its more popular sense of inhabitant, as it frequently was, for instance, by Vitruvius, who, speaking of the inhabitants and buildings in Rome, says, " *In ea autem majestate urbis, et* civium *infinita frequentia innumerabilis habitationis opus fuit explicare.*" But whether we take the sum stated by Tacitus as the number of Roman citizens throughout the empire, or as the number of the inhabitants of Rome and its suburbs, including all classes both free and slave, we shall arrive at nearly the same result.

But the population was not at its height when this census of Claudius was taken; it continued greatly to increase even to the days of Aurelian, and perhaps to those of Honorius.

"Speaking even of London," says Mr. De Quincey, "we ought in all reason to say, the nation of London, and not the city of London ; but of Rome, in its meridian hours, nothing else could be said in the naked rigor of logic. A million and a half of souls, that population apart from any other distinction, is *per se* a justifying ground for such a classification. *A fortiori*, then, will it belong to a city which counted from one horn to the other of its mighty suburbs not less than four millions of inhabitants, *at the very least*, as we resolutely maintain after reviewing all that has been written on that much vexed theme, and not impossibly half as many more."*

This is also the number reckoned by Lipsius as the probable population of Rome in its flourishing Cæsarian days.

* The Cæsars, p. 1.

A number so enormous as this could not of course be included within the walls of the city as they now exist; but it must be remembered that the walls once probably enclosed a far larger space. Yet setting this consideration aside, Rome the city was no more circumscribed by its walls, in its real meaning, than is the city of London by its actual limits of Temple Bar. When London is spoken of, we do not mean the city proper, but all that agglomeration and mass of houses extending over miles. In like manner Rome, overrunning its walls, spread itself in every direction; so that for a diameter of some ten miles at the very least the houses were closely compacted together. Dig where we will on the Campagna between Rome and the Alban Hill, or down in the direction of Ostia, we turn up the substructions of ancient buildings. We have the testimony of Pliny, and Dionysius, and Venantius Fortunatus to the enormous extent of country covered by buildings. "If any one," says Dionysius, "be desirous to measure the circumference of Rome by the walls, he will find it hard to discover them, on account of the buildings by which they are closed in and surrounded."* And in the banquet of Athenæus occurs a remarkable passage, fully bearing out these statements: "Rome," he says, "may be fairly called the nation of the world; and he will not be far out who pronounces the city of the Romans an epitome of the whole earth; for in it you may see every other city arranged collectively, and many also separately; for instance, there you may see the golden city of the Alexandrians, the beautiful metropolis of Antioch, the surpassing beauty of Nicomedia; and besides all these, that most glorious of all the cities which Jupiter has ever displayed, I mean Athens. And not only one day, but all the days in an entire year would be too short for a man who should attempt to enumerate all the cities which might be enumerated as discernible in that *uranopolis* of the Romans, the city of Rome, so numerous are they; for indeed some entire nations are settled there, as the Cappadocians, the Scythians, the people of Pontus, and many others."† To what modern city would such a description as this apply, after making all allowances for poetic exaggeration?

Besides, the name Rome did strictly and legally include not only the buildings within the walls, but those beyond the walls as well; while to those within the walls was applied the term "*urbs*," precisely as London is distinguished from "the City." "*Urbis appellatio muris; Romæ autem continentibus ædificiis finitur*," says Paulus; ‡ and in the 87th Law, "*ex Marcello*," according to Alfinus, "*Urbs est Roma, quæ muro congeretur; Roma est etiam, qua continenti ædificia essent.*" And again, in the 147th Law, "*ex Terentio Clementi*," "*Qui in continentibus urbis nati sunt, Romæ nati intelliguntur.*"

* Lib. iv. ch. 13.
† Deipnos, Book i. chap. 36, translated by C. D. Yonge.
‡ Digest, lib. i. tit. 16, de Verborum Significatione.

Nor do the walls as they at present stand probably afford a correct indication of the enclosed city in its most flourishing period. Vopiscus says that the walls of Aurelian were nearly fifty miles in circumference, while the present walls are only about thirteen, and his account would seem to be borne out by Claudian. According to Pliny, however, the walls were only 13,200 fathoms, which is about the measure that they now have, if he meant their circumference and not their diameter. Lipsius, in a discussion of this question, states that this measure is manifestly incorrect and inadequate, and reckons it to have been about forty-two miles: and Nibby is of a similar opinion. M. Ampère, while inclining to an opposite opinion, seems to hesitate in rejecting this estimate, and answers one of the objections to it, that no traces of such a wall now exist, by saying, " Thebes had an enclosure (*enceinte*) at least as considerable. Yet I do not know that a brick of this enclosure has ever been found."

At all events, we know that the Pomerium, which was the actual boundary of the city, in which no houses could be built, was repeatedly removed beyond its original limits, and specially by Augustus and Claudius, clearly showing the constant growth of the city and the demand for additional space.* And Strabo tells us that the actual limit of Rome was at a place between the fifth and sixth milestones, where the Ambarvalia were celebrated. This measure is from the column in the Forum, and if the distances were equally great in all directions, we have a diameter of the city at about eleven miles.

The enormous population of the city of Rome may also be inferred from the accommodation required by the spectators at the theatres, amphitheatres, and baths. There were no less than 9,025 baths, of which those of Caracalla afforded baths for no less than 1,600 persons at a time, and those of Diocletian for 3,200 persons. Three aqueducts now supply Rome with more water and fountains than are to be found in any other city in Europe. Yet, in its best days, no less than fourteen, and, according to some accounts, twenty aqueducts were needed to supply the demands of the population, and to feed more than 13,000 fountains. Look, then, at the theatres. The wooden theatre of Emilius Scaurus contained no less than 80,000 seats. The theatre of Marcellus seated 20,000 persons. These were found too small, and the Colosseum was constructed to seat 87,000 and to afford standing space to 22,000 more. The Circus Maximus was enlarged from time to time to meet the demands of the public, and under the emperors it would hold no less than 385,000 spectators. The population which required such accommodations as these must have been enormous. Reckoning it at four millions, and subtracting one-half as being slaves, we have two millions of free people at Rome; and in the Circus Maximus alone we have pro-

---

* See Tacitus, Ann. xii. 23; Dion. lv. 6; Vopiscus, Aurel. 21; Aulus Gell. xiii. 14; Senec. de Brev. Vit. 14; Strab. lib. v. ch. 3.

vision made to seat about one in five of the free population. But would not this be an enormous proportion to attend at any one spectacle?

Look, again, at the loss of life in the arena. At the triumph of Trajan 10,000 gladiators fought; and 60,000 fell under Spartacus; and 1,000 knights and senators fought in the Campus Martius at one spectacle given by Nero. There were also 10,000 combatants in the Naumachia on Lake Fucinus, under Claudius. These numbers surely indicate a great population.

Consider also this statement of Eusebius. On the occasion of a great epidemic in Rome, he says, for many days 10,000 dead were reported in the journal: "*Ingentem Romæ luem factam ita ut per multos dies in ephemeridem, decem millia mortuorum referrentur*"—that is, if there were 4,000,000 of inhabitants, one in four hundred died daily, for many days; and if those "*multos dies*" were ten, the city lost 100,000 persons. This would be an enormous mortality even in such a population.

Long after its great imperial days were past, the remains of Rome attest its former grandeur. Even as late as the sixth century, and after the passage of Alaric and Genseric, it must have been a wonderful city, as will be seen by the following statistical statement found by Cardinal Mai, and descriptive of this period.

This document, which dates from the middle of the sixth century (540), was written by a certain Zacharia, and begins thus:—" This is a brief description of the beauties of the city of Rome. Its abundance in everything and its tranquillity are great; its delights and comforts (*commoditates*) are marvellous, and such as conform to this admirable city. And first for the richness of the ornaments: I do not speak of those which are in the interior of the houses, as columns of porticoes, of their elegance and *height*. There are 384 large and spacious streets; two capitols; 80 great golden statues of the gods, and 66 ivory statues of the gods; 46,603 houses; 17,097 palaces; 13,052 fountains; 3,785 bronze statues of emperors and other generals; 22 great horses in bronze; 2 colossi; 2 spiral columns; 31 theatres; 11 amphitheatres; 9,026 baths; 274 bakers, who furnished bread to the inhabitants, without counting those who circulate in the city in selling it; 5,000 burial-places (*fossi*) where dead bodies are placed; 2,300 shops of perfumers; 2,091 prisons."*

Taking the numbers here given of the houses and palaces as a basis of calculation, we shall see that we cannot have over-estimated the probable population of Rome.

"We must remember," says Mr. De Quincey, " that feature in the Roman domestic architecture (so impressively insisted on by the rhetorician Aristides) in which Rome resembled the ancient Edinburgh, and so far greatly eclipsed London, viz., the vast ascending series of storeys,

* This will be found in " L'Histoire Romaine à Rome," by M. Ampère, Revue des deux Mondes, vol. xii. p. 332, November, 1857.

laying stratum upon stratum, tier upon tier, of men and women, as in some mighty theatre of human hives. Not that London is deficient in thousands of lofty streets, but the storeys rarely ascend beyond the fourth or at most the fifth; whereas in old Rome and the old Edinburgh they counted at intervals by sevens and even by tens."

A similar statement is also made by Desobry in his " Rome au Siècle d'Auguste" (p. 223):—" The houses of Rome," he says, " are of a height so prodigious that in many places the city is tripled, quadrupled, even sextupled ;" and this is fully confirmed by the ancient authorities. And it is also to be added that not only were the houses exceedingly high, but the streets were exceedingly narrow. Cicero describes Rome as " placed upon mountains and valleys, uplifted and suspended with attics or garrets, with not good streets, and with very narrow alleys" (*in montibus positam et convallibus cœnaculis sublatam et suspensam non optimis viis, angustissimis semitis*).* So also Plutarch speaks of the houses as "*ædificia multa nimio pondere et domiciliorum multitudine corruere.*"† Claudian also speaks of Rome as a city :—

> " Qui nihil in terris complectitur altius aer
> Cujus nec spatium visus, nec corda decorem
> Nec laudem vox ulla capit."

And again, not to multiply quotations, Vitruvius, speaking definitely, and as an architect, says, " On account of the majesty of the city, and to accommodate the infinite crowds of people (*civium infinita frequentia*), innumerable dwelling-places were required. But as the actual plane area of the city could not afford space for such a multitude of habitations, it became necessary to obtain it by the height of the houses. Therefore, by means of stone pilasters, constructions in terra cotta, and plaster walls, the upper storeys were built out and supported by numerous beams, which were utilized for attics hanging over the streets."

This condition of things had got to be so intolerable in the time of Augustus, that he was obliged to fix 70 feet as a limit above which they should not be built for the future. This height was afterwards reduced by Trajan to 60 feet. Such indeed was their height that the streets were completely darkened and overshaded by them; and one of the great improvements introduced by Nero in rebuilding the city was to enlarge the squares and streets and let in more light.

Now in the list just cited there are no less than 46,603 houses, and 17,097 palaces. Counting each of these houses as containing five storeys, and five persons on an average to each storey, we should at once have a population of 1,165,075. We then have the palaces. No person living in a palace in Rome during its days of greatness could at the

---

* De Leg. Agr. Orat. § 35.

† Crassus, § 2. See also Tacitus, Ann. lib. xv. § 47; Suetonius in Neron. 38; Juvenal. Sat. vi. 78; Diod. Sic. xiv. 324; Tit. Liv. xxi. 62; Strabo, v. 235; xvi. 257.

very least be supposed to have less than 100 persons in his employ, and this alone would add 1,709,700, bringing up the population to 2,874,770. Yet this calculation as to the household of the noble Romans is manifestly far too low, when we consider the statements of Athenæus, to the effect that many Romans had 10,000, 20,000, and even more slaves; "not," he adds, "to draw from them a revenue like Nicias, the rich Greek, but the greater part of the Romans have a very large number to make their *cortège* when they go out." In this passage, Larensius is replying to the statement of Marsurius, that "Aristotle reported of the republic of Egina that it possessed 27,000 slaves; that Agatharchides relates that the Dardanians had some a thousand slaves, some more;" and at this point Larensius interrupts him to say, "but every Roman, as you know, my dear Marsurius, possesses infinitely more slaves."

But if this be strictly true, consider what a number of slaves must have been in these 17,097 palaces. His words are undoubtedly not to be taken in the letter, but only in the spirit. Yet let us suppose that one-fourth of the owners of these palaces had 200 slaves, or one-half the number which we know Pedanius Secundus had in his house when he was murdered, viz. 400, and that the other three-quarters had one-fourth the number, or 100 slaves each, we have the astounding number of 2,125,000 to add to those of the free population. Yet if a freedman, in the time of Augustus, after suffering heavy losses by the civil wars, could leave 4,116 slaves, this calculation does not, to say the least, seem excessive as applied to the nobles.

This calculation is borne out by other facts which we know. Rome was divided by Servius Tullius into four regions. But under the Empire Augustus made a new arrangement, dividing the whole city within and without the walls of Tullius into fourteen new regions.

Each Augustan region, according to a survey made in the time of Vespasian, contained 19, or, according to a later account, 22 *vici*, with as many *sacella*, in places where two streets crossed each other.

Each *vicus* contained about 230 dwelling-houses. If there were 22 *vici* to each region, the city must have contained 75,000 houses. Of these, we know by the list already cited that 17,000 at least were *domus* or palaces, &c. Reckoning each of these to have contained 200 persons, including family, freedmen, and slaves, we have 3,400,000 persons; and considering the remaining 58,000 houses to have been *insulæ*, and to have contained 25 persons each, we have in them 1,450,000. This would give an entire population of about 4,850,000 persons, without counting those who were in the Pretorian camp and elsewhere.

Mr. Brottier, in his edition of Tacitus, has devoted a long note to the examination of this vexed question as to the population of Rome, which he places at 1,188,162 persons. He reasons that the number of persons in Rome will bear the same relation to the houses in Rome that the persons in Paris will to the houses in Paris. Now, in Paris at the time when he wrote there were 30,000 houses, of which 500 were hotels. The hotels he reckons to hold 42 each, and in each of the houses he reckons that there are 3½ families, or 21 inhabitants. This would just make the population of Paris as it then was, or 640,500.

This rule he then applies to Rome. On the authority of P. Victor, "*De Regionibus Urbis*," he says that there were in Rome 46,602 *insulæ* or houses, and 1,780 *domus* or hotels. The *domus* he reckons to have contained 84 persons each, and oddly enough cites in support of this statement the fact that in Pedanius Secundus's house were 400 slaves, not counting the freedmen, which seems a curious reason for estimating the whole household at 84. The *insulæ* he supposes to have held only 21 persons each. On this calculation there were in the *insulæ* 978,000, and in the *domus* 149,520; to these he adds 60,000 for those in the Pretorian camp and elsewhere,—thus bringing the total population to 1,188,162.

But instead of 1,780 *domus* or hotels, there were in fact, if we credit the list discovered by Cardinal Mai, 17,097—an error or misprint having occurred in the statement of P. Victor, by which thousands are changed into hundreds. If this be so, even on Mr. Brottier's calculation, the total population, instead of being 1,188,162, would be 2,473,896. That there is a mistake is plain from the fact that the two accounts concur in stating the number of *insulæ* at almost exactly the same figure; and if hundreds be changed to thousands, the number of *domus* will very nearly correspond. And besides, there seems to be no reason for estimating these *domus* or palaces as containing only 84 persons. His calculation is, that each of the private so-called hotels in Paris contains 42 inhabitants; but certainly a private hotel in Paris does not represent a palace in ancient Rome, with its retinue of freedmen and slaves. In what private hotel in Paris, for instance, would 400 persons be found? Yet these were the slaves only of Pedanius Secundus, not reckoning the family or freedmen; and if one takes into account the statements of Athenæus, or the fact of 4,116 slaves left by one freedman, we shall see that this calculation is simply absurd. We must therefore either utterly reject the statement of Athenæus, and in fact all ancient writers, as pure fictions, and suppose all the cases of which we have exact data to be purely exceptional, or we must consider the calculation of Mr. Brottier as manifestly wrong, erring as much in under-estimating the population of ancient Rome as others perhaps have in over-estimating it. While putting forward his own views, he says: "Lipsius thought that Rome contained four millions of persons; others believe that it contained eight millions; and still others have not been ashamed to estimate its inhabitants at fourteen millions."*

Yet while thus setting aside the conclusion of Lipsius as untenable, he does not attempt to answer his arguments, nor to dispose of his facts. He contents himself with a sneer, and, like a true Frenchman, cannot admit that Rome could be much larger than Paris, or that any ancient palace could contain more inmates than a Parisian hotel.

* Brottier's Tacitus, vol. ii. p. 379.

Again, this calculation of Mr. Brottier would not apply to Paris at the present time. Though its population has more than doubled since his time, the number of houses has by no means increased in the same ratio; and if the rule adopted by Mr. Brottier of calculating the inhabitants of Paris by the number of houses were now applied, he would find that he must allow a much larger number to each house, and this immediately would greatly increase his own calculation of the population of ancient Rome.

But in presence of these facts, which have been stated, let us now briefly consider what would be the result if we take the estimate of Mr. Merivale that the population was about 700,000. The Circus Maximus could seat considerably more than half of it. But did half of any population ever go to any single game in the known world? When the old men and women, the children, the decrepit, the sick, the slaves, and all those who had business elsewhere, or who cared not to see any game, are subtracted, if one in twenty went, it would be a large proportion. Suppose one in ten went; we should have a population of four millions. But that more than half should go, and that a building should be made sufficient to accommodate such a proportion of the inhabitants of all classes, is incredible. Then, again, the Colosseum would hold nearly one in six of the whole population.

Take, then, the number of houses and palaces. This would allow an average of twenty persons in each palace, and less than eight persons in each house. There were even in the 6th century 17,097 palaces, which, multiplied by 20, gives 341,940 persons in the palaces. Then there are 96,603 houses; and if there were eight persons in each house, there would be 372,824—which would give 14,760 persons above the calculation of 700,000. Yet after the descriptions we have of the houses, storey above storey, and of the numbers of slaves, is it possible to believe that a palace contained only twenty persons, and a house not so many as eight? In the house of Pedanius Secundus there were 400 slaves, not to speak of the family; or as many as there would be in fifty of these houses, or in twenty palaces. Or take the case of the *freedman* in the time of Augustus, who had 4,116 slaves; he would alone have taken more than 500 houses, or more than 205 palaces to house them. But if each palace has only twenty persons, what becomes of the *agmina* of gladiators that lived in them? the 10,000 and 20,000 slaves owned by some rich men, of which Athenæus speaks? Now, in one palace in Rome of the present day, of which I can speak with knowledge, there are housed 115 persons, yet there are no slaves, of course; the family is small, and the household is by no means considered large in Rome, and in the palace there is much unoccupied room. As for the ordinary run of houses in Rome, I do not believe one can be found with so few as eight occupants, even in the meanest quarters.

Take, again, the statement of Eusebius as to the famine. If 10,000 persons died each day for many days, and this mortality lasted ten days,

100,000 persons would have perished, or one in seven of the whole population if that were only 700,000. This is an impossible proportion.

Again, in the time of Augustus, when the population was by no means at its height, there were 320,000 *plebs urbana*, not including women, senators, knights, children, strangers, and the "*plebs honestas*." As for every man at least there is a woman, we have at once 640,000, without counting children, senators, knights, and strangers. Shall we admit that in a population of 640,000 men and women there are only 60,000 children? Why, the very freedmen alone, as early as the year 364, numbered no less than 152,580. What must they have been then at the time of Claudius, when the city had so enormously increased?

But let us go back a little. Eleven years after the expulsion of the Tarquins, when there were no Roman citizens except those in the city of Rome and its vicinity, the census gives the Roman citizens between fifteen and sixty years of age at 150,700. Then Pliny gives as the freedmen at about this date as 152,580. Here we have at once a total of 303,280, which must be doubled for the women, making it 606,560. Then again we have the children under 15 years of age, which must be equal to the number of the men, and raises the population to 909,840, without considering the slaves and the strangers, and all other persons. Even at this low reckoning we far exceed Mr. Merivale's amount as early as the year 364. But let us go back even further, to the days of Servius Tullius in the year 197. In his reign we have the first regular registry of the people of Rome, and we find that there were 80,000 citizens able to bear arms. Now, what proportion of a population are able to bear arms? Shall we allow the enormous proportion of one-tenth? This at once makes the whole population 800,000. Now there can be no doubt that this census by Servius Tullius applied solely to Rome and its immediate vicinity. And yet at this early date, by the narrowest reckoning, we have a population exceeding by 100,000 that which Mr. Merivale assigns to Rome in the height of its power and grandeur.

But let us see how Rome grew. In 64 years after the first census, we have, instead of 80,000 citizens able to bear arms, 110,000, which, if they formed one-tenth of the population, raises the number of inhabitants to 1,100,000. Rome is evidently increasing with rapidity. In a few years more this number of citizens between fifteen and sixty, and able to bear arms, has risen to 150,700; and Dionysius says that 133,000 registered their own names and fortunes and the names of their sons who had arrived at manhood, which makes 266,000. Let us now suppose that these were only one-sixth of the whole population, we have at once 1,596,000. At this early period, then, we have a population more than double that estimated by Mr. Merivale.

The subsequent registers of the census are not so definite as to the city, because the Roman citizenship became so greatly extended. But still it is probable that the statement of Livy that there were 270,000 Roman citizens able to bear arms in the first quarter of the 6th century refers to those furnished by Rome itself; the total number of the whole population of the kingdom being, according to Polybius and Eutropius, from 750,000 to 770,000.

But, setting this aside, we see by the preceding facts that, in less than a century, Rome had more than doubled its population. After this we have no exact means of estimating the relative proportion of the census to the total inhabitants of Rome. But certain facts are clear. In the year 197, the census was 80,000; in 683, it had risen to 450,000; in the time of Augustus, it had become more than 4,000,000; and in the reign of Claudius, it was 6,000,000. Here is a steady and enormous increase, which still continued certainly to the time of Aurelian. Taking the rate of increase as indicated by the census, we have more than seventy times as many citizens in the time of Claudius as existed in the time of Servius Tullius.

In the mean time, undoubtedly, Roman citizenship had been greatly extended throughout the provinces, so that we cannot take this ratio of increase and apply it to the city of Rome. But suppose that one in five of the population under Servius Tullius could bear arms, and was between the ages of fifteen and sixty (a proportion impossible, in fact, but taken for argument), we have at his time 400,000 inhabitants of Rome and its vicinity; and, as the census increased seventy times, let us suppose the population of the city increased ten times, we have as the result 4,000,000 of persons in the time of Claudius.

Does this increase seem large? It is nothing like the increase of New York, nor even of London and Paris. Yet none of these cities is the centre of a gigantic empire like that of Rome, from which everything issued and to which everything flowed.

Pliny, who has given us descriptions of Nineveh, Babylon, and Thebes, confidently states that no city could be compared in size with Rome. "If," says he, "any one considers the height of the roofs, so as to form a just estimate, he will confess that no city could be compared with it for magnitude." "*Si quis altitudinem tectorum addat, dignam profectò æstimationem concipiat, fateaturque nullius urbis magnitudinem potuisse ei comparare.*"

On the whole, then, it would certainly seem that the estimate of Lipsius and of De Quincey, among others, that the population of Rome, at its height, was at least four millions, is not an exaggerated one—nay that it is within all the calculations which we can make upon known facts. The probability would seem to be that the population was greater rather than smaller.

THE END.

www.ingramcontent.com/pod-product-compliance
Lightning Source LLC
Chambersburg PA
CBHW020910230426
43666CB00008B/1391